The
Madness
of Art

The Madness of Art

A guide to living and working in Chicago

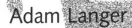

Adam Langer

CHICAGO
REVIEW
PRESS

Library of Congress Cataloging-in-Publication Data

Langer, Adam.
    The madness of art: a guide to living and working in Chicago/
Adam Langer.
        p.   cm.
    Includes index.
    ISBN 1-55652-286-1 (pbk.)
    1. Arts—Information services—Illinois—Chicago—Directories.
I. Title.
NX192.L36   1996
700'.9773'11—dc20   96-15362
                                                                          CIP

The author and the publisher of this book disclaim all liability incurred
in connection with the use of the information contained in this book.

Note: The 312 area code in Chicago will change in October, 1997.
For information about the change or to confirm telephone numbers with
the 312 area code, please contact your local telephone company.

© 1996 by Adam Langer
All rights reserved
First edition
Published by Chicago Review Press, Incorporated
814 North Franklin Street
Chicago, Illinois 60610
ISBN 1-55652-268-1
5 4 3 2 1

To Beate (natch).

To my folks (I mean, how could you not?)

To Amy at CRP for agreeing to publish this thing.

To the ducks at Indian Boundary Park, 39 Brusseler Strasse, the Man in the Mac with all the shirts, Hartzell Street, Lake Michigan, the miso soup at Sai Cafe, everyone at the *Reader* and *Subnation*, the coffee soda at Urbus Orbis, my sis and bro, the Jackson Generals, WXRT, Richie Allen, the fiction section at Waterstone's, and anyone or anything else who's provided inspiration, support, or whatever.

And to my Ford Escort, which has held up without forcing me to wear out my bicycle. Fixed at last, fixed at last, thank God almighty, it's fixed at last . . . I think.

Contents

Introduction

There was a time when we all were artists, at least for a couple hours of the day. In kindergarten at Daniel Boone School we drew during the free Crayola drawing period. At JCC and YMCA day camps we performed the saga of Prince Charming and Sleeping Beauty for our tolerance-award-winning parents. We sang hippie songs in grade school, joining tortoise-shell-glasses-sporting Mrs. Lazar on choruses of "Ride Captain Ride," "Get Back," "Guantanamera," and "Where Have All the Flowers Gone?" We took arts elective courses in high school, maybe joined the drama club, maybe sang with the chorus. And even if we weren't in that official legion of granola-crunchy artists, we managed to express our creativity somehow. Maybe by tie-dyeing a T-shirt and writing "sold out" on it to give it an air of authenticity. Maybe by inscribing original limericks on the walls of the john next to the "Do bongs" graffiti. Maybe through adding our own unique variation to the Chicago Hustle, the Bump, the Bus Stop, and whatever else it was that Ms. Mandell made us do in gym class when she had suddenly decided that square dancing was out of vogue and disco was the cat's pajamas.

As the years went by, though, the arts became so much more distant and segmented from our everyday behavior. Of course there's artistry in every profession. Whoever designed my futon could have been the next Louis Sullivan. It must have taken some real creative writing ability for my realty company to put together my lease agreement. And, if you ask me, the guy who put together the recipe for the onion bagels at New York Bagels and Bialys on Touhy is one of the great unheralded artistic visionaries of the twentieth century. Sure, some of us have become artists and inherited a new cliquey set of friends who eye establishment folks either as bores, traitors, or ready reservoirs of cash. We have also had to endure the difficulties of cocktail parties at which some new swaggering jamoke fresh out of Chicago-Kent Law School, one of the many who left art behind with that final dreadful Noel Coward senior play, would peer down at us through superfluous Armanis and ask that question, the bane of all artists' existences, "But what do you do for money?"

Well, this book isn't about money. Well, not really. Because being an artist isn't about making a living as an artist. Yeah, it's nice. Finding a healthy check in the mailbox or an envelope filled with bills for something that you created is certainly better for the ego than receiving your pittance from a job typing labels for wigs at a beauty manufacturer, hawking tour brochures for downtown double-decker buses, or learning how to put new toner into copier machines. And, as you read along, you'll know dozens more ways to convert your creativity into cold, hard cash (or cold, hard coins at least). But, more than that, hopefully, you'll learn the ins and outs of this city's artistic communities, understand where to practice your art, and discover how to get it out in front of people.

Sure, you might play a mean guitar, but if screeching your homespun lyrics into the Walkman microphone isn't quite getting it done for you, you had better know how to get gigs, where you can rehearse, how you can get a band together, and who'll stock your CDs and vinyl. Writing in a journal is all right for the time being, but you might want there to be a day when someone else is reading your insightful prose other than that lunkhead who shares the pillow next to you. Do you know where to exhibit your paintings, how to get your photographs published, where you can present your poetry (in front of a supportive crowd), how to produce your play, or get someone else to?

This city is one of the great artists' cities in the world, but navigating it can sometimes be difficult. It ain't Paris, and it ain't Soho. Many have called this city one of the most segregated in the country, and though they weren't talking about artists, I think I know what they mean. Artists exist in tiny pockets of the city, in perfectly hermetic outposts, sealed off like unwittingly tinned King Oscar's sardines. Walk around Lakeview and you'll think everyone's an actor. Take a stroll through Wicker Park and everyone's a painter or a musician. But stroll through Sauganash and try to sell a painting that isn't of a sad clown and they'll cart you off to the Joliet correctional facility. Ask if they know where *Triple Fast Action* is playing and they'll to send you to the paint department of the True Value on the corner.

But it's a great artists' city nonetheless. As the legacies past and present of Nelson Algren, Louis Armstrong, Junior Wells, Buddy Guy, Charlie Chaplin, Douglas Fairbanks Jr., Mary Pickford, Ed Paschke, Studs Terkel, Ruth Page, Willard Motley, John Dos Passos, Nathan Lerner, Benny Goodman, Bill Murray, Gilda Radner, Elaine May, Mike Nichols, William Friedkin, Laurie Metcalf, John Malkovich, Liz Phair, The Buckinghams, and God knows who else can attest, if you can make it here, you can make it anywhere. What makes a great artists' city? Opportunity, plain and simple. It is possible, and (once you've finished this book) even easy to live, work, and create as an artist in this city. It has more galleries than you can shake a stick at. It has more places to show off your new tunes. It has more theaters, dance companies, film making resources, and art schools than one human could afford to use in a lifetime.

Consider this book your ticket, your hitchhiker's guidebook, your compass as you stroll out from oblivion and into the furthest reaches of that mystical artistic netherworld known simply as Chicago.

PART I

The Arts of Chicago

ONE

Art, and Why Not Architecture?

The average soul off the street doesn't immediately think of Chicago as a city where great artists worked; it's so much more natural to think of it as a place where the greats dropped off their stuff and cruised. Miro, Picasso, DuBuffet, Chagall, and Nevelson plopped their sculptures smack dab in the center of the Loop and then went on to enjoy the fruits of their fame and fortune elsewhere, and, in the case of Chagall, to chill out with a certain Rolling Stones guitarist along the southern coast of France. The rich and not-so-famous snarfed up the works of the great impressionists and dabbled with the surrealists, bringing their works back to adorn the walls of the exclusive Art Institute of Chicago and the Near North galleries.

With rare exception, the major artistic institutions of Chicago were never ardent supporters of city artists. The culture honchos of Chicago have been far more willing to embrace New York and international artists than to appear provincial by giving preferential treatment to the locals, and have either ghettoized them in "local artist" nooks in the Art Institute or the Museum of Contemporary Art or simply ignored them. Even today, the Art Institute manages to virtually ignore the world around it with its never ending fetish for those same damned impressionists ("Hey, I got your haystack right here, pal").

In Chicago, we've always been taught to think of our artists as our architects. Using the sky as their pallet and streaks of black, white, and silvery metal as their brushes, architects have scratched out the imprint of their artistry against the Chicago sky. The city's skyline is a frozen display of intellectual

3

fireworks carved out by geometric sculptors. Since the excesses of the eighties, there has been a trend toward slightly more dull and retro-heavy buildings (the big clunker of the Harold Washington Library; that repulsive Nestlé Crunch–colored mausoleum known as Comiskey Park), but this is still very much the city planned by Daniel Burnham and handed down through the generations from Louis Sullivan and Holabird and Roche to Mies Van Der Rohe and Helmut Jahn, who, even if his work is often despised, has been the topic of cocktail conversations for years.

Unfortunately, becoming a master architect is not something that can be accomplished on a quick whim and a desire to change one's career. A part-time sketch artist can turn her back on her copy shop employer and decide to pursue her artistry full-time. If you're really the next Ed Paschke or Chicago's answer to Magritte or some other such budding genius, read on. If you want to become the next Mies Van Der Rohe, it's grad school for you, buddy.

(Warning: cliché coming.) As far as artists go, Chicago's history has always been a divergent one. Although attempts have been made to categorize artistic groups and movements, these rubrics are often far more useful to exhibition curators and guidebook scribes than to, well, reality. Any city that can produce the expressionistic works of Ivan Albright, the landscapes of D. F. Bigelow, and the cartoonish humor of Jim Nutt can't exactly be said to have a coherent heritage. This is, after all, the city to which the supremely rationalist Bauhaus moved under the leadership of Lazslo Moholy Nagy. Chicago soon developed the Institute of Design which, among many other accomplishments, gave birth to Chicago photographic pioneer Nathan Lerner's earthy Maxwell Street portraits and luminous experiments. Lerner, even after seventy years with a camera at his side, is still working as a sympathetic and compassionate artist here in Chicago. The Institute of Design also helped launch Chicago as a major center for graphic design, a reputation that persists even today because of visionary graphic artists based here like Rick Valicenti of Thirst Design.

The School of the Art Institute has produced world-renowned artists like Robert Indiana, Red Grooms, Claes Oldenburg (who left us a big baseball bat downtown, perhaps as a token of his appreciation), and Leon Golub. Golub, as a member of the so-called Monster School of Chicago artists here in the fifties, produced grimly affecting postwar works, depicting neurasthenics and other human forms devastated by the physical and emotional ravages of war. Such issues also informed H. C. Westermann's death ships.

Yet, this is also the city that fostered the revolutionary talents of peculiarly named groupings of experimental and irreverent artists like James Nutt, Gladys Nilsson, Karl Wirsum, Art Green, James Falconer, and Suellen Rocca who formed the Hairy Who, a playful sextet of so-called Chicago imagists who gained notoriety in Hyde Park in the sixties, and The Nonplussed Some, led, most notably, by lifelong Chicagoan Ed Paschke. The imagists continue to this day with the works of many original members of the aforementioned groups and other artists, like the comic-book-influenced Ray Yoshida and Roger Brown, a so-called false imagist whose politically charged sense of satire is perhaps summed up in his self-explanatory work *Shit To Gold*, which describes the relationship between the artist, his public, his critics, and his dealer. At the same time, Chicago has been home to a bevy of self-taught "outsider artists," who have been represented by such individuals as Lee Godie and Henry Darger and who are perhaps best emulated today by noted artist and boulevardier Tony Fitzpatrick, who joins a long list of current Chicago artists making national names for themselves. These include whimsically naive yet emotionally wrenching painter Hollis Sigler and abstract expressionist Wesley Kimler, whose recent exhibit at the Museum of Contemporary Art suggested that the movers and shakers of civic thought are finally taking a closer look at the local crowd.

It's been said that the era of the Chicago artist reached its peak during the eighties, but this is really true only from the standpoint of the gallery owner, the dealer, and the artist rep. True, many a River North gallery has shut down. But art is not necessarily something snooty that happens right around Wells Street. There is a burgeoning underground, from cartoonists like Chris Ware and Terry LaBan to spray can artists like D-zine. And the world of small, offbeat galleries is thriving. Opportunities are abundant, especially for the newcomer whose works undercut the market.

Getting Schooled

Jane Addams Center Hull House, 3212 N. Broadway, Chicago, IL 60657 (312) 549-1631
It's not exactly for the accomplished professional, but relatively cheap classes are offered for the dabbling shutterbug eager to brush up those flagging photography skills. An eight-week darkroom course costs $120.

American Academy of Art, 332 S. Michigan, Chicago, IL 60603 (312) 461-0600
Founded in 1923 by advertising design pioneer Frank Young Sr., the academy offers two-year associate's degree programs in painting, design, and illustration. Emphasis is given to the commercial and business aspects of the art world with a staff composed largely of professional, working artists.

Artworks in Oak Park, 246 Chicago, Oak Park, IL 60302
(708) 524-1422
Artworks offers pottery classes, teaching anything from the basic techniques (throwing) to the more specialized (how to make a seder set out of clay). Three-hour weekly classes run eight weeks and cost $180. Also affiliated with Expressions Graphics Workshop, which teaches printmaking techniques for $90 per three-hour session.

Beacon Street Gallery, 4520 N. Beacon, Chicago, IL 60640
(312) 561-3500
For younger folks but not just toddlers, this longtime community art gallery in the Uptown Hull House offers *free* classes in mural painting and photography.

Beverly Art Center, 2153 W. 111th, Chicago, IL 60643
(312) 445-3838
Probably not worth the drive or bus fare if you don't live in the area (unless you're shopping for bargains at Evergreen Plaza along the way), but there are good workshop opportunities here in photography, textiles, and jewelry. Six-week classes never cost more than $100.

Chicago Printmakers Collaborative, 1101 N. Paulina, Chicago, IL 60622 (312) 235-3712
Founded in 1989, this full-service printmaking workshop rents press time to printmakers and offers classes and workshops in lithography, woodcut, letterpress, monotype, and etching. The small Workshop Print Gallery attached to the Collaborative exhibits printmaking and works on paper. One-day workshops cost $45. Eight-week classes (3 hours a week) are $195.

Clayworks, 1405 W. Lunt, Chicago, IL 60626 (312) 262-2522
Storefront studio and workshop under the Morse el offering classes in wheel throwing and hand building for $80 a month. Classes meet two to three times per week.

Contemporary Art Workshop, 524 W. Grant, Chicago, IL 60614
(312) 472-4004
Founded in 1949 by John Kearney as a training and exhibition center for young and emerging artists, among them Leon Golub. Currently offers one sculpture class which costs $110 for ten sessions. Also rents out twenty-one studio spaces, which generally run $100 and up per month. Gallery artists chosen by jury must pay $300 per exhibition and help design and pay for promotional mailers.

Creative Claythings, 3412 N. Southport, Chicago, IL 60657-1420
(312) 472-5580
A small pottery gallery housing an even smaller pottery training center. Eight weeks of hour-long classes run $65.

Evanston Art Center, 2603 Sheridan, Evanston, IL 60201-1799
(847) 475-5300
They're still offering classes here, even though I practically ruined the kiln with some monstrous creation I sculpted some twenty years ago. Nowadays, they offer safer drawing, painting, and quilt-making classes, which generally run for eight weeks at approximately $10 a shot.

Harrington Institute of Interior Design, 410 S. Michigan, Chicago, IL 60605-1498 (312) 939-1475
Founded back in the thirties and located in the Fine Arts Building, this undergraduate institution offers both bachelor's and associate's degree programs in interior design that prepare students for careers in window display, historic restoration, and commercial interior design. Tuition runs approximately $4,700 per semester for day students, $220 for night students. Financial aid and grant programs are available.

Hyde Park Art Center, 5307 S. Hyde Park, Chicago, IL 60615
(312) 324-5520
Founded in 1939, this now-rather-staid-looking gallery was once the epicenter of artistic invention in Chicago. It still supports local, emerging artists in its exhibits but is as much an instructional facility as it is a gallery space. Offers classes and workshops in oil painting, jewelry, nature drawing, and ceramics. A ten-week course of one class per week generally runs in the $100 range.

Lill Street Gallery, 1021 W. Lill, Chicago, IL 60614 (312) 477-6185
Founded in 1975, this arts-and-crafts gallery/training center/knickknack shop remains as a holdover from the time when this neighborhood was home to more than a few folks with macramé belts and earth shoes. Eight weeks of small group classes (no more than sixteen students) in ceramics, tile making, metalsmithing, and jewelry making meet once a week for three hours. Cost is $220.

Lincoln Park Cultural Center, 2045 N. Lincoln Park West, Chicago, IL 60614 (312) 742-7726
Neighborhood park district arts center offering cheeeeeeeeaaaaaaaaap classes in drawing, painting, jewelry making, and woodcraft.

Old Town Triangle Art Center, 1763 N. North Park, Chicago, IL 60614 (312) 337-1938

Founded in 1955, this mellow community arts center offers training for professional and nonprofessional artists. Hosts twelve shows per year, two by students. Offers classes in watercolor painting ($120-$125 for ten weeks), yoga ($40 for five sessions), which should get you in the mood for painting, and self-defense ($40–$70 for a four-week course), which should get you ready to face your critics.

Palette and Chisel Academy of Fine Art, 1012 N. Dearborn, Chicago, IL 60610 (312) 642-4400

Founded in 1895 by some snobs at the Art Institute who sought to get away from the tired old world of charcoal drawings and landscape sketches, the academy still maintains an old-fashioned, almost stodgy artists' salon atmosphere while offering exhibits of its members' work and training artists in the basics of watercolor, sculpture, oil painting, and life drawing. Annual dues of $240 entitle members to workshops, class discounts, exhibition opportunities, and the opportunity to rent studios that cost $50–$250 a month. Poor, nonmember scrubs will have to cough up approximately $175 for eight three-hour, weekly sessions.

Francis W. Parker School, 330 W. Webster, Chicago, IL 60614 (312) 549-5904

Adult education classes in painting, pottery, jewelry design, and textile arts are offered at this institution, where, years ago, a six-year-old doofus once said, "My dad makes $100,000 a year. I make $25,000 from TV commercials. How much does *your* dad make?" Class sessions run about $10 a shot. Commercial residuals not included.

Ray College of Design, 401 N. Wabash, Chicago, IL 60611 (312) 280-3500

A small, undergraduate institution offering degree programs in advertising, fashion, illustration, and interior design, as well as in fashion merchandising and management. Tuition tends to run $3,000–$4,000 per semester.

South Side Community Art Center, 3831 S. Michigan, Chicago, IL 60653 (312) 373-1026

Founded in 1941 with the financial support of the Works Progress Administration as a training and exhibition site for black artists, the center has played host to the works of legendary artists like Gordon Parks and Archibald Motley. Poet Gwendolyn Brooks even took classes here. Now one of the only remnants of a mid-South Side artists' neighborhood in a still-deteriorating area, the center continues to offer exhibits and classes from a mysteriously talented teacher who claims he can teach anyone to draw. Private classes are given only if the arrangement is agreed upon with the instructor.

Textile Arts Center, 916 W. Diversey, Chicago, IL 60614
(312) 929-5655
Billing itself as the Midwest's primary source of fiber exhibitions and programs, TAC hosts exhibits and classes for would-be textile artists. Classes are offered in silk screening, beads, jewelry making, basket making, and yarn. The price schedule is highly variable, but six weeks of two-and-a-half-hour sessions generally run about $100.

Triangle Camera, 3445 N. Broadway, Chicago, IL 60657
(312) 472-1015
A Lakeview photo shop offering classes in basic photography (three classes for $49) and color and black-and-white darkroom skills ($125-$175 for five sessions). Also offers critiques, and a gallery is available for members of Triangle Photography Club.

Major graduate and undergraduate institutions with highly reputed programs in the field

Columbia College, 600 S. Michigan, Chicago, IL 60605-1901 (312) 663-1600

School of the Art Institute of Chicago, 280 S. Columbus, Chicago, IL 60603 (312) 899-5219

University of Illinois at Chicago, School of Art and Design, 929 W. Washington, Jefferson Hall, Room 106, Chicago, IL 60607 (312) 996-3337

Getting Paid

Getting into the galleries

It doesn't take much to get your work out there. It's all a matter of luck, networking, and having the invitations to the right parties. If all that doesn't sound much like being an artist, well, welcome to the nineties. And welcome to your press/marketing/self-promotion kit. You mean you don't have one? Get one. Now. Start off by finding a good photographer. (Well, actually, start off by being a good artist. The better the artist you are, the less talented a photographer you'll need.) You know photographers, don't you? Of course you do—you're an artist, damn it.

The best way to get into a gallery is, of course, to have a gallery owner in your immediate family. The next best way is to have your own. The next best method is to get drunk with a gallery owner at an opening, converse over toothpicked cubes of Swiss cheese, and gradually reveal that you're an artist. If none of these apply, you're going to wind up knocking on a lot of doors and sending out a lot of slides. But having a glitzy press packet with your résumé, artistic statement, and a plastic folder of your slides is a tricky business. If you're dealing with one of the top-of-the-line galleries who will only see artists this way, fine. Send these folks a letter with all the relevant information and, of course, the ever-requested self-addressed, stamped envelope. And then, if there is no response after a week or two, begin to make regular, polite, businesslike phone calls. But if you're dealing with some of the smaller galleries, being overly professional might be a detriment. Small gallery owners frequently like to boast about having discovered this or that artist and like to pass their time by talking about how the best artists have the poorest business skills. If you are a true artist, some think, you wouldn't even be able to spell your name, let alone design stationery, develop a résumé, and produce a professional looking package.

You should probably start off by touring galleries pertinent to your particular genre, not only to find out if your work is appropriate (or, if it's a tiny gallery, whether your paintings are too big to fit on the walls), but also to gauge the attitudes of the gallery owners and managers. Most galleries are open most weekday afternoons, and business is almost invariably slow. Taking some time to feel out whether the gallery you're looking at is the kind where the bored owner talks to you for hours on end about her artistic philosophy or where the manager does not even look up from his mag when you walk in the door should give you a hint as to which approach you should take. The city's galleries have more attitudes and atmospheres than our tempestuous weather system. Walk into any of the Uncomfortable Spaces collective of forward-thinking, intelligent galleries and you'll be greeted with a refreshing unpretentiousness and openness to new concepts in art. Walk into some River North joints and you'll wonder if they've heard of any artist who isn't dead.

I have enclosed a list of some of the galleries in Chicago most suited to taking on newer or lesser known artists. Not every gallery is included here; some of them are too snooty for our consideration. Some just might not be open in a couple months. I also have provided a snob rating to give you a handy, uncomplicated way to gauge the atmosphere of a particular gallery. This is, of course, a highly subjective listing, but it should indicate whether you should come in with a suit and tie and a résumé or with dreadlocks, a joint, and a jar of rye whiskey.

Snob Rating Key to the Galleries

0/4: My God, how hip, how cool. Almost too much so. You could wear ripped jeans, smoke, and have a sandwich with the owners in here and they wouldn't mind.

1/4: Quietly and unpretentiously sophisticated. Very helpful and polite people and very clean floors.

2/4: A bit snooty, but not out of spite. Friendly, but with a definite, unstated concept of the difference between high class (gallery owner) and low class (you).

3/4: "Excuse me? Who let *you* in here? I'm just going to keep talking on the phone to *real* people, and if you ask me a question, I may deign to respond while speaking in a slight British accent and peering at you suspiciously through my bifocals."

4/4: "Get out. Now. Don't ask me any questions. Is your name Andy Warhol? No. Can you make me a big pile of money? I didn't think so. I only work with major, established artists or members of my immediate family or rich boys with whom my daughter went to college. Why are you still standing here breathing my air and soiling my carpet, you troll?"

A cross-section of galleries that every artist should know about

Ab Imo, 804 W. Randolph, Chicago, IL 60607 (312) 243-8395
Alternative furniture design gallery hyping local artists in a mellow, unpretentious loft district. Also cofounded the Chicago Furniture Designers' Association, which exhibits annually. Advice: send slides of innovative furniture or lighting work. Snob rating: .5/4.

Jean Albano Gallery, 215 W. Superior, Chicago, IL 60610
(312) 440-0770
Rather stuffy atmosphere here belies the cheerful, whimsical, and colorful mood of the artwork often displayed. Snob rating: 2/4.

ARC Gallery, 1040 W. Huron, Chicago, IL 60622 (312) 733-2787
Standing for Artists, Residents of Chicago, this not-for-profit gallery is geared primarily toward women artists but also features experimental and emerging artists regardless of gender. Special invitational showings cost $600 for the big room, $350 for the smaller one. For the fee, you get your work listed in all the major publications, a selection of postcards announcing your exhibit, and 100 percent of any sales the gallery makes. For qualified, chosen artists, the

"rawspace" installation space is free. Contact the gallery for specific application procedures. Snob rating: 1/4.

Artemisia, 700 N. Carpenter, Chicago, IL 60622 (312) 226-7323
Named for Italian Renaissance painter Artemisia Gentileschi, this spacious, not-for-profit, cooperative gallery showcases lesser known women artists selected by a jury. Works range from painting and sculpture to printmaking and performance. Exhibiting opportunities are available to members for a small fee. Snob rating: 1.5/4.

Artisans 21, 5225 S. Harper, Chicago, IL 60615 (312) 288-7450
A remnant of the time when Hyde Park was still thought of as an artistic community, this cooperative space is taken up primarily by artsy-craftsy stuff, though the occasional photograph or sculpture does crop up every now and again. A very friendly sort of place run by the helpful artists themselves, Artisans 21 is unfortunately probably better for selling than for exhibiting or for acquiring a reputation in the arts scene, especially since most of the customers ask questions on the order of "Got any wind chimes?" Snob rating: 0/4.

Beret International, 1550 N. Milwaukee, Chicago, IL 60622
(312) 489-6518
Founded in 1991, this whimsical, anti-art-establishment gallery run by social worker Ned Schwartz is part of the renegade group of galleries known as Uncomfortable Spaces which embraces progressive, conceptual artists who challenge mainstream notions of art. Hilariously offbeat, establishment-skewering group shows have included "The Woolworth Show," featuring artists who work with Woolworth products; "The Free Show," in which all artworks were "auctioned off" for free; and the self-explanatory "Worst Show." Beret rarely works with painters and leans toward artists who wouldn't want to be exhibited in "status quo galleries." Artists exhibited here include Marc Alan Jacobs, Paul Kass, Jno Cook, and Allison Ruttan. Gallery takes 30–40 percent commission. Snob rating: .25/4.

Calles y Sueños, 1900 S. Carpenter, Chicago, IL 60608
(312) 243-4243
A small, storefront gallery in the heart of Pilsen showcasing the works of Latino painters, often with an eye toward magical realism. Snob rating: .5/4.

Circa, 1800 W. Cornelia, Chicago, IL 60657 (312) 935-1854
Founded in 1993, this cooperative living/work space in the Cornelia Arts Building focuses on emerging young Chicago artists. There are sixty-five raw and

relatively secluded artists' studios in this rather abandoned industrial neighborhood off of Ravenswood, offering occasional exhibits of artists who live here. Snob rating: 1/4.

Creative Artists Salon, 1561 N. Milwaukee, Chicago, IL 60622
(312) 278-7784
Founded in 1993. The only combined hair salon/art gallery in Chicago. Wide range of artistic styles, including violent and blatantly sexual work that would offend hair clients. Artists rotate every two months. The gallery takes a 30 percent commission on artwork. A lot of artists are hair clients, but you don't need to be to exhibit here. Stop by with work and get a haircut if you want or meet the gallery owner at a neighborhood party. That always helps. Snob rating: 0/4.

Eastwick Art Gallery, 245 W. North, Chicago, IL 60610
(312) 440-2322
One of the closest things to an actual museum in the gallery world, this deceptively large and classy space juxtaposes the works of modern eastern European artists with contemporary, cutting edge Chicago painters. Viewing spaces range from those with paintings hung on traditional brick walls to a cozy back room resembling either an artist's boudoir or the VIP room in a high-class bordello. Snob rating: 1/4.

Catherine Edelman Gallery, 300 W. Superior, Chicago, IL 60610
(312) 266-2350
This gallery is dedicated solely to photographers and usually ones with national reputations. Snob rating: 2.5/4.

Exhibit, 724 W. Washington, Chicago, IL 60610 (312) 382-0400
No set method for approaching this friendly, almost "aw shucks" gallery located in a strange, untraveled block by the expressway. It will exhibit anything, but leans toward painting and sculpture, with the occasional photographer thrown in. Group shows change often and tend to have a slightly Midwestern sort of feel rather than a Chicago one, perhaps because the curator–assistant director comes from Cincinnati. Advice: bring slides, get to know the curator, or just stop by—it ain't crowded. Snob rating: 1/4.

Ezell, 954 W. Washington, Chicago, IL 60607 (312) 563-0305
A tiny but comfortable and only slightly pretentious West Side gallery with a predilection for photography. Features the work of lesser known photographers as well as longtime, renowned Chicagoans like Barbara Crane. Snob rating: 1/4.

Fassbender, 415 N. Sangamon, Chicago, IL 60622 (312) 421-3600
Gallery dedicated to fostering exchange between German and American artists. Leans more toward the abstract than the literal. If the planned international distribution of this book has gone through, Hans, this is a great gallery for you. Snob rating: 2/4.

Feigen, 742 N. Wells, Chicago, IL 60610 (312) 787-0500
This upscale River North gallery tends to have a more adventurous, Wicker Park-y, on-the-edge feel. It also has the reputation of being *the* most innovative and daring in the neighborhood. Far more willing to take risks than most of its neighbors, Feigen inadvertently made headlines in '95 when one of its artists, Gregory Green, was arrested and his work confiscated. Snob rating: 1.5/4.

Gallery A, 300 W. Superior, Chicago, IL 60610 (312) 280-4500
This relatively new River North gallery, though it still may seem a bit stuck up, is more willing to take risks than your usual Superior Street establishment. Has exhibited the likes of the much-seen Red Grooms but also has pushed the envelope with on-the-rise Wicker Park artist Alan Gugel. Snob rating: 1.75/4.

Gallery E.G.G., 216 N. Clinton, Suite 300, Chicago, IL 60601 (312) 879-9667
An "environmental art" gallery. Looks for artists in all mediums who show a reverence for nature or use found objects and natural items, such as tree branches and so forth. Stop by, send slides and an artist's statement, or look for calls for entries in the Chicago Artists' Coalition newsletter. Snob rating: .5/4.

Gallery 1756, 1756 N. Sedgwick, Chicago, IL 60614 (312) 642-6900
A quiet, reserved Old Town gallery with a dignified, hushed ambiance well suited for River North. It began as an architects' gallery but has also started to highlight local artists who have some sort of quirkiness or attitude. Tries to combine established artists with emerging ones and artists who just happen to work in the neighborhood. Snob rating: 1.5/4.

Gallery 1633, 1633 N. Damen, Chicago, IL 60647 (312) 384-4441
Not a place that gets reviewed often but not a bad place to start out and to be seen. Gallery 1633 has been around for ages, long before anyone thought Wicker Park was cool. Features a rotating series of exhibitions by eclectic in-house artists but also offers small amounts of wall space for rent. Space is also available in the ultracool Berlin-style sculpture garden. Snob rating: 1/4.

Gallery 312, 312 N. May, Chicago, IL 60607 (312) 942-2500
Unlike many of the better known not-for-profit galleries in town, this one is more museum and less store or "anybody can paint" in atmosphere. Dedicated primarily to hyping unknown Chicago artists, although Chicago stalwarts like Irene Siegel and Aaron Siskind have exhibited here. Not in the business of making hefty bucks; all profits go to charity. Snob rating: 1/4.

Carl Hammer Gallery, 200 W. Superior, Chicago, IL 60610 (312) 266-8512
An outsider art gallery. But there's a term that's rather redundant, I always thought. What artist doesn't consider himself or herself an outsider? And then again, if you're a true "outsider artist," should you be reading this book? Shouldn't you be at home (if you have a home) working on refining your craft? Well, maybe you happened on this book by accident, and maybe you should happen on this gallery, the city's preeminent outpost for outsider art, too. Snob rating: 1.5/4.

Idao, 1616 N. Damen, Chicago, IL 60647 (312) 235-4724
A daring gallery guarded by its owners' friendly dogs, Idao has showcased a wide array of local and international contemporary artists. And any gallery that has the chutzpah to feature a show titled "The Fall and Rise of the Big Pussy" is likely to give your work the right amount of hype to attract the groovy off-the-street crowd as well as rich men in raincoats. Snob rating: .75/4.

Illinois Art Gallery, 100 W. Randolph, Suite 2-100, Chicago, IL 60601 (312) 814-5322
Founded in 1985, this exhibiting organization showcases artists who live in the state. Although there's always been something a tad Midwestern-provincial about the gallery itself, the many artists who've exhibited here over the years range from quiltmakers and experimental video artists to Chicago's top practitioners in photography and painting, such as Harold Allen and Ed Paschke. Tough to get your work in because shows are frequently guest curated. But curators on staff will look through your stuff and recommend it if they dig it. Snob rating: 1/4.

InsideArt, 1651 W. North, Chicago, IL 60622 (312) 772-4416
Seemingly most concerned with showcasing "affordable art" and combating the pretensions of the nose-in-the-air gallery scene, InsideArt naturally gravitates toward lesser known, up-and-coming artists, though frequent seminars about how to collect and how to get comfortable with art suggest an approach geared more toward the desires of novice collectors than toward those of novice

painters. The gallery takes a 35 percent commission on sales, and preference is given to women artists. Snob rating: 1.5/4.

Phyllis Kind Gallery, 313 W. Superior, Chicago, IL 60610
(312) 642-6302
One of the long-standing fixtures of the Chicago gallery scene that has been affiliated with the Chicago imagists since the late sixties. Work in here tends to focus on the surreal with elements of pop culture and the carnivalesque. Gallery artists include Roger Brown, Howard Finster, Gladys Nilsson, Jim Nutt, and Ed Paschke. Obviously not the easiest place to break into, but its success has bred its ability to take risks with younger, daring artists from the Chicago area. Snob rating: A surprising 1/4.

Lydon Fine Art, 301 W. Superior, Chicago, IL 60610 (312) 642-6302
A very cheerful and warm, open space despite the River North location. No specific style or subject matter; artwork exhibited ranges from abstracts to landscapes and even the occasional sculpture. Focuses on lesser known artists, about a third of whom come from Chicago. A large number of artists shown here come via word of mouth, but slides always receive a good look and a personal response. Snob rating: 1/4.

MWMWM, 1851 W. Chicago and 1550 N. Milwaukee, Chicago,
IL 60622 (312) 666-0204
Whimsical, irreverent gallery associated with the Uncomfortable Spaces collective. Snob rating: 1/4.

N.A.M.E., 1255 S. Wabash, Chicago, IL 60605 (312) 554-0671
Long known as an alternative gallery before alternative was cool, N.A.M.E. still plays host to emerging and experimental visual and performance artists. Snob rating: 1/4.

Ann Nathan Gallery, 210 W. Superior, Chicago, IL 60610
(312) 664-6622
Though the owner's fascination with some untrained and found-object artists has given this gallery a reputation as an outsider gallery, the main focus here is on established sculptors. And lest anyone make that mistake again, one gallery manager said, bristling, "Most of our artists have master's degrees." Feel free to send slides of your work and, of course, your curriculum vitae. Snob rating: 2/4.

One Touch of Nature, 5208 N. Clark, Chicago, IL 60640
(312) 561-3300
This nature store in the heart of Andersonville sells lots of Audubon prints and local artists' paintings (often watercolors) of standard natural fare: birds, water, pebbles, etc. Snob rating: -1/4.

Aron Packer, 1579 N. Milwaukee, Suite 205, Chicago, IL 60622
(312) 862-5040
Rather informal, quirky policy for trying to get your work into this small outsider art gallery. The artists this gallery seems to favor most are those without the wherewithal to read a book and call up the gallery with an eye toward marketing their work. But the gallery does feature "blur artists," too: those who use the elements of outsider art (folk traditions, found objects) and have a concept of art history and the gallery scene as well. Being college educated doesn't necessarily disqualify you, either. Snob rating: .75/4.

Perimeter, 750 N. Orleans, Chicago, IL 60610   (312) 266-9473
Founded in 1982 and begun with regional artists. Features contemporary painting, sculpture, drawings, ceramics, fiber, and metalsmithing. A full stable of twelve craft artists and twenty-five "fine artists" are on staff. Tastes run to the abstract. Not looking to take on anyone new or review slides but will look at slides if you send them. Snob rating: 2.5/4.

Portia, 1702 N. Damen, Chicago, IL 60647   (312) 862-1700
Glass, glass, and more glass (furniture, paperweights, and just plain nonfunctional art). Only a few Chicago artists are represented (we're not exactly the glassblowing capital of the world) in this specialized gallery. Snob rating: 1/4.

The Renaissance Society, 5811 S. Ellis, Chicago, IL 60637
(312) 702-8670
Don't be fooled by the name or the gallery's proximity to the University of Chicago. Though the gallery was founded in 1915, it still tries to maintain a hip, modern view featuring top-of-the-line local and national artists. Artists who've exhibited here include Ed Paschke, Rodney Carswell, and Louise Bourgeois. Snob rating: 2/4.

Byron Roche Gallery, 1446 N. Wells, Chicago, IL 60610
(312) 654-0144
Founded in 1994 as an artists' salon as well as a gallery. Artwork exhibited runs the gamut from Mexican folk art to pottery to wood to, of course, painting. Uncommonly open-minded folk singer-gallery owner with eclectic,

hard-to-pin-down tastes, Roche favors Chicago-based artists who are guided by the need to create rather than the need to profit. He likes to see "a creative purity and spiritual quality" running through their work. If that doesn't narrow things down (you are creative and spiritual and pure, aren't you?), maybe this will: artists exhibited here include Steven Halvorsen, Nicolas DeJesus, David Stull, Chuck Walker, and Benjamin Varela. Advice: be a cheerful painter, or at least not a morbid one (gallery owner hates grim, nasty stuff). Snob rating: 1/4.

Space, 314 W. Institute, Chicago, IL 60610 (312) 440-3222
This successful, adventurous Wicker Park gallery has headed east to tonier headquarters while still focusing on cutting edge area artists. Snob rating: 1/4.

Ten in One, 1542 N. Damen, Chicago, IL 60622 (312) 486-5820
Begun as a cooperative venture among art school graduates, this airy, pleasant, and friendly gallery remains dedicated to promoting local artists by embracing what has been called too often in press clippings "warm conceptualism." Still, it does favor conceptual art that isn't solely intellectual but also has a personal, humorous touch. Looks for new, emerging artists whose work is, according to owner Joel Leib, "sharply witty and intelligent, not merely decorative." Part of the Uncomfortable Spaces gallery coalition. You'll get a good feeling for the eclectic and edgy atmosphere of the gallery by the CDs Leib chooses to play—Tom Waits, The Beatles, Eric Dolphy, and Sonic Youth. Snob rating: .5/4.

Tough Gallery, 415 N. Sangamon, Chicago, IL 60622
(312) 733-7881
A member of the Uncomfortable Spaces collective focusing largely on minimalist, conceptual sculpture while attempting to eschew anything that seems too commercial and veers toward the provocative and the controversial. Reverse snob rating: 2/4.

Woman Made Gallery, 4646 N. Rockwell, Chicago, IL 60625
(312) 588-4317
As one might expect from its self-explanatory name, this gallery, tucked away in a mostly residential North Side neighborhood, focuses on promoting the works of emerging and unknown women painters, sculptors, and photographers. It features works that often, though not exclusively, carry a strong feminist slant. Shows change often and require a small entry fee for participating artists. Snob rating: 1/4.

Woman Wild, 5237 N. Clark, Chicago, IL 60640 (312) 878-0300
A New Age-y kind of store/gallery selling the handicrafts of many local women artists, ranging from jewelry to scarves to nonfunctional art pieces. Snob rating: 0/4.

Wood Street Gallery, 1239 N. Wood, Chicago, IL 60622
(312) 227-3306
Founded in 1992 in a former orphanage and Polish army veterans' home. Very cool melding here of both emerging modern artists and producers of folk handicrafts. Sponsors an annual exhibit of artist-made kites. Snob rating: 1/4.

Non-traditional galleries: pros and cons of the bar/ restaurant scene

If your salesmanship skills match your abilities at the easel, then sometimes the best way to get yourself into a gallery is by approaching a restaurant, a café, or a bar with wall space to spare and asking if they'll let you exhibit your work there. Some places will work out a consignment deal with you. Others might just let you do it gratis so they'll have something cool on their walls. Some might just show you the door. The hell with them—they just don't know talent when they see it. A number of cafés, bars, and the like already let artists exhibit there and are listed below. These will probably be more receptive to you than the local tavern owner who has bare walls and likes them just fine. But there might be more competition at these places, too.

The downside of showing in a restaurant or bar is certain places aren't as respectful of your work as a regular gallery might be. Who's to say that a plate of cold linguini won't wind up decorating your latest mixed media piece? There's also a good chance that your work won't be insured by a restaurant owner in case of theft or damage. And fat chance getting any critics to come see a café showing. Here's a list of places that have been known to feature local artists on their walls. Try your luck with these twenty-five suggestions to get you started.

Artful Dodger Pub, 1734 W. Wabansia, Chicago, IL 60622 (312) 227-6859

Buddies', 3301 N. Clark, Chicago, IL 60657 (312) 477-4066

Cafe Jumping Bean, 1439 W. 18th, Chicago, IL 60608 (312) 455-0019

Cafe Voltaire, 3231 N. Clark, Chicago, IL 60657 (312) 528-3136

Cairo, 720 N. Wells, Chicago, IL 60610 (312) 266-6620

Club Foot, 1824 W. Augusta, Chicago, IL 60622 (312) 489-0379

The Dome Room, 632 N. Dearborn, Chicago, IL 60610 (312) 266-1944

The Eccentric, 159 W. Erie, Chicago, IL 60610 (312) 787-8390

Ennui Cafe, 6981 N. Sheridan, Chicago, IL 60626 (312) 973-2233

ETA Creative Arts Foundation, 7558 S. South Chicago, Chicago, IL 60619 (312) 752-3955

Guthrie's Tavern, 1300 W. Addison, Chicago, IL 60613 (312) 477-2900

Heartland Cafe, 7000 N. Glenwood, Chicago, IL 60626 (312) 465-8005

La Piazza Cafe, 3845 N. Broadway, Chicago, IL 60613 (312) 868-0998

The Local Option, 1102 W. Webster, Chicago, IL 60614 (312) 348-2008

Neo-Futurarium, 5153 N. Ashland, Chicago, IL 60640 (312) 878-4557

The Rainbo Club, 1150 N. Damen, Chicago, IL 60622 (312) 489-5999

Roscoe's Tavern, 3356 N. Halsted, Chicago, IL 60657 (312) 281-3355

Roy's Bar, 7006 N. Glenwood, Chicago, IL 60626 (312) 338-3396

Sheffield's Wine and Beer Garden, 3258 N. Sheffield, Chicago, IL 60657 (312) 281-4989

Silver Cloud Supper Club, 1700 N. Damen, Chicago, IL 60647 (312) 489-6212

Star Top Cafe, 2748 N. Lincoln, Chicago, IL 60614 (312) 281-0997

The Third Coast, 888 N. Wabash, Chicago, IL 60611 (312) 664-7225

Transient Theatre, 1222 W. Wilson, Chicago, IL 60640 (312) 514-1802

Urbus Orbis, 1934 W. North, Chicago, IL 60622 (312) 252-4446

Wild Onion, 3500 N. Lincoln, Chicago, IL 60657 (312) 871-5113

About neighborhood art fairs

Every summer, every Podunk town and every neighborhood in Chicago usually features some sort of art fair. Of course, chief among these are the annual May "Art Chicago" exposition at Navy Pier and the infamous "Around The Coyote" festival in and around Wicker Park in September. The May festival at the pier, organized by Chicago's Thomas Blackman Associates (230 W. Huron, Chicago, IL 60610 (312) 280-2660) is a massive undertaking and a wonderfully eye-popping trip in which a number of the city's and the world's

Name	Location	Approximate date	Contact	Entry fee
57th Street Art Fair	Hyde Park	First weekend in June	(312) 293-3247	$100
Wells Street Art Festival	Old Town on Wells from Division to North	Second weekend in June	(312) 951-6196	$150 for a booth
Old Town Art Fair	Lincoln Park West, Wisconsin, Menomonee, and Orleans Streets	Second weekend in June	(312) 337-1938	Donation of a piece of your art
Gold Coast Art Fair	River North gallery region	Second weekend in August	222 W. Ontario, #502, Chicago, IL 60610	$70
Bucktown Arts Fest	Uh, maybe Bucktown?	Last weekend in August	(312) 489-4662	$75

strongest galleries participate, and it's a great place to schmooze your way around gazillions of gallery owners, collectors, and dilettantes.

In addition to these, however, there are a number of neighborhood, drink-a-lemonade-and-wear-a-sunhat-while-you-look-at-art fairs. These are not a bad way to get people interested in your work and maybe sell a few paintings (or a couple of glasses of Country Time at the very least), but a lot of them are more trouble than they're worth. First, most of them charge entry fees. Second, you have to go through the hassle of renting some kind of display setup. And third, if you're the least bit avant-garde, you might very well strike out at the "Long Grove Fine Art Fest" or the "Streamwood Summer Celebration" unless you do the most basic of watercolors of ships, birds, or idyllic country houses. Probably the best of these are in the accompanying table.

The Illinois Arts Council in the State of Illinois Center offers a far more comprehensive and far less selective guide, the *Art Fair Directory*. Make sure, though, if you use it that you research the fair you want to participate in so you don't wind up with the local American Legion branch picketing your work and, consequently, wasting your time.

About artists' reps

Unlike the motion picture and industrial film worlds, visual artists don't necessarily need agents or artists' representatives to get their work out in front of the public. With a little moxie and savoir faire, you're probably your own best agent. After all, people usually want to buy your artwork more because of who you are and what you represent than what some suit says about you. If you want to get corporate clients and have your works exhibited in boardrooms or have your illustrations used for things like textbook covers and so forth, you might need a rep. The Chicago Artists' Coalition publishes a list of such representatives, which you can pick up from them for just a couple of bucks.

Ten Overused Subjects That You Might Want to Keep Away From

1. Sad clown
2. Sunset
3. Your dog
4. Mean-spirited depiction of your parents
5. You with a brush in your hand painting you with a brush in your hand painting you with a brush in your hand painting you with a brush in your hand

6. Basket of fruit
7. Cultural icon: Marilyn Monroe, James Dean, Elvis Presley, Jesus Christ, Winona Ryder
8. Famous asshole: Jesse Helms, Bob Dole, Oliver North, Hitler, Manson
9. One square of solid color
10. Any of your body fluids

Publications and Other Resources

Around The Coyote, 1735 N. Paulina, Chicago, IL 60622
(312) 486-4000
Annual, massive autumn Wicker Park art showing and gallery walk, which has lately inspired much controversy over whether it helps artists to hype their careers or just nudges them out of the neighborhood to make way for wealthier collectors.

Art Encounter, Noyes Cultural Center, 927 Noyes, Evanston, IL 60201-2705 (847) 328-9222
Community arts center sponsoring gallery walks and tours of artists' studios and private collections, as well as artist critique classes, to which you can come to criticize and be criticized.

Art Now Gallery Guide, 97 Grayrock, PO Box 5541, Clinton, NJ 08809
Essentially a playbill of sorts for the arts scene featuring listings of openings and showings for the more mainstream Chicago galleries as well as others in the Midwest. Of more use to the novice collector and/or gallery hopper than to the artist. But what the hell, you can get it at most any gallery and it's free.

Chicago Art Dealers Association, 730 N. Franklin, Chicago, IL 60610
(312) 649-0065
A networking organization for approximately thirty-five River North member galleries (usually the more entrenched or well-endowed ones). The association offers occasional seminars and exhibitions, but many hip artists tend to find it way out of the groove.

Chicago Artists' Coalition, 11 E. Hubbard, Chicago, IL 60611
(312) 670-2060
A multifaceted not-for-profit networking resource with its own artists' slide registry and discount service for artists' supplies. The coalition publishes a pretty informative monthly newsletter, which provides illuminating profiles

of and interviews with artists and a good selection of want ads for loft space, exhibiting opportunities, grant information, and so forth. The coalition also publishes the very comprehensive, if somewhat pricey *Artists' Yellow Pages* as well as information on basic things such as health insurance, tax filing, etc.

Chicago Gallery News, 107 W. Delaware, Chicago, IL 60610
(312) 649-0065
Basically a listing of all the galleries that pay to be listed in it, as well as ultrapositive up-with-galleries fluff articles. Includes free listings for not-for-profits. You probably won't find your ultracool renegade artists' collectives in here. Sometimes a sign of a gallery's coolness is the fact that they're not listed in here. Useful more for gallery hoppers than for artists.

Chicago Public Art Group, 3942 W. North, Chicago, IL 60647
(312) 227-0209
Arts organization dedicated to the production and promotion of murals and other public art displays. Offers youth programs and exhibitions and publishes a comprehensive, if somewhat insidery, newsletter.

Chicago Women's Caucus for Art, 700 N. Carpenter, Chicago, IL 60622 (312) 226-2105
Billing itself as the largest multidisciplinary organization for women in the visual arts, annual dues of $45 entitle members to networking sessions and the ability to participate in membership showcases.

Fort Dearborn Camera Club, 47 W. Polk, Chicago, IL 60605
(312) 922-0770
Founded in 1895, it's the country's oldest camera club, which has featured exhibits and lectures by the likes of Edward Steichen, Alfred Stieglitz, Ansel Adams, and Margaret Bourke-White. The club also sponsored a photo exhibition at the 1933 World of Progress Exposition in Chicago. Dues of $25 a month entitle members to use of two darkrooms, classes, lectures, and other events.

Illinois Arts Alliance, 200 N. Michigan, Chicago, IL 60601
(312) 855-3105
Advocacy group promoting state arts funding.

Lawyers for the Creative Arts, 213 W. Institute, Chicago, IL 60610
(312) 944-2787
Provides free legal advice to artists and arts groups. Staffed by volunteer lawyers with time on their hands. No personal injury cases, please.

Near Northwest Arts Council, 1579 N. Milwaukee, Chicago,
IL 60622 (312) 278-7677
Founded in 1985, this exhibiting, networking, and community art resource
center is dedicated to promoting awareness of local artists and developing
community-based arts programs. Offers workshops in art techniques including kite making, doll making, and etching, as well as grant writing. Publishes
Context, a better-than-usual organizational newsletter which includes information on arts programs and exhibition opportunities, as well as observations
on the local scene.

New Art Examiner, 314 W. Institute, Chicago, IL 60610
(312) 649-9900
An excellent monthly publication in which well-researched feature articles
provide comprehensive coverage of local and national artists in regional gallery reviews. The $4.75 cover price won't help you get exhibited anywhere,
but it should help make you the erudite, well-informed artist you need to become.

You'll Need

Beret
The calling card for all artists and poseurs. In fact, it's so poseury, you can be
an artist again and look cool wearing one. Snag one at *Army-Navy Surplus
USA, 3100 N. Lincoln, Chicago, IL 60657 (312) 348-8930.*

Big dog
There's something unseemly about spending a lot of money for the creature
who's going to be your best friend and the guardian of your fine artwork as
well as your symbol of grooviness. Screw the fancy pet stores and pop into
one of the local shelters to pick up your trustworthy pup. *The Anti-Cruelty
Society, 157 W. Grand, Chicago, IL 60610 (312) 644-8338,* and *Save-A-Pet, PO
Box 193, Highland Park, IL 60035 (847) 943-7788* will be able to supply you
with your hound and most honest critic. Please try and feed him or her better
than yourself, though. Artists may survive on fast-food takeouts sometimes,
but dogs tend to get cranky.

Camera
I'm not talking about a new camera. It's not the cost of the equipment that
makes the photographer, anyway. Nathan Lerner took his most famous shots
with a camera that fit into his pocket and probably cost about a buck. Really

cool vintage, oddball camera and movie equipment (as well as weird old Super 8 movies) can be found at *Ambers Camera Store, 4036 W. Armitage, Chicago, IL 60639 (312) 252-2205.*

Canvas
You stretch it or they stretch it. Either way you paint on it. Try *Chicago Dropcloth and Tarpaulin Company, 3719 W. Lawrence, Chicago, IL 60625 (312) 588-3123.*

Clay
Or Play-Doh for sculptors. Get a nice big clump at *Genesis Creative Oasis, 2417 N. Western, Chicago, IL 60607 (312) 738-5300.*

Fabric
Whether you're a textile artist or just a painter who needs his or her couch reupholstered, you can't go wrong at some of the city's biggest fabric suppliers like the daunting *Fishman's Fabrics, 1101 S. Desplaines, Chicago, IL 60607 (312) 922-7250*, or Evanston's huge *Vogue Fabrics, 718 Main, Evanston, IL 60614 (847) 864-9600.*

Film
Well, I suppose you could just buy it at Walgreen's. It's the artist and not the film that makes the photograph, but if you're looking to buy in bulk or just feel like a pro, you're better off at *Helix, 310 S. Racine, Chicago, IL 60607 (312) 421-6000*, or *Calumet Photographic, 520 W. Erie, Chicago, IL 60610 (312) 440-4920*. For processing work, professional photographers also tend to favor *Helix; Gamma Photo Labs, 314 W. Superior, Chicago, IL 60610 (312) 337-0022; Ross Ehlert Photo Labs, 225 W. Illinois, Chicago, IL 60611 (312) 644-0244; or LaSalle Photo Service, 1700 W. Diversey, Chicago, IL 60614 (312) 327-6402.*

Frames
Somehow it never seems real until it's surrounded on all sides by wood. What's true for houses is true for paintings and photographs. *Artists' Frame Service, 1915 N. Clybourn, Chicago, IL 60614 (312) 248-7713* is the biggest, but *Lakeview Art Supply, 3359 N. Lincoln, Chicago IL 60657 (312) 296-6696; Rich's Art Supply & Framing Shop, 3838 N. Cicero, Chicago, IL (312) 545-0271; or Good's of Evanston, 714 Main, Evanston, IL 60202 (847) 864-0001* will also get the job done.

Groovy van
You're going to have to carry your supplies from one place to another, and you're best off doing it in style. If you can find a VW Vanagon from the seven-

ties or anything that once belonged to the military, you're in serious luck. Pick up a copy of the *Auto Trader* at your local convenience store.

Kiln
The toaster oven you have left over from college is not an acceptable sculptor's tool. Get ahold of Hansel and Gretel's least favorite bit of artistic equipment at *A.R.T. Studio Clay Company, 1555 Louis, Elk Grove Village, IL 60007 (847) 593-6060*, or *Chicago Metropolitan Ceramic Supply, 940 W. Lunt, Schaumburg, IL 60193 (847) 893-8701.*

Paint, pencils, a pallet, and a paintbrush
If you're a painter, you need them. Deal with it. Good deals are available at any of Chicago's well-stocked art supply stores like my personal favorite, *Brudno Art Supply, 601 N. State, Chicago, IL 60610 (312) 751-7980.* There's also *Flax Company, 62 E. Randolph, Chicago, IL 60601 (312) 580-2535; Stairs Paint Center, 3801 W. 63rd, Chicago, IL 60629 (312) 767-5355;* and *Pearl, 225 W. Chicago, Chicago, IL 60610 (312) 915-0200.*

Rope
Not to hang yourself if things get rough, more to solidify your career as a textile artist. Buy some at *Consolidated Hardware, 3256 N. Pulaski, Chicago, IL 60630 (312) 685-2100.*

Sketch pad
What may have been a doodle pad destined to become background for drawings of superheroes or cartoon characters in your youth is now the rough draft tool for your career. Snag one at any of the art supply stores listed above or at *Paper Source, 232 W. Chicago, Chicago, IL 60610 (312) 337-0798.*

Welding and metal materials
You can find all kinds of metals at *Gordon Brothers, 1340 W. 43rd, Chicago, IL 60609 (312) 927-1800.* Welding supplies may be had at *Wisco, 2200 N. Western, Chicago, IL 60647 (312) 384-7622.* Contact the Chicago Artists' Coalition for their pamphlet about insurance for bodily damage.

Interviews

Tony Fitzpatrick on Artistic Integrity and Colossal Pains in the Ass

In this era of specialization, the outspoken Tony Fitzpatrick shines as a risk taker, a jack-of-all-trades, and master-of-plenty. As a fine artist and former head of the late lamented World Tattoo Gallery, he's developed a national reputation for his self-styled emulation of outsider art. Jonathan Demme, Johnny Depp, and Penn Jillette are proud collectors of his work. As an actor, he's won a Joseph Jefferson Award and appeared in films by Jonathan Demme and John McNaughton. As a radio performer, Fitzpatrick lent a touch of intelligence and humor to the eternally sophomoric WLUP-FM. And, though few people know about it, some of his best artistic skills can be found in his writing. But we don't talk about that here.

Location: Big Cat Studios, 2124 N. Damen

AL: What should artists know about the business in Chicago?

TF: You don't wait for anyone's stamp of approval—that's stupid. Artists that wander around this town bitching about not getting the breaks are a colossal pain in the ass, and they usually don't deserve the breaks and lack the will and the intellect to govern their own destiny. They won't go out and do it for themselves. I have no pity for them.

AL: You've been quoted a lot about your disdain for the gallery scene and dealers here in Chicago.

TF: What's lacking here is a symbiosis between artists and the people who make money off art. That's the big problem. And then the dealers get really pissed when you don't stay on the plantation. I went out and bought my own equipment so I wouldn't have to be indentured to somebody who owned the equipment and I really, honest to God, didn't feel that here in Chicago I should be giving away half my living. The dealer I was with did not buy my ink or pay my printers. I did all that myself, so why should I cut them in? Every time you tell them it's about art, they tell you it's about money, and every time you tell them it's about money, they tell you it's about art. It's bullshit.

What has to happen for this arts scene to become a community again is for it to act like one, and self-reliance is how you start. These kids who come out of school now, they're like, "Okay, I'm here. I got my degree. I'm ready for that major career." I didn't go to art school, so I wasn't synthesized that way.

I went around River North with slides, and a lot of them would not even look. This was in the mid eighties. They didn't have to. So I went to New York; somebody looked, and they gave me a show, and the show sold well, and you know, I had a career.

AL: A lot of galleries aren't making as much money in River North as they did in the eighties. Some have even closed up. Who's responsible for that?

TF: What's happening in River North, they did to themselves. It's very easy for them to say, "Well, I blame the public." And that's ugly, that's stupid, that's pejorative, and it isn't true. The worst thing is that it's a lie. The public never stops buying art. They never stop supporting art. It's just that you have to make it accessible to them, either financially or just spiritually, just by virtue of welcoming anyone who comes through the door and saying, "You know what? This is a part of your life. Come in here and look at this, enjoy this." That's kind of been my one piece of gospel. I'm not missing any meals. I do real well. This is a slow, bad economy for the arts? You could've fooled me. I don't think people have gone off of art; I don't believe the public is not buying it. I believe they're not buying stuff that's masquerading as art.

AL: I took a walk through the River North area, a gallery walk, and some places are just a real turn off.

TF: Did you get greeted at the door? Did anybody say "Hi, welcome?"

AL: No, it was a "What are you doing here?" look.

TF: Exactly. I had a kid working for me when I first opened World Tattoo, a bright guy. This kid knew everything you had to know about art history. One day I'm standing in there and I'm watching him as people walk into the gallery, and he wouldn't even look up from his *Vanity Fair*. So I said, "What are you doing?" I said, "I greet people, I tell them hello, I introduce myself, I offer them a drink. What are you doing?" So I fired him that day. He said, "Well, I worked in New York. We don't do that in New York." I said, "Go back to New York."

I lack a certain breeding in all this. If you want people to know more about art, you goddamn well better contribute to their education and their understanding of it. It is the fault of the artist and the fault of art dealers, the idea that art is private property and not accessible to people. We take the blame for that and we should. And, as artists, what do we do? Where do we define our larger place in the community? Do we get out to the schools? Do we talk to the kids? Do we show them what we're doing? Or do we just sit there with the blind arrogance of entitlement and say, "Well, I'm entitled to this because I'm creative." Fuck that noise. We should have to define our larger place in the community like anybody else, just like a plumber, just like a cop, just like a fireman, just like somebody who waits tables, just like somebody who washes windows. I always say that's what the art world forgot, but I'm not sure they ever really knew it.

I was lucky. I was brought up very working class. I didn't go to art school. I barely got out of high school. I never thought I'd have a career at this. The fact that I have a career is really more because of a few lucky accidents than anything by design or by intention. Once it became a career, I treated it very seriously. I get here every day at eight o'clock. I work here all day. I don't work on just one thing. I look at it as being a perpetual student. Picasso on his deathbed said he was still a student. A good artist will tell you that he's still learning. The hurdle's still there. That glass ceiling you try to break through is still there. It might be a little higher now.

What's happened here in Chicago is that we didn't throw the money changers out of the temple. We just stood in line and hoped like hell that some of the coin would run down our way. And artists are feeling all indignant, and they're pissed off at collectors. They're the last people they should be pissed off at. You should never be pissed off at the public because you didn't do your job. Everybody thinks that I'm decidedly antidealer and that's not true. There are some dealers who do it right.

AL: What's doing it right?

TF: They offer real representation instead of just turning the fucking lights on, aspiring to a better and higher understanding of the art that they sell or they show rather than trying to become one of the pictures of the people in the back of *Interview Magazine.* An act of dialogue.

AL: Sometimes it seems like those making the decisions in the art community are such a small group.

TF: Oh yeah, it is. It's tiny. Four or five people. Talk to Alan Artner. He said it only takes three or four people to make an art movement.

AL: So, what's a young, unestablished artist in Chicago to do?

TF: Find others like him or her. Get together, pull some money, pull some resources. Okay, the guy who knows how to light work, lights are his job. The person who has a flair for writing writes the press releases. The person who has a flair for business keeps the books and arranges the sales. The person who has a good, pleasant demeanor, a good bullshitter, a good welcoming person, runs the gallery, and everybody takes turns, and when they make a few bucks, they invite somebody else in.

AL: How much of this job is self-promotion and business savvy?

TF: I've never had a publicist, never called a reporter. I don't buy ads. They eventually find me. I've never sent out a press release for one of my own shows. I think there is a way to get noticed, and that's to work real hard and show every opportunity you have. I also very early on was offered an illustration job for a magazine. I took it, because it was exposure and because it was being paid to do what I did, which is paint pictures. And, because of some of those illustrations, I got the Neville Brothers album cover. And because of the Neville Brothers album cover, a bunch of movie stars started buying my work. But never once have I ever spent a dime on an ad or a publicist or a PR firm or any of that kind of shit, because I don't have money to spend on that shit; I spend it on art.

AL: Do you think there's a place for publicists and PR and all that, or that it's unnecessary?

TF: I think it's unnecessary for one reason. If I'm doing my job right, you're gonna notice me eventually, whether you like what I do or not. You're gonna know who I am eventually. What I try to tell artists is you make your career in your studio, not at parties. I don't hang out at bars, I don't go to parties, I don't drink. I come here and make images every day, and people come here and they buy them, and luckily, some of them happen to be famous people. When I see an artist with a publicist, I see an artist who's going about it the wrong way. I think there's a troublesome circle jerk that goes on between artists and the press, too, that can be dangerous.

AL: Does what you read inform what you paint?

TF: Very much. More so than what I've seen. Samuel Beckett, Nelson Algren, A. J. Liebling. I'm more interested by writers. One of the big problems with artists is that they don't read. They're all informed by shit like MTV, which is interesting and you can learn something there, but we've become a culture of vidiots. I trace most of my education to things I've read. Reading is like heroin; the more you read the more you want to read. I read books on baseball, on beekeeping, on quantum physics.

AL: Do you pay attention to criticism of your work?

TF: No.

AL: Do you read it?

TF: No. Why let them into your game? When Tommy Hearns started losing fights, it was when he started reading what people thought of his fighting.

Don't let anybody in your game. A lot of guys will write it because they have a personal issue with you, because they genuinely don't like you, but who fucking cares? I've never responded to anything ever written about me. I don't let anyone else into my game. I just go to my sketchbook, and nobody's allowed in. You notice with playwrights, they get awful skittish, awfully defensive. Particularly Edward Albee, so he writes a fucking critic-pleasing play.

AL: He's pretty much a jagoff.

TF: He's a fucking asshole. Him and Lanford Wilson. Same shit. He's a stroke. Self-important douche bag, and he wrote a play to please his critics because they were hacking apart his other work. I think Mamet listens to people too much. You know who my hero is, the biggest influence on me as an artist? Samuel Beckett. He had the courage to look stupid. He showed absolutely reckless courage. You think he listened to critics? You think he let them in? The best ones don't. You think Picasso did? I'm not saying I'm him. I'm just saying that the minute you let people start dictating or interfering you're in trouble. You don't like the way I use color? Hey, find somebody whose color you like. This is America. Go look at any fucking art you like.

Rock and Roll Photographer Philin Phlash on How to Capture a Moment in Time

If you've been to a big party or rock concert in Chicago, you've seen Philin Phlash. Camera always at his side, Phlash has been the city's nightlife photographer for years. Speaking as fast as he clicks his camera, he's worked for the *Boston Globe*, the *Chicago Tribune*, and *Subnation*. A friendly paparazzo, he's photographed the likes of Courtney Love, Kurt Cobain, Michael Jordan, and any other celebrity you could possibly imagine. He has had retrospectives of his work exhibited in Germany and in Chicago, and he is represented in Chicago by the David Leonardis Gallery.

Location: Home of Philin Phlash

AL: How do you become a great photographer?

PP: To become a photographer, a great teacher once taught me that you have to be a good salesman. Timing is everything, being at the right place. One photograph can change your life, getting that great photo that's gonna do something for you.

AL: Is there any photograph that changed your life?

PP: My photograph of The Jam from 1978 with the two guitarists jumping up in midair with shoes flying next to each other was my first famous photo and that kind of changed things for me.

AL: Do you get the same thrill as an artist when you're shooting for daily newspapers?

PP: Sure. The thrill is getting the best possible photograph and publishing it and seeing it the next day in the paper. That's what keeps you going.

AL: How do you develop a style?

PP: You need to have a name for yourself, a name people won't forget. I carried my camera with me every night for fifteen years, and I've shown in laundromats and basements. Any place I could possibly have an exhibit, I would show my photography and people always came to see the photographs, because they were real life. The posed kind of photograph isn't really what I find extremely important; I like the decisive moment, the in-between. I photograph interaction and expression—between the photographer and the people being photographed, between people themselves. It's something only photography can do–freezing time so you can examine it. My goal in life was not to be a rich and famous photographer, just to be a photographer who would be in the history of photography.

AL: To capture those in-between moments, those decisive moments, how much of your art is dependent on luck?

PP: There's a percentage there, I'm sure, but for me, when I'm on and I'm aware, sometimes it's a vibe you can feel and you know something's going to happen. You have to be 360 degrees wise to what is going on, and sometimes I feel it's a whole power or weird sort of thing that's out there, and that's where a lot of great photographs have come from. I think there's technical skill, there's focus, there's film, but then there's the unknown factor.

AL: Is the sort of material you photograph not always taken seriously by the snooty high art aficionado? Are you too raw?

PP: Yeah, but some people like that. It's making a statement about the times. I basically photograph my life and the times that we live in here and now. Looking back at my photography from the punk rock days, you see some pretty outrageous things. It's the difference between being a documentation photographer and a commercial photographer. Documenting life doesn't tend to be as sellable.

AL: When you go out, are you consciously trying to document life or photographing what you see and hoping it's an accurate reflection?

PP: It is a reflection. I don't carry my camera in the daytime. I'm not a tourist, but I don't go out at night without it. It just seems like the situations arise and, having a camera, it puts you in places that you wouldn't be. For me, it's kind of a shield against the world. Nothing can touch me. Being aggressive has a lot to do with it. I never got into photography to make pretty pictures. I don't really think that pretty pictures are what photography is about. I love looking at photographs from the twenties and the thirties. They show the style of clothes or the way things looked back then, and eventually my work can be looked back on in the same way. I don't think I get a lot of respect as of yet, but maybe as an old man, I will. People just see you as a guy with a camera. Someone will say "Oh, are you a shutterbug?" I don't know how to explain what I am. For me it's not just the picture, it's the whole process of making the photograph, developing the film, making the print. Everybody earlier in their lives tries to figure out what their purpose is in life. Once I discovered photography, I didn't have that question anymore. I know what I'm supposed to do. It has something to do with the combination of art and science. It's not like anything else. Taking a blank piece of paper and making an image on it is still magic to me.

AL: Were you always only interested in photographing people?

PP: I didn't photograph people. I was afraid to photograph people at first. That sort of changed. Probably the only great advice my mother gave me was that people will always be your most interesting subjects. For me, when I started, I was just like any other photographer, taking pictures of pretty sunsets and flowers, all the bullshit photography that most people do. Finding my own niche was something about the flash. It freezes life and gives it its own kind of look.

AL: Is there any violence to the act? People have written about the language of photography—*shooting* and *capturing*. Is there an aggressiveness to it?

PP: I would say there is. I always say "I gotta shoot this." It makes you really alive; it makes you really aware; it makes you really look at things differently. When I put my camera on, it's different. I view life differently and it has something to do with that. It's a superhero kind of thing. A blind man can hear better. Maybe a photographer does see things differently. I'm not a critical person, and that has something to do with photography. I don't judge people.

AL: Aren't you a judge or critic in the sense that you choose what to photograph or not to photograph?

PP: I guess so. That's truly hard, because you carry a camera and people say, "Oh, take my picture." And you're like, "Well, no, I don't see something interesting here."

AL: Was there ever a time when you didn't bring your camera or you forgot it?

PP: Oh, no. I never forgot it.

AL: Or, maybe they wouldn't let you in with a camera?

PP: Yeah, that's always been a problem.

AL: Does it feel like your armor's gone?

PP: In those situations, I don't feel like I'm doing what I'm supposed to. I don't want to be just an observer; I'm a participant. I like to put myself in a performer's shoes and feel that vibe and capture it for that person so it's the greatest photograph ever taken of them. That's always the goal, that the next photograph you take is the greatest one you've ever taken. You can't stop. It's like being a collector or a drug addict. People are into what they're into and I'm really into what I'm into. It gives me a reason for living.

AL: How do you approach a subject who doesn't want to be photographed?

PP: I never wear a camera strap. I carry it down by my side. When people see the camera, their defenses are up, and the best way to avoid that shield everybody has is not to be too obvious about it. You can get that picture that everyone wants to show of themselves, that posed sort of thing, or you can capture something that's different.

AL: I gather from your work, your photographs of Peter Max or Courtney Love, for example, that sometimes you have to forget everybody's inhibitions and their defense mechanisms and get the picture you want, no matter what they care about.

PP: Oh yeah, you take the picture and worry about the consequences later, and sometimes the consequences have been bad. I've gotten beat up plenty of times for doing it. I used to say I was the most often beat up photographer you'd ever know. No one's ever gotten my film, though. No one's ever been able to get my camera away from me.

AL: Is it hard to run with a camera that size?

PP: Yeah. You gotta have good legs. You gotta run fast. I've never been a good spy.

AL: Do you know what you have on the film before you develop it?

PP: Sometimes I can feel a power surge, a great high if I can get there and get that photograph. But still, something can go wrong. I never tell someone I have a great photograph because something can go wrong. You can scratch a negative, bad chemicals, it can fall on the floor, and it's useless.

AL: Do you have a different personality when you have your camera?

PP: Once the camera's in my hand, it's like I have a job to do. It's why God put me on the earth. It's something that I can't explain. It's the difference between having your camera in the photo bag and having it out or having your flash ready or not. It does change things.

There's nothing more important than that moment in time that no one else has. It's up to me. I don't carry my camera during the day, because I would be totally burned out if I was always on. That's the difference. When I have the camera, I am just like a flashbulb or a battery pack. There's a switch, and you turn me on or turn me off. If I'm on, I'm on. If I'm not, I'm just like everybody else. I'm an observer instead of a participant. Right now I'm sitting here observing and reflecting, but when I have my camera on, I have it for a reason, like I'm waiting for something to happen. A lot of times you just run into things. It could be a beautiful child, the innocence of life, or who knows? You never know when that head-on car collision is going to happen.

TWO

Comedy

Stand-up comedy an art? Well, maybe not as it's been practiced over the past few decades. One would hardly call the dick-joke-spouting sleazeballs I shared the stage with in the late eighties in Rosemont and Elmhurst artists. Then again, one could hardly call the impudent schmuck with whom the dick-joke-spouting scumsuckers had to share the stage an artist, either. The comedy club boom of the eighties effectively ruined for a time any pretensions that this art form may once have had. No longer were the carefully honed styles of folks like Woody Allen, Richard Pryor, Lily Tomlin, and Robin Williams something toward which one could aspire. For a couple of years, any fool who could memorize an act, tell a few sleazy jokes, tell off a few sleazy hecklers, and hold the stage for ten to fifteen minutes before the red light flashed in their faces could have something vaguely approaching a career in show business. Granted, this form of show business involved more than a few nights spent entertaining the whiskey-sodden clientele of the Travel Lodges and the Howard Johnsons outside of St. Louis and Pawtucket, but hell, it was better than working at Chuck E. Cheese.

Like singles bars for the couch potato generation, comedy clubs sprouted up, a welcome relief for the uncreative swinging single who sought to entertain a date without the arduous process of coming up with his or her own jokes. Clubs were omnipresent, and not just near airports. Aside from the roadside yuckhouses in Palatine and Cicero, Chicago was blanketed by places with names like Giggles, Titters, and Chuckleface. Every bar with a stage in it played host to a comedy night or two. In the back of places like Lounge Ax on Lincoln and the "world famous" Apple Pub west on Irving Park, if you were a date-seeking comedian you'd go with your ten minutes of material, collect your beer money, and cruise out into the audience, thinking that, having braved the role of stand-up comedian, you could now wow any potential date with your newly oiled comedy techniques in everyday cocktail conversation.

Of course you were wrong. You were just another bozo in the litany of bozos striving for their five-minute spot on David Letterman or Johnny Carson, where such homegrown talents as Emo Phillips, Jeff Garlin, Mark Roberts, Anthony Griffin, and Ted Holum enjoyed their eight to twelve minutes of fame. The guys who used to smoke cigars in the green room of Elmhurst's Who's On First? left Chicago and found surprising success on both coasts as Bob Odenkirk joined the writing team of *Saturday Night Live*, Ken Campbell joined the cast of *Herman's Head*, and the comedy team of Steve Rudnick and Leo Benvenuti, who never managed to raise more than a whimper or a chuckle out of the Elmhurst faithful (or just whiskeyful), must have had something going for them, as they succeeded in achieving Tinseltown glory on the ill-fated NBC TV series *The Second Half* and the inexplicable box office smash *The Santa Clause*. The few comedians with more than just a gimmick or a dick joke seemed to dry up quickly, leaving any number of shuttered or razed comedy clubs in their wake.

Many who continue to ply the trade in town seem to have forgotten that comedy is more than technique. If scripted and performed properly, a comedy act can be the ultimately challenging art, combining the rigors of acting with the difficulties of scriptwriting. The best comics are, in essence, playwrights in miniature, whose structure and content must not only be flawless but ingenious if they hope to do more than appear as a contestant on *Star Search*. Such was not the case when the comedy boom went bust.

Who's On First? is gone now. So too are the Comedy Cottages (perhaps notable as the chain where one of the managers used to congratulate comedians on the success of their acts over a quick whizz at the urinal). Catch a Rising Star was ill named. And I don't remember the last time I saw a comedian in Lounge Ax, although a couple of the bands I've caught there over the years might be more successful as comedy acts. Such a crash in the popularity of an art form (yes, art form) might lead a potential comic to despair, discouragement, or Los Angeles, which is, of course, a combination of both of these. But, in fact, the disappearance of the surfeit of comedy clubs indicates a rise in national standards. The talent pool has grown more selective, and quality is on the rise. Imagine, if you will, what the National Hockey League used to be like when there were only six teams or when baseball was such that every American city with a population of over 200,000 didn't have a major league squad. These days, if you want to get booked, you have to be decent, and while scummy joke emporiums lorded over by mustachioed goons with wide collars have gone by the wayside, an entire new venue has opened for the stand-up comedian.

So if you get really good and start to wow the crowds at places like Zanies and the Funny Bone, you might want to stop calling yourself a comedian. Call it performance art and damned be the Chuckleheads of the world; as the ultimate, back-to-basics, low-budget act, if you can stretch your ten to fifteen minutes into an hour or two's worth of anecdotes and entertainment, soon the Goodman, the Organic Theater and the purveyors of Hollywood sitcoms will come a-knocking.

Getting Schooled

You think there's a school for this? Sorry. Next chapter for you, buddy.

Getting Paid

All Jokes Aside, 1000 S. Wabash, Chicago, IL 60605 (312) 922-6030
Successful club for primarily black audience and comedians. Your best chance to break in is at the Wednesday "Best of Chicago" showcase.

Barrel of Laughs, 10345 S. Central, Oak Lawn, IL 60453
(708) 499-2969
Booked in tandem with Fun Seekers by professional comedian Bill Brady. Longest running comedy house in Chicago area, since 1977. Open six nights a week. There's a language restriction: say beyond *hell, shit,* and *damn,* and you're out of there. If you've done some work around town, talk to the booker; he might arrange for you to do a ten-minute personal guest set on a Wednesday night. Will hire with a professional recommendation. Payment varies based on experience, minimum $25 for a beginning opener or MC. Arsenio Hall played here in 1979.

Comedy Womb, 8030 W. Ogden, Lyons, IL 60534 (708) 442-0200
Once-proud comedy club above The Pines Restaurant, which hosted the likes of Emo Phillips and Judy Tenuta way, way back in the day. It's now very hard

to get booked here since it does only Friday- and Saturday-night shows. Once in a while will have a new comedian do a showcase on Friday night gratis. These are mostly the result of recommendations from comedians and other club owners. Rarely hires acts sight unseen, especially after a horrific experience with a neo-Nazi taking the stage. Payment information: Keep your day job. Beginning acts get gas money.

Fun Seekers, 684 W. North, Elmhurst, IL 60126 (630) 993-0423
Comedy, improv, and pop music (rock, rockabilly, R & B) club at the site of the old Who's On First. Newcomers occasionally do showcase openings or MC work. Newcomers get three to five minutes, but it's usually a volunteer gig. Takes recommendations from other comedians. "A person who can be very funny at work might just go onstage and bomb." Won't hire someone fresh off the street, need a little open mike work, at least, behind you. Occasionally hires off opening acts when they're "ready to move up." Features three shows per week. Cagey about payment information.

Funny Bone, 1504 Naper, Naperville, IL 60565 (630) 955-0500
This local branch of a national chain takes very few newcomers. Books primarily people they know or folks recommended by other comics and Funny Bone managers around the country. Occasionally will look at video tapes or have someone audition at a show, but "ninety-nine out of one hundred usually suck." Doesn't like either blue or squeaky clean acts. Main concern: can you put people in the seats and get them to buy drinks? "I like acts that draw people," the owner explains. They do five shows a week; opening acts get $50 a show; middle act: $75; headliner: $150.

Hitchcock's, 1157 W. Wrightwood, Chicago, IL 60614
(312) 963-3760
Once prevalent, open mikes in the industry are now a rarity. Here you can rise to the stage before a surprisingly supportive audience on Wednesday evenings with a number of novices and semiprofessionals and even get a videotape made of your performance. No one of note in the industry will see you here, but it's good practice anyway.

KJ Riddles, 15750 S. Harlem, Orland Park, IL 60462 (708) 614-6336
Standard touring acts and longtime Chicago area comedians. Booked through "Johnny." Call him in the evenings after 7:00 P.M.

Zanies, 1548 N. Wells, Chicago, IL 60610 (312) 337-4027
Zanies Mt. Prospect, 2200 S. Elmhurst, Mt. Prospect, IL 60056
(847) 228-6166
Zanies Pheasant Run, 4051 E. Main, St. Charles, IL 60174
(847) 513-1761
Zanies Vernon Hills, 230 Hawthorn Village Commons, Vernon Hills,
IL 60090 (847) 549-6030

The flagship Wells Street location was founded in 1978. Zanies is one of the only relatively successful comedy chains still in existence after the comedy boom turned into the comedy bust. Has no new talent nights. If you've been playing around for a year or two, a booking agent will set up a Tuesday showcase night at the Wells Street location. Don't try to get booked at one of them unless you have at least ten minutes of material. The odds aren't with you: out of every eight showcases usually only one act gets booked. Most of the headliners are established or booked through word of mouth from people that the booking agent trusts. Don't bother sending a video; the agent's sick of looking at them. Biggest pitfall, says agent, is comics thinking they can use four-letter words when, in fact, you'll rarely go any further than the club circuit if you do. Says a booker, "You can't say it in Las Vegas. The only place you can say it is in the comedy clubs. But I'm not stupid; I give the people what they want. You book the comics people want. Dick jokes will never go out. Dirty jokes will never go out. Women talking bad about men, blacks talking bad about themselves, they'll never go out. But clever comics they won't ever go out, either." Headliners and middle-tier acts can expect to make between $50 to $100 a show. An MC should still keep his day job.

Twelve Overdone Topics to Avoid in Your Comedy Act

1. Differences between cities (New York and L.A., Chicago and L.A., etc.)

2. Jokes about presidents (Political jokes haven't worked since Nixon.)

3. Your car, driving, bad drivers

4. Dick jokes

5. Hackneyed imitations of celebrities: Robin Leach, John Houseman, Bill Clinton, Jack Nicholson, Arnold Schwarzenegger, Sylvester Stallone

6. Hackneyed imitations of celebrities in compromising situations: "Here's Sylvester Stallone in bed with Jack Nicholson"

7. Hackneyed imitations of ethnic groups (Believe me, your jive accent ain't as good as you think.)

8. Fat people jokes (even if you are fat)

9. Your crazy family

10. Jokes about the comedians who preceded you: "Hey, didn't that last guy suck?"

11. "I can't get a date" jokes (You won't get one even if you tell them.)

12. Differences between ethnic groups: "White folks be walkin' like this. . ."

You'll Need

Assertiveness training books
It ain't easy getting up in front of a posse of hostile drunks. If you don't feel like paying for a shrink or figuring out self-hypnosis, get a copy of seventies feel-good-about-yourself manual *I'm OK, You're OK*. You can probably find a copy in the recesses of *Powell's Bookstore, 1501 E. 57th, Chicago, IL 60637 (312) 955-7780.*

Boxing lessons
Maybe that nasty drunk doesn't exactly like that joke you made about his toupee and he's waiting for you out in the parking lot. Learn how to deck his ass at *Degerberg Academy, 4717 N. Lincoln, Chicago, IL 60625 (312) 728-5300,* or *Windy City Boxing Club, 4401 W. Ogden, Chicago, IL 60623 (312) 277-4091.*

Gasoline
On the road again—that's where you'll be spending most of your life, living out of a suitcase and a Days Inn. My favorite gas stations in the city are *Phil and Son's Gas for Less, 4201 N. Lincoln, Chicago, IL 60618 (312) 477-9877; D'Agostino's, 841 W. Irving Park, Chicago, IL 60613 (312) 477-2210,* and the Amoco station right across the street from the Chicago Historical Society parking lot. I can't tell you why.

Legal pad
You'll have to keep one of these at your side to jot down all of the brilliant notions you're having during the day. Screw all of those new, faceless office supply outlets that look like K mart. Buy one at *Randolph Office Supply, 1025 W. Belmont, Chicago, IL 60657 (312) 348-2700.*

Mints
No one likes a comic with halitosis. Go to my favorite deli counter, at *Manny's Coffee Shop & Deli, 1141 S. Jefferson, Chicago, IL 60607 (312) 939-2857* and

stock up on some weird ones from Switzerland. Come to think of it, have a kishke, too, while you're at it.

Mirror
If you don't have friends with inordinate amounts of patience, practicing in front of a mirror is one of the necessary evils of the comedy rehearsal process. Don't bother buying one. Just take over a fancy bathroom for as long as you need. My personal favorite is the women's at the Drake Hotel by the Palm Court. Don't ask me how I know; it's a long story.

Pocket tape recorder
The most painful part of comedy is listening to your act once it's over, even if you got good laughs. Still, if you want to learn from your mistakes and practice your rhythm, you'll have to listen to yourself over and over. Ninety-nine percent of these jobs suck, so just snag a cheapo at a *Radio Shack* outlet, e.g., *1273 N. Milwaukee, Chicago, IL 60622 (312) 278-9668.*

Stopwatch
Club owners get pissed off if you go over the time limit. First they shine the lights in your eyes. Then they get the hook. And if that fails, then come the cement shoes. Keep yourself punctual with an athlete's timepiece from *Sportmart, 620 N. LaSalle, Chicago, IL 60610 (312) 337-6151.*

Trickbag
When all else fails with your humor, wow them with your physical talents like juggling balls and performing card tricks. The best place for these is *Magic Incorporated, 5802 N. Lincoln, Chicago, IL 60659 (312) 334-2855.*

Whistle
Maybe those boxing lessons didn't turn out so well. Try and get somebody's attention with a piercing tweet. Pick one up at *Woolworth's, 18 N. State, Chicago, IL 60602 (312) 236-9265.*

Interview

Aaron Freeman on How to Develop a Comedy Act

Freeman achieved his moment of glory in Chicago in 1983 when he coined the term *council wars* for his now legendary comic lampoon of Chicago race politics. Since then, Freeman has become a successful comedian on the convention circuit, a noted actor with roles in Northlight Theatre shows and the

Second City mainstage company, an acclaimed writer-performer for hit shows including *Do the White Thing*, and a host on WBEZ-FM.

Location: Urbus Orbis, 1934 W. North

AL: Is stand-up comedy still alive in Chicago? Can you still make a living from it?

AF: Sure can. I make most of my living from it.

AL: Here in Chicago?

AF: Yeah, and around. More than half of my work is in Chicago doing conventions, dinners, but what is dying, thank God, are the clubs. I never did the clubs, never liked the clubs, they never liked me. Comedy in clubs is an excuse to sell pitchers of beer to teenagers. It was all so formulaic. There got to be so many clubs with such a huge need for comics that anyone could do it. Anyone who wanted to put together five minutes of material or half an hour worth of relationships, airlines, and Reagan jokes could do it.

AL: That's the best of it sometimes. For a while, Rosemont was Dick Joke City.

AF: Okay, I was giving people the benefit of the doubt. You know the difference between an improviser and a comic? An improviser tells a dick joke because he has to; a comic tells a dick joke because he wants to. That's the big thing. At Second City, we only told dick jokes when things were going really badly.

AL: Are there any golden rules to succeeding in comedy?

AF: I discovered a very simple rule and I would tell it to anybody who wanted to get into comedy. If you can make strangers laugh for ten minutes, you can make three hundred dollars and that's true here and it's true anywhere in the world.

AL: What impulse is it that drives you to comedy?

AF: Desperate insecurity, self-loathing. No. For me, it was very simply a way to make a living. I just learned that funny is money. I could do whatever the hell I wanted, say whatever the hell I wanted, be whoever the hell I wanted, and make my own money and be a self-supporting grown-up. Comedy is one of the few jobs on earth where you can legitimately say "Gotta go to work. Be right back." A big, long, heavy stand-up gig is maybe ninety minutes. And that's hell. And that's when you're working. You're really busting your chops if you gotta work for ninety minutes. More often, it's fifteen minutes to a half hour. And you'll make anywhere from five hundred to five thousand dollars.

AL: Do you see it as an art form?

AF: Modern stand-up is. Prior to Lenny Bruce and Will Rogers, you'd get your act and you would do that same act for the rest of your career. Lenny Bruce and Mort Sahl came up with the comedy of catharsis where it was no longer sufficient to do the jokes. You had stand-ups becoming a cross between a poet and a clown. You were expected to express what you were about and your own unique take on the world in a much more didactic kind of way. Dickens used comedy to make his points about evil and empathy and society, and certainly Chaplin did, *The Great Dictator* being the grand, classic example of them all. The idea of modern comedy is an art form to the extent that you create a persona around your own neurosis and you mine that persona. Modern audiences want to think they know you. They look to the arts, they look to a comic for something that has a ring of truth, not merely your act.

AL: When you go about constructing a persona, is it just a matter of extending and exaggerating what's already there?

AF: Absolutely. But that's not how I do it. That's not my approach. My approach is I start with the basic assumption that I'm a funny guy and that I will make jokes about my world. So, I decided back when Harold Washington was in power that I was going to make my world politics, and if I made my world politics and I made my vocabulary the stuff of politics, the polls, the charts, the numbers, from that, jokes would emerge. The notion of Aaron as erudite, intellectual comic I made up.

AL: But it comes out of you.

AF: Sure, but it's the biggest shock in the world to people I went to grade school with that I'm a comedian. In fifth grade when Monsignor Bryant came by, I hid under my desk. I couldn't bear the notion of saying my name aloud in public. But just as I learned that if you can make three hundred dollars if you can make people laugh for ten minutes, I learned that you had to develop a gregarious personality. I developed a personality that allows my brain to hide the rest of me.

AL: How do you approach creating an act?

AF: You try to figure out what's worth saying. What's out there that I care about? What do I care about? And you try to do your homework on it and see why the hell this is and why it's happening and again, the base assumption that I make is that I'll be funny, that whatever I do, I'll be making jokes.

AL: The process involves a lot of reading.

AF: A lot of reading, a lot of homework, watching old tapes of *Nova*, or whatever I feel like doing. What I learned from doing Council Wars is that whatever people care about, you can make them laugh at.

AL: It's kind of a hidden career, all these corporate events and industry gigs. It's very separate from what one imagines when one thinks of the public nature of show business.

AF: Yeah.

AL: But you have to succeed at the first level in order to jump to that one.

AF: I don't have any desire to. I wouldn't mind having a sitcom, but I have no desire to do clubs. I have a desire to make a lot of money, which this allows you to do.

AL: But you had to be known as a comedian in the public sphere before you could approach this industry career.

AF: Yeah, you've got to be known as a funny guy.

AL: How does one start out in this business now?

AF: Go to the clubs. What I always recommend to people is find the comedian you like and steal their material.

AL: Is that what you did?

AF: No.

AL: Oh.

AF: Over the course of my career, I've occasionally lifted other people's jokes, much to my regret, but no, that's not what I did, really. But it's easier. I did it the hard way, and I don't recommend it. It's not necessary. It's too much time and trouble, and who needs it? Go and steal someone else's material. Go and find old Dick Gregory records or Richard Pryor records and steal their material and spend some time getting laughs. Don't worry about the material; the material will come. Spend some time getting laughs and getting used to being up there being a funny person. And take material that you can count on, so you won't have to worry about that. Don't be obsessed with the writing stuff.

AL: Now, you have a scientific background. Did you study rhythms and patterns of how a joke works?

AF: Yeah. You don't have to study comic timing too long to realize that clearly the rhythms of your lines and the patterns of your jokes are going to get you laughs. You can get timing laughs without ever saying anything even moderately humorous if you've got your rhythm going. If you steal material from anyone, you can see the one-two-three punch clearly.

AL: Do you often keep going with a joke that isn't necessarily working for an audience? Do you keep plugging away at it?

AF: Yes. Sometimes there will be things you think are really worth saying, and those will hang in there a while, and then I find that I get bored not getting laughs. Even if I think it's really important, if they're not laughing, I get bored. I want them to laugh. I want them to like me.

AL: Did you or do you sit down with tapes of your performance to try to figure out what works and what doesn't?

AF: I should. But I never did. I should. I just write, and I read them over and over to people and edit them that way. And you cut lines that don't work in the performance of them. I don't listen to the tapes; it's so painful. It's so miserable, because all you ever see are your mistakes and they depress you so much.

AL: How do you rehearse?

AF: All you've got to do is remember it. Ultimately, it just matters that the audience laughs in real life. There's no way to tell ahead of time what's going to work. There is certain stuff that has worked forever. The classic kinds of jokes, classic setups. Dick jokes would be the obvious example. But, when you're trying to do something interesting and different, there's no way of telling. For a long time, I did this joke on the international monetary fund. Who would have figured that you could get drunks at a nightclub to laugh at the IMF? But you try it.

AL: Are you cognizant of the kind of laugh you're getting or why you're getting a laugh?

AF: Yes. There are some laughs that I'm really proud that I got after I got them, and there are some laughs you only get when you're desperate, and there are laughs that are the equivalent of dick jokes. Like Schaumburg.

AL: Schaumburg is the intellectual dick joke.

AF: Some are there to keep the act going between nifty points you want to make. But there are some laughs like the IMF stuff that I'm really proud of. I can make Jewish audiences laugh at Farrakhan and I'm really proud of that. The secret of great comedy is that it's serious.

The people I think are wonderful are really trying to tell you something and do something with it. You know what I love about Whoopie Goldberg and Charles Dickens? These are hugely funny people, but they're not just trying to make you laugh. They're trying to use their comedy to do something worthwhile in the world and those are the people I respect. Like Chaplin, who used that great sense of humor to make the world a better place and promote decency and empathy and compassion and the kind of stuff that we all want to promote, and comics are privileged enough to do in a special kind of way.

AL: How do you deal with an audience that's not responding?

AF: You die. You try everything you can. You pull your dick jokes out. You do the best you can, you try to make them laugh, you try to win them. But at a certain point, you've got to say they don't like it. And it's really horrible. What do you do? You pick yourself up and you do it again next week. You just have to keep going. You work on the material. You cast it out there and you see what happens. Annie Dillard said "At its best, the sensation of writing is that of any unmerited grace. It is handed to you, but you have to look for it. You work, you sweat, you break your heart, you wrack your brain, and then and only then, it is handed to you." Henry James said, "We work in the dark, we do what we can, we give what we have. Our doubt is our passion and our passion is our task. The rest is the madness of art." Or you slog around there and hope you get lucky. That's my version.

THREE

Dance

There was a time when dance in Chicago was performed either before the snooty clientele of an exclusive arts club or the Iowa conventioneers in a Las Vegas–style hotel floor show. Not anymore. For years, Chicago dance was ballet, and ballet was pretty much synonymous with one woman, Ruth Page, whose influence is still felt at her dance school and every Christmas when parents drag unwilling tots and tots drag unwilling parents to the Arie Crown Theater for the annual performance of *The Nutcracker*. But then, in dance (as in everything else), the world changed markedly in the sixties.

In many ways, the growth of dance in Chicago during the sixties and seventies mirrored the explosion of Chicago theater around the same time. What once was a rather unpopulated cultural landscape soon became peopled with experimental, fledgling dance companies renting out storefronts. When Shirley Mordine founded Mordine and Company in a Lincoln Avenue storefront as well as the Dance Center for Columbia College in the late sixties, about the only lights on Chicago's dance horizons were choreographers like Sybil Shearer and Maggie Kast. Mordine's company would later give birth to MoMing. Around the same time came Nana Shineflug and her Chicago Repertory Dance Company. And, by the mid-seventies, dance companies like Hubbard Street and Shineflug's Chicago Moving Company had sprouted.

These days, though notoriously underfed, underfunded, and underattended, the dance world is still surprisingly eclectic and vast. From the more mainstream and traditional companies like Ballet Chicago and the Boitsov Classical Ballet Company to the avant-garde and iconoclastic troupes like Abiogenesis Movement Ensemble and Hedwig Dances, this is a very differentiated community.

Dance, unfortunately, is not one of the more profitable art forms in this city, despite the fact that New York's prestigious Joffery Ballet finally decided to set up shop here. With the exception of the company members of Hubbard Street, precious few dancers can make their living solely off the slim checks they cash from their dance performances. Even at some of the other top companies in the city, dancers have to make their money by teaching classes or doing music videos, or, if they're lucky, snagging a part in the touring company of *Les Miz*. And then, of course, there's that heinous activity called *waiting tables*. The delineation between school and company is not so clearly defined in Chicago. Probably the best way to get involved with a dance company is, in fact, to take one of its classes and make yourself known.

Getting Schooled and Getting Paid if You Can

Abiogenesis Movement Ensemble, 606 W. 18th, Chicago, IL 60616 (312) 733-2246
A highly daring and innovative company in the midst of transition (read: not regularly performing but hopes to soon), Abiogenesis attracted attention in the late eighties and early nineties with their guerrilla performances, doing modern dance under Wacker Drive and under the Dan Ryan Expressway off of Eighteenth Street. Offers classes sporadically.

Ballet Arts Studio of Wilmette, 719 Lake, Wilmette, IL 60091 (847) 256-6614
Suburban studio offering ballet classes for the kiddies but specializing in Flamenco and Spanish dance for the oldsters. Classes run $105 for fifteen hour-long, once-a-week sessions.

Ballet Chicago, 185 N. Wabash, Chicago, IL 60601 (312) 251-8833
Founded in 1987, emphasizes both classical and neoclassical ballet and pursuing the time-honored technique of using movement to tell stories like*Hansel and Gretel* and *Coppelia*. Multiple levels of classes in classical ballet training run no more than $10 per class session.

Beverly Art Center Dance Studio, 3324 W. 111th, Chicago, IL 60643
(312) 238-9283
This community arts center offers hour-long classes in ballet, jazz, tap, and African dance. Thirteen weeks of one-hour classes run $105.

Boitsov Classical Ballet School, 410 S. Michigan, Chicago, IL 60605
(312) 663-0844
For the few remaining dancers who see their future in *Swan Lake* and *Giselle* instead of hip-hop videos, this classical training center led by a graduate of Moscow's much-ballyhooed State Bolshoi Theatre Choreographic University might provide the perfect opportunity.

Chicago Moving Company, 3035 N. Hoyne, Chicago, IL 60618
(312) 880-5402
Founded by quirky veteran Chicago choreographer, mystic, bodybuilder, and personal trainer to the stars (well, star . . . well, Burgess Meredith), Nana Shineflug, CMC teaches an idiosyncratic dance technique incorporating elements of yoga and weightlifting. Shineflug teaches modern dance classes at the Joel Hall Studios as well as free classes for young'uns and adults through the Chicago Park District during the summer.

Lou Conte Dance Studio, 218 S. Wabash, Chicago, IL 60604
(312) 461-0892
Probably the first step toward or the next best step to dancing with Chicago's premier dance company, Hubbard Street Dance Company. Rigorous, professional-minded attitude here—auditions are required for both dance (jazz, ballet, tap, hip-hop) classes and choreography workshops. Prices tend to run a little less than $10 a class session.

Dance Center of Evanston, 610 Davis, Evanston, IL 60201
(847) 328-6683
Aside from offering Tippy Toes classes for the youngsters, modern dance, jazz dance, musical theater, and ballet instruction is also available for teens and adults. Figure on spending about $40 per class.

Dancespace, 410 S. Michigan, Chicago, IL 60605 (312) 939-0181
Verrrry reasonably priced dance classes offered by the School of the Chicago Dance Medium, a dance company dedicated to demystifying the art of dance through the incorporation of ethnic history and abstract art and architecture into its performances. Classes ranging from contemporary ballet to jazz to Argentino tango tend to run about $8 for a ninety-minute session.

Sammy Dyer School of Theater and Dance, 2411 S. Michigan, Chicago, IL 60616 (312) 842-5934
The oldest dance school in the city of Chicago. Established in 1930. Offers ballet, tap, jazz dance for all ages. Four-session classes are $30 a month.

Gus Giordano Dance Center, 614 Davis, Evanston, IL 60201
(847) 866-9442
Founded in 1963 by Giordano, this jazz company began choreographing for WTTW specials as well as industrial shows and soon grew to become a major touring company showcasing the work of new or unsung choreographers.

Joel Hall Dance Center, 934 W. North, Chicago, IL 60622
(312) 587-1122
One of the preeminent contemporary African-American choreographers, Hall and his troupe have won accolades for their socially conscious and funky fusion of jazz, modern dance, and ballet in London, New York, and the former Soviet Union. Classes in all styles relevant to Hall's choreography are a maximum of $10 per shot.

Hedwig Dance Incorporated, 4753 N. Broadway, Chicago, IL 60640
(312) 907-2192
Founded in 1985, it's one of the few companies in town that tries to blend text and visual art with seemingly divergent forms of dance. Rather eclectic in its array of classes, Hedwig cheaply offers everything from modern to African to improvisation to tap, as well as instruction in holistic body training. The most intense three-a-week sessions for twelve weeks run $270.

Betsy Herskind School of Ballet, 2740 W. Touhy, Chicago, IL 60645
(312) 973-6446
Founded in 1969, this West Rogers Park dance school offers basic training in ballet and tap. Hour-long class sessions are $28 if you take one per week and about $16 if you take five.

Joseph Holmes School of Dance, 410 S. Michigan, Chicago, IL 60605
(312) 986-1941
Under the leadership of Kevin Iega Jeff, the Joseph Holmes Chicago Dance Theatre has maintained its powerful jazz-influenced sense of artistry and social conscience with an emphasis on highlighting the struggles of the socially and racially disenfranchised even after Holmes's untimely death in 1986. Instruction in ballet and jazz runs $6–$8 per chance.

Mayfair Academy of Fine Art, 1025 E. 79th, Chicago, IL 60619
(312) 846-8180
Offers beginning classes in ballet, tap, jazz, and modern dance. It's $85 for ten weeks of weekend classes.

Mordine and Company, 4730 N. Sheridan, Chicago, IL 60640
(312) 271-7804
This dance company was founded in 1969 by Shirley Mordine, who was the 1994 winner of the Ruth Page Award for outstanding artistic achievement. This company has endured because of its founder's uncompromising eclecticism, using elements of jazz, classical ballet, abstract movement, multimedia presentations, and sometimes startling costumes to explore social issues, such as the role of women in society, racial prejudice, and xenophobia. Or one can study at the Dance Center of Columbia College, 4730 N. Sheridan, Chicago, IL 60640 (312) 271-7804, which Mordine also founded in 1969.

Muntu Dance Theatre of Chicago, 6800 S. Wentworth, Chicago, IL 60621 (312) 602-1135
Founded in 1972, Muntu specializes in African-American dance, incorporating traditional styles from the Caribbean and Africa as well as contemporary America. The company tries to include elements of history and folklore in its performances with an eye toward demonstrating the history and development of African and American dance. Beginning dance classes tend to run about $9 per session. (It's cheaper for kids, but this ain't a kids' guide.)

Najwa Dance Corps, 1900 W. Van Buren, Chicago, IL 60612
(312) 921-4722 or (312) 850-7224
Founded in 1977, this company is dedicated to preserving the African-American choreographic heritage by blending together ritualistic African dance with more modern forms. Classes and workshops are offered irregularly.

Old Town School of Folk Music's School of Planetary Dance,
909 W. Armitage, Chicago, IL 60614 (312) 525-7793
Not for serious professionals but a good way to get to know your neighbors and other folks who like sandals, socks, and Bob Dylan's *New Morning* LP. Offers beginning classes in African dance, salsa, flamenco, Irish stepdancing, and tap. Eight once-a-week, hour-long classes run $100. See listing in music section for further information.

Outabounds Performance Company, 3319 N. Berwyn, Chicago,
IL 60625 (312) 463-3956
A unique dance company combining elements of theater, movement, and
voice with principles and techniques of improvisation based on audience suggestions. Offers semiregular workshops and classes.

Ruth Page Foundation School of Dance, 1016 N. Dearborn, Chicago,
IL 60610 (312) 337-6543
Named for its founder, Chicago ballet legend Ruth Page, this center has provided training for dancers who have wound up in many nationally reputed
dance companies including Hubbard Street. Classes, generally taught by instructors who've danced with Page's ballet companies, are offered in ballet
(of course), jazz, and tap. Tuition for eight ninety-minute classes runs $74
with discounts for professional dancers or people who want to take more.

Zephyr Community Center, 4401 N. Ravenswood, Chicago, IL 60640
(312) 275-5651
Dance studio in the heart of a slightly spooky industrial building. Offers classes
in flamenco, ballet, and modern dance that generally run $7 per session.

Major graduate and undergraduate institution with highly reputed programs in the field

Dance Center of Columbia College, 4730 N. Sheridan, Chicago, IL 60640
(312) 271-7804

Publications and Other Resources

Chicago Dance Coalition, 200 N. Michigan, Suite 404, Chicago,
IL 60601 (312) 419-8384
A networking not-for-profit for Chicago-area dance companies. Also publishes
the slim newsletter *Dance News*, which lists upcoming performances and comments briefly on the Chicago scene.

Chicago Dance Coalition Hotline, (312) 419-8383
This listing of upcoming dance performances as well as auditions, most often
for industrials and commercials, is updated weekly.

Six Things Not to Say to Your Fellow Dancers at an Audition

1. "You want some of these fries?"
2. "What happened to your hair?"

3. "I never knew you had a limp."

4. "I admire your courage for making it."

5. "What is this, *Flashdance*?"

6. "Oh, I didn't realize this was an open call."

You'll Need

Apple
Unlike most art forms, which not only sustain but sometimes even foster an unhealthy lifestyle, dance requires a balanced diet. Start with a nice, juicy, red apple, the kind that would even make Snow White succumb to her evil stepmother. I'm into the organic thing; I'd pick it up at *Whole Foods* in the shopping center at North and Wells.

Cutoff sweatshirt
Why not? It worked for Jennifer Beals. Get a pack of ten from any local K mart and cut them yourself. See the next edition of this book for where to buy scissors.

Dance bag
Perfect for enclosing your togs and bouncing against your hip as you saunter in and out of class. Try *Leo's Dancewear, 1900 N. Narragansett, Chicago, IL 60639 (312) 745-5600.*

Health club membership
You get obsessive when you're a dancer. If seven days a week of practice and performances still hasn't given you the stamina you need (or it's off-season), feel free to join a work-out emporium. But please, not one of those expensive neon meet markets. You can get basically everything the slick places offer at your local YMCA or *Lincoln Turners, 1019 W. Diversey, Chicago, IL 60614 (312) 248-1682.*

I'm Dancing as Fast as I Can, by Gelsey Kirkland
You get obsessive when you're a dancer. If you begin to get too obsessive, this is key reading material. You don't need to buy it, though. Check it out from a Chicago Public Library branch (not the downtown branch; that one's gross).

Leotard
Required apparel, like stripes for prisoners. Try *Motion Unlimited, 218 S. Wabash, Chicago, IL 60604 (312) 922-3330.*

Spring water

Following a healthy workout and before the apple, there's nothing more replenishing than fresh water from the spring or the pump. There aren't many natural water sources in the Chicago area, but you can pump or ladle your own at Caldwell Woods or in Joliet at the natural springs.

Tap shoes

Clickety clickety click. Clickety clickety clack. Clickety clickety click. Yes, these and other sounds are available at *Kling Theatrical Shoe Company, 218 S. Wabash, Chicago, IL 60604 (312) 427-2028.*

Tinsel

Not so much to look at in daylight, but in a darkened auditorium, with you shimmering as you leap across the stage, it's cool, cool, very cool. Try the *Dance and Mime Shop, 643 W. Grand, Chicago, IL 60610 (312) 666-4406.*

Interviews

Lou Conte on Becoming a Successful Dancer

Born and raised in southern Illinois, Lou Conte with his unique eye for talent and what the mainstream public wants, did the unprecedented by creating the most successful dance company in Chicago history, Hubbard Street Chicago. His company continues to thrive and grow in its athletic, energized jazz style, nabbing plum grants, garnering amazing reviews, and attracting the likes of world-renowned choreographers like Twyla Tharp.

Location: Lou Conte Studios, 218 S. Wabash

AL: When you look at something like visual art or music, people say you can start at pretty much any age. It doesn't really matter if you have enough commitment, but in dance, that doesn't work. You have to start out early.

LC: It definitely helps to start out when you're young. Dancers' careers are short. Dancers' careers are over sometimes when other people's careers are just starting. By forty, you're pretty much an old person, and also, the physical thing. Your bones, when you start training at nine or ten years old, still haven't formed. It's easier to train a person so that they develop with the kind of anatomy that you need. When you start older, your bones are pretty much set, so that's a big thing. And, people just move differently.

I had this conversation the other day with the studio manager about how I can pretty much tell dancers that started late and dancers that started young.

There's just a quality about the way they work. If they start out young, it takes away the inhibitions, and it helps to start them off emotionally right. I think dancers feel insecure sometimes simply because they started late.

AL: What is "emotionally right"?

LC: There's a constant sense of rejection when you're a dancer. You take class every day and every day you don't do most things right. It's like "No, stretch your foot higher. Move your leg higher. No, you're timing is off. Your rhythm is no good. Do this, do that." Every day you go in and do your daily routine and you have to face this rejection thing and, after a while, you adapt to that and you're secure enough as a person to know that it's not personal. Some dancers, if they're really insecure, they just can't take that. They give up. But it's a hard thing. Artists in general are a neurotic lot and sensitive to everything, so the early training has to prepare you for what this is all about and what the focus is, and you will handle it better when you get older. I know some principal dancers of a major American ballet company who are fabulously successful and very wealthy. They make a lot of money, but they're messes personally.

AL: So, it's possible to succeed in this business and still not be quite ready to take the rejection anyway?

LC: Oh yeah. Like Gelsey Kirkland. There's a case of an incredibly gifted and talented person who couldn't handle all the stuff surrounding dance. She couldn't handle it. It wasn't just dance for her, though. She just happened to be a dancer, and she had a real rough time, became anorexic.

AL: That's not particularly uncommon in the dance world.

LC: As an artistic director, my biggest job here is psychiatrist, which I am completely untrained for.

AL: Do you need to be incredibly mature at a very early age to pursue this work and take this kind of criticism, incredibly focused?

LC: Focused? Oh yeah. You can't go to class every other day. You have to go to class every day. That comes with part of a dancer's or any successful person's life. You can't come at your whim. You have to come every day. I'm not saying be obsessed, but you have to have a passion for it that you just wake up and want to do it, and even some days when you don't feel like doing it, you still go ahead and do it because you know that you have to. You have to be able to have that to be any sort of artist. You can study and learn and whatever, but if you really want to be good you have to have that passion.

AL: How did you discover that you had that passion?

LC: I never did. I came from a small town and no one in my town, no little boys, danced. I don't know why I ever wanted to do it. My parents certainly weren't involved in it. It was just something I wanted to do. I often wonder about that, like where did that come from in southern Illinois? It was sort of Jungian. It was there planted generations ago.

Take Twyla Tharp. I went to New York and we went to ABT and New York City Ballet; so we're sitting there at intermission, and I ask her "What do you like to do? What do you do for fun?" She says "Work." That's all she does. She's here at 8:30 in the morning reviewing videotapes from last week. She goes in there and works on choreography and phrasing and stuff on her own until noon when the dancers come in. She works from noon to 5:30 with no break. All the dancers get their hour lunch break, but she just shovels some food down here and there. Then she goes into the room in the back with her assistant, does the schedule and everything else, and continues working until about 8:00 at night and then goes home and reviews more videotapes. That's what she does for entertainment. She has a passion and a focus like nobody else, which is one of the reasons why I believe she is one of the best choreographers working in the world today. That's what it takes, that kind of focus.

AL: How rigorous is the physical training regimen for dance that you personally recommend for members of your company?

LC: Everybody takes class in the morning. They do that from 10:00 to 11:30. Then, they have like a fifteen-minute break, and then they start working. Some days it's more rigorous than others. Last week, they were in there working all day, nonstop, very tiring. There'll be days when the choreographer is doing something simpler with a couple of people here, a couple of people there, and then the rest of the day is the easy schedule. Last week, it was five and one-half, six hours solid.

AL: How many days a week?

LC: Five days a week. When we're on the road, it's up to ten days without a day off.

AL: And do you use nutritionists, massage therapists?

LC: We have chiropractors, massage therapists if you get a crick in your neck. You need to take care of it. It's like maintaining a car or something. You can't just let it go.

AL: Is there a specific diet as well?

LC: You have to eat healthy. You can't live on junk or your body won't function. Some dancers are real good about eating really well. But then, you get guys who go out and eat McDonald's every day and milkshakes and cheeseburgers and come in and take class. Most people can't get away with that. You need complex carbos to sustain you through the day, so your blood sugar level stays and you have a constant, even flow of energy so you don't get those highs and lows. I used to eat Fannie May peanut clusters and Coca-Cola and get these incredible highs and then have to come in and take a nap.

AL: One talks about a Chicago school of literature, of theater. Is there a Chicago voice in the dance scene?

LC: There's a Midwestern work ethic that goes on here. There's a little less jaded behavior among the dancers, a more down-to-earth willingness to just work and not be concerned about union rules. They're just dancing for the right reasons. Some people call us a jazz company, but I don't. I think in the dance world, when you say jazz, people think of *Solid Gold* and splayed hands. The jazz we work on comes from improvisational roots and alienation, all the kinds of things that jazz music comes from, a much more sophisticated approach. And that's what most people associate with jazz.

We were in Frankfurt, and this one company out there was doing the most bizarre things—I don't know if you call it avant-garde or what you call it. To me, it's crap. Really. It's like making a joke that as long as it's different, it's good. Well, I don't buy into that. I like physicality, movement, the quality of movement, the control of it, being able to do the tricks, the turning, the jumping with ballistics and agility and using good music and creating the kind of environment to present on stage to an audience. I am not into solving human condition problems and making social statements through pretentious acting stuff. I've seen ballets where they're wandering around and they're shaking their hand and they're looking at the floor, and I'm like, "What is that? What does it mean? What is all that?" Nobody knows what they're doing.

AL: That's your Midwestern mentality.

LC: I'm not saying you can't do something serious and you can't be an abstract artist, but I think there's a lot of pretentious silliness that goes on that people try to sell as art.

AL: Have you found yourself at any disadvantage by being in Chicago?

LC: New York is the center; it's the mecca where everybody goes. Most companies in Chicago do not provide a living, so you dance three days a week and then you go wait tables.

AL: Your company's the exception.

LC: Absolutely. You can't do this and expect the company to grow if you dance eight hours a day and then you go wait tables two hours a night and then come in exhausted in the morning. We were lucky to get living wages for the dancers.

AL: How do you find them?

LC: I have formal auditions in New York three times a year. I put ads in the trade papers, *Backstage* and *Variety*. You see all these dancers, and then dancers come to the studio to take class. They'll say, "I'd like you to see me," so you look at them in a ballet class or a jazz class. If they look like they have the right combination and technique and whatever, then we give them a formal audition. But the best way and the way we started was that all of the dancers came through the school. Everyone who was in the company had studied with me.

AL: So, let's say I'm fifteen or sixteen years old, I've taken some classes, I've been in my high school dance show, I decide I want to make a career out of it. What do I do?

LC: You want to do musicals?

AL: No, I want to be a serious dancer. I want to work for you.

LC: Get somewhere where your training is good, and study hard, and get with good teachers and good mentors, and make sure you're trained properly.

AL: How do I know who a good teacher is?

LC: Do your homework. Look at the dancers they've turned out. A big school isn't necessarily the earmark of a good teacher.

AL: If someone is auditioning for you, what do they need to prepare?

LC: You give them material to see how they handle it and check out their technique and see how they do your material. The individual company has certain styles and ways of giving their audition. If you've been studying a Graham technique, go off and audition for Martha Graham. If you've just studied Graham and you come to audition for Hubbard Street, it's a waste of your time. It's like studying French and going off to China, a different language.

AL: How long does it take you to know in an audition if someone has what you're looking for?

LC: You can tell right off the bat if they have the potential. What you can't tell is how they'll develop, because you don't know if they have the passion, you don't know about their discipline, you don't know about their state of mind. Do they let all kinds of garbage get in the way of their progress? I've had dancers that I thought were going to be sensational who just don't work out, and then I've had dancers who seemed mediocre, but through sheer determination, they became very successful company members.

There's a big difference between people who are well trained in their technique and people who move naturally. You need both. If I think you have the potential, I'll have you spend a week here, watch you with the material, see how you develop over the period of a week. You can tell a lot from a week, but in a one- or two-hour audition, I won't hire people like that. You may be having the worst day of your life. I don't know that. I don't know what kind of day you're having.

Nana Shineflug on Becoming a Successful Human Being in the Dance World

Nana Shineflug is one of the pioneers of the Chicago dance scene. A dancer, a choreographer, a bodybuilder, and something of a mystic, she has managed to keep the Chicago Moving Company afloat for nearly twenty-five years.

Location: Hamlin Park Fieldhouse, 3035 N. Hoyne

AL: What drives you to choreograph?

NS: I wasn't originally driven to be a choreographer. I'm a dancer; I love dancing. I just *am* a dancer. I don't know what that means. It's just that I need to do it, and I've recognized that need all my life. When I was real little, I signed up for dance class, came home, and gave my father the bill and told him, "Here, pay this." Dance is the one place where I've been able to figure out who I was.

AL: So the passion for dance isn't the same as the passion for choreography.

NS: No, I don't think it's ever been. I'm a good choreographer, but I'm not a great one, and it's okay with me. I'm not a great dancer, but I love to dance. Choreography doesn't consume me all day, every day, all year long, year after year.

AL: But it does have an obsessive quality.

NS: I'm a trained mathematician, and so I have this thinking mind that likes to work with patterns and things like that. Always before if I created a piece from my thinking mind, I didn't like it, and if I created a piece out of my intuition, it was so scary. I was never able to put the two together.

AL: How can you separate the mathematical part from the intuitive part?

NS: Because when I'm thinking mathematically, I sit down with a piece of paper and write the dance before I ever start doing it, making it all up before I do it. And intuitively, I get ideas. When you choreograph intuitively, it's like looking into a window. You start to see it before you. You don't think about it; you just see it and you know what to do. It's another way of knowing, because before you say it, you don't know it. It forms itself somewhere else like in a big cloud and all of a sudden it starts pushing at you, but it isn't anything that you cogitate about. It's like being a channel for something.

AL: What do you try to achieve while creating a dance? Is it to educate or to comment on something or just to express?

NS: I always wanted to express spiritual things, because dance is where I live with my spirit. And the first piece I did that I liked was called "White River Forest." And it was a piece that I wanted to do, because that was the place where I figured out that I didn't have to kill myself. And I wanted to do a piece to say thanks to the forest. I didn't really know how I was going to do it, but that was what it was going to be about.

AL: That's when you realized your dance was a step toward self-knowledge?

NS: Dancing is the place where I know I am myself and where I explore my life, and so I learn from every piece about who I am and what I feel and what I'm concerned with. It's like any other form of meditation. You do it over and over and over again in the process of rehearsing it and performing it, and it changes you. It alters you. It's like those people who say, "Stand in the shower every day and say 'I'm healthy. I am healthy. I am healthy.'" And eventually you become healthy, because it changes your life.

Since I'm growing older, I'm very interested in dying well. I've watched a lot of people die into the darkness and I really don't want to do that. I would really like to go into the light, and I think part of that is really coping with everything that happens in the process of your life. I think it's an essential part of your living to understand how you're going to die, and I understand that there are people who never even think about it. Maybe if they see it in a performance and it's not so scary, they'll be able to cope with it.

AL: Is it a very cathartic process to see what you've envisioned enacted on stage?

NS: It's the process of doing it. Once you see it at the end, what you want to do is change it. You see the places that you failed. It's always full of flaws. It doesn't always work.

AL: How do you know if something's not working?

NS: It can happen because the dynamics of it aren't quite right. It can be the wrong image. It can be the wrong step, the wrong costume, the wrong person, the wrong form. It can be lots of different things.

AL: Is that something that's immediately recognizable?

NS: You can feel it in your energy field. You stop responding aesthetically to what's going on. I used to be able to tell what was wrong, but I didn't know why it was wrong. I think when you're in your whole self, there's a whole self that knows. It's the same place that you choreograph from when you're doing intuitive choreographing, and that self can tell you a lot if you listen to it.

AL: Can you be a very guarded, defensive person and still be an effective, expressive dancer?

NS: It depends on the form you're dancing in. If you're interested in athletic dancing, where skill is the primary asset of that performance, and that's a valid thing to do for a lot of people, you can be a terrific dancer and still be closed off, guarded, and totally screwed up. And there are also people who, in their ordinary life, cannot connect to what I call the God force, but when they get involved in their art form, they are completely connected to the God force, so they have kind of a split personality. They're connected on channel one, and on all the other channels they're not connected. Then there are other people who are connected on all channels and those are the extraordinary dancers.

AL: How can you recognize someone who is connected on all channels?

NS: I don't hire anybody I don't know. I do some auditioning, but I won't dance with people unless I know them. In five minutes you can find whether someone's heart is open or whether it's not. If people ever treat anybody like they don't matter, I won't deal with that person. I used to try to take people that were quite far away and help them grow spiritually, but I don't want to do that anymore. I don't want to mess around with people who don't have love in their hearts, who are so screwed up and neurotic that they have to be a prima donna. I don't want to have to deal with that.

AL: One of the things Lou Conte told me was that the trouble with being a dancer is that you have to deal with a world that's rejecting you 95 percent of the time, that every time you go to dance class you do something wrong, and to survive, you have to cope with that. Do you accept that?

NS: There is an old-line attitude that you have to be tough and survive rejection and people telling you you're a shithead. I think there's a whole other way of being in the world. If you're in the world to get ahead, if you're in the world to make money and be a commercial success in a big, huge way, then maybe you have to do that. But I think there are other ways of being in the dance world when you go to class and it's not about rejection—it's about loving.

AL: But at the same time, what you're doing requires a lot of rigor, a lot of discipline.

NS: Devotion, absolutely. If you have devotion then you have discipline and you have rigor. You don't have to look at the world from a punitive frame of mind, but if you say that life is not worth living without devotion, then all of that falls into place, but from another place, and that's from love. I think each person in their lifetime is given something that they're supposed to learn. Each of us is supposed to take a look at all of the things we've learned and done and put them all together in a really unique way that no one has done before and contribute that thing to the rest of us.

AL: So should anyone go into this art with the goal that this is how they're going to make their money in their career?

NS: I happen to come from the school of living that what you should do as a human being is try to figure out who you are, what it is you've been gifted with. What is it that makes you excited? What is it that makes you want to wake up in the morning? What is the path that you can perceive that can make you grow in your lifetime? And then, whatever it is that you figure out you are, you become devotional to that thing.

You can't approach it from making the decision to do or not do something. It's not a process of striving to do anything. It's about staying alert and devotional and exploring everything and trying to develop whatever the possibilities are, and that's a much more happy way of going about it, because there's not this whole thing of failure.

In the old days, you were born and your mother and father said, "You're going to be this person." And in the process of your life, as an actor would on stage, you created this person to the point where you can no longer find out who you are because you're so far away from your true identity and your authentic self and you can't access yourself anymore. I think that's a very dangerous place to be, where you're no longer connected to yourself or anybody else.

FOUR

Media of the Twentieth Century: Film, TV, and Radio

Part I: Tinseltown Midwest

For a city that played a major role in the birth of American cinema, there sure wasn't a hell of a lot going on here in terms of movie making for decades. But that's all changed over the past twenty years or so. Once again Chicago has become an outpost for both major studio productions as well as a burgeoning independent film movement, recalling the days of nearly a century ago when this town was the Hollywood of the Midwest, even before there was a Hollywood of anywhere.

For a city as loud-mouthed as ours, it may be surprising to note that Chicago was a major hub for silent film production. Most historically noteworthy was the legendary Essanay Studios, founded by film exhibitor George K. Spoor and G. M. Anderson, a famed actor, who appeared in the 1903 *Great Train Robbery*, as well as in the then-popular Bronco Billy cowboy series. Their initials gave the company its name, and the terra cotta facade may still be seen at Essanay's original location at 1333 W. Argyle. Interesting as a sidepoint for cocktail conversation is the fact that Spoor and Anderson hired two techies to work for Essanay by the name of Donald Bell and Albert Howell, who left the operation in 1907 to start the film equipment manufacturing company Bell and Howell. Essanay's first Chicago production, *An Awful Skate, or The Hobo on Rollers* featured mustachioed, gangly actor Ben Turpin rolling down Wells

Street in a simplistic slapstick farce, which basically consisted of Turpin bumping into people. Essanay produced countless melodramas (some written by Ring Lardner) and cowboys-and-Indians flicks, many of which were filmed in Rogers Park. Around the same time, Carl Laemmle, who had owned a clothing company in Oshkosh, Wisconsin, came here to open a nickelodeon on Milwaukee and Ashland but later headed west to start Universal Pictures.

The Chicago silent film era reached its apex in 1915 when Charlie Chaplin was wooed to make films with a cushy $1,250-a-week salary. In truth, he only made one, *His New Job*, which was released in February of that year and featured then-unknown Chicago film actress Gloria Swanson in a walk-on role as a stenographer. Chaplin, according to biographer David Robinson, purchased his trademark tramp costume in a shop on State Street. Local legend has it that Graceland Cemetery served as a motion picture backlot for Essanay's films and that Chaplin used to get wasted at the Green Mill with fellow famed silent stars Douglas Fairbanks and Mary Pickford.

Regrettably, a year later, in 1916, Chaplin cruised out of town and, for the most part, the rest of Chicago's silent film industry closed up shop, following him to California. During the early years of motion pictures, Chicago was notable for the role it played in the African-American film industry. Black pioneer Oscar Micheaux's films were shown on the South Side at silent movie houses like the Garfield on 51st and Michigan, sandwiched in-between vaudeville acts. Beyond that, any book on the Chicago film industry when sound films rolled around would have to be a very thin one. If you can find any major film produced or filmed in Chicago between the twenties and the early sixties that wasn't an industrial or stag film, please bring it to my attention. Word on the street during the fifties and sixties was that hizzoner Mayor Richard J. Daley despised the idea of having films produced in this city, believing that somehow it would cheapen our image. Maybe so, but whatever the reason, for eons, Chicago was a cinematic ghost town. And the fact that *Mickey One* was filmed here doesn't change that fact all that much.

The seventies and the mayoral regimes of Michael "Snow Job" Bilandic and Jane "Bread and Circuses" Byrne slowly awakened the sleeping cinematic giant. The beginnings of what would become the Chicago cinema boom were inauspicious with films like *Silver Streak* (Pryor and Wilder before the chicken suits), *Looking for Mr. Goodbar* (sexual violence and singles bars), and *Damien: Omen II* (the one where somebody's head *doesn't* explode) representing Hollywood's increasing interest in Chicago. But by the seventies and early eighties, it was difficult to go down a street in this town without finding a Hollywood film crew in the parks, in the alleys, or in the sewers.

For children of the seventies, it became a kind of game to walk around town and find where the latest flick was being filmed. We went downtown and peered under Wacker Drive to try and get a glimpse of Dan Aykroyd and John Belushi filming *The Blues Brothers*. We watched as Steve McQueen's car crashed through the Marina City parking lot in *The Hunter*. We waited until the wee hours of morning in the Budlong Woods area to see James Caan and Tuesday Weld walk down Catalpa and witness the facade of a house exploding in Michael Mann's *Thief*. It was at this time that I also realized that the girl I had a crush on from K.I.N.S. Hebrew School was dating somebody else and the necklace I had given her for her bat mitzvah had not succeeded in wooing her.

By the time high school rolled around for me, everyone knew someone who had a bit part in some movie. My brother's friend purchased the gold Porsche that fell in the lake in *Risky Business*. Our authoritarian drama teacher told us that John Cusack would be unable to perform his assigned duties in our school play because he'd secured a plum part in *Class*. And anyone who lived on the North Shore was bound to wind up with a cameo role in *16 Candles* or some other John Hughes film with clean-cut kids wreaking havoc in the city and its suburbs. Whenever there was a high school party north of Touhy, there was always a rumor that Molly Ringwald would show up or that Rob Lowe was in another room getting laid. And who could forget running into a young Charlie Sheen, in town shooting *Lucas*, at Evanston's Lighthouse Beach boasting about the drinking capacity of his buddy Adam Rich from seventies TV classic *Eight Is Enough*.

From that time on, Chicago has survived as a sort of second-string film center, usually showing up in a dozen or so major flicks every year and helping the local film folks to have something approaching steady employment. It's been rather shaky of late, and lots of highly talented crew members have very few scraps of work to pick up throughout the year. But homegrown directors like Andrew Davis and Chris Columbus and their ilk have assured that this city will continue to be at the forefront of non-L.A.-based films. Brian DePalma's *The Untouchables* and Davis's *The Fugitive* are the best of the filmed-in-Chicago projects, although we still get our share of questionable endeavors like *I Love Trouble*, *Little Big League*, and whatever gigantic blockbuster film John Hughes happens to be making this week.

But what's more exciting than the stray dozen or so films that Hollywood deigns to film here is the emergence of Chicago as a prominent center for independent made-in-Chicago films featuring largely local talent. As I write this, while Hollywood continues to churn out the same old detritus, the

American independent cinema is experiencing something of a renaissance. The indie scene in Chicago had long been the playground for experimental 8-millimeter films that would only be seen in local cinema showcases at places like Chicago Filmmakers or once a week on PBS's *Image Union.* For years, folks like Tom Palazzolo and Jim Sikora would have their own cult followings, selling their pictures through indie distribution mags like *Film Threat,* but remaining in national obscurity. Now, however, as low-budget indie films (like Richard Linklater's *Slacker,* Hal Hartley's *Trust* and *Amateur,* and Steven Soderbergh's *Sex, Lies, and Videotape*) have captured the national wine-and-cheese crowd's imagination and major festival awards, Chicago, too, has entered the fold.

After a long stint as a midnight feature at the Music Box, John McNaughton and Steve Jones's gritty, documentary-style *Henry: Portrait of a Serial Killer* gave the pair the credibility to work from Chicago on Hollywood features like Eric Bogosian's *Sex, Drugs, Rock & Roll* and *Mad Dog and Glory.* South Side filmmaker Darryl Roberts scored big with the independent hit *How U Like Me Now* and continues to work here. The technically suspect but ultrahip lesbian romantic comedy *Go Fish* proved a boon to the career of director Rose Troche. Columbia College–bred director George Tillman and producers Robert Teitel and Jason Novak secured a million-dollar deal with Hollywood-based Savoy Pictures for their urban trilogy *Scenes for the Soul.* Joe Chappelle's *Thieves' Quartet* gave the local director a Hollywood calling card, allowing him to work on such pictures as *Halloween VI* (really). And, of course, *Hoop Dreams,* one of the most unlikely cinematic success stories of the decade, finally gave a healthy dose of respect to long-standing but still highly unknown Kartemquin Films and the film's team, Peter Gilbert, Steve James, and Frederick Marx. Presently, Chicago is awash in indie film projects, as directors like John Covert, Mick Napier of the Annoyance Theatre, Robert Munic, Phil Koch, Jim Sikora, and a host of others ready their projects to follow in the footsteps of their worthy predecessors.

The film community in Chicago is probably the least competitive and most hospitable group of artists in the city, probably because it's, in many ways, the newest and the smallest. Telling most anyone in the community that you have an idea for a film will get you not only oodles of support but also a list of names of people who might want to work on your crew. The city is filled with camera operators, directors, editors, and any number of other talented folks who've been working their asses off on industrials and commercials and are longing to break into something artistic. Once you know they're out there, they're not all that hard to find.

Part 2: Radio and TV in Chicago, or How to Be a Chewing Gum Producer

Soap operas started here. You can't find them here anymore, but sixty to seventy years ago on radio you could. Chicago pioneered the format of the radio serial at NBC Studios, where fifteen-minute melodramas like *Bachelor's Children*, *Houseboat Hannah*, *Working Wife*, *Scattergood Baines*, and *Stepmother* were performed in front of live audiences and broadcast nationally. Chicago scriptwriter Irna Phillips created *The Guiding Light* here and wrote for the radio and TV versions of it for decades. Radio comedies were also created here, including the infamous *Amos 'n' Andy*, in which white comedians Freeman Gosden and Charles Correll, broadcasting from the Edgewater Beach Hotel starting in 1928, trafficked in racial stereotypes, doing their patented blackface comedy routine as the proprietors of the Fresh Air Taxi Company. The rural cowpoke comedy of *Lum 'n' Abner* and the by-now-legendary cluttered closet of Fibber McGee and Molly were also Chicago NBC creations. Round about the forties, though, radio theater shows began to skip town for New York, and, over the years, aside from news and music broadcasts, nothing major originated out of here, unless you want to count Dick Orkin's *Chickenman* serial, Don McNeill's *Breakfast Club* in the fifties, the *National Barn Dance* show, Steve Hart's WBEZ children's theater programs like *Audio Jam*, WFMT's live broadcasts of Chicago theater companies in *Chicago Radio Theatres on the Air*, Yuri Rasovsky's 1970s radio experiments, or Tony Green's black radio soap operas *Grand Boulevard* and *East 47th Street* (still running on WBEE in Chicago). Probably the most successful, long-running radio drama out of Chicago is *Unshackled*, featuring "true stories" of Christian conversion, performed by Chicago actors on WMBI locally and on hundreds of stations worldwide. Seeing the weekly Saturday live performances complete with sound effects at the Pacific Garden Mission on South State Street is probably the only way to still get a glimpse of the way shows used to be made here in the golden age of radio.

Television has hardly been an industry in Chicago, let alone an art form. No offense to the hosts and crews of such outstanding offerings as *Kukla, Fran, and Ollie* and *Studs' Place*. No offense to Milton Berle, who experimented with the TV format by doing a closed circuit broadcast here in 1929. No offense even to the individuals who began launching national TV careers from here like Lincoln Park Zoo's Marlin Perkins, who left *Zoo Parade* to do *Wild Kingdom*, or Dave Garroway, who followed his locally based *Garroway at Large* with the *Today* show. Every once in a while, a creative show gets based here, as was the case with *The Untouchables* or the short-lived *Jack and Mike*. Other network shows that got filmed here (why did most of them involve some dumb cop plot and all of them only last a season or two?) include the Robin Givens vehicle *Angel Street*, and *Chicago Story*, *Crime Story*, *Lady Blue*, and *Sable*. Most of what little we have here amount to late-night community affairs broadcasts (read: some guy sitting in a chair talking about Chicago's sports teams or neighborhood beat policing to an audience of about four) or talk shows. We have lots of them. From *Jerry Springer* to *Jenny Jones* to (okay, I guess I can get away with only mentioning her name once in this book) *Oprah*, we seem to have cornered the Midwest market on cheap-to-produce sleaze entertainment. Too bad Phil Donahue left town in the eighties and Morton Downey in the nineties, otherwise we could be the Big Mouth Capital of the Western Hemisphere.

Crap aside, however, TV does offer certain opportunities for the artist if you're willing to nose out the few existing outposts of decidedly unlucrative but incorrigibly creative video production available amid the nether regions of incessantly beleaguered television (ye Gods), local access cable, and even network TV. You'll have a head start if you like Sunday mornings or late, late, late nights, or if you want to write scripts for the Jewish children's TV show *The Magic Door*. If visibility is your main goal, however, you stand a better chance of success if you like producing sports shows. Chicago Bears pregame show, anybody?

Ten Films That No Human Should Be Allowed to View (except that they were either made by a Chicago filmmaker or feature cool parts of Chicago)

1. *Continental Divide*
2. *Doctor Detroit*
3. *Ferris Bueller's Day Off*
4. *Grandview USA*
5. *The Hudsucker Proxy*
6. *The Hunter*
7. *Lucas*
8. *I Love Trouble*
9. *The Package*
10. *Things Change*

(Author's query: why did I actually see these films?)

Getting Schooled

Center for New Television, 1440 N. Dayton, Chicago, IL 60622
(312) 951-6868
The most reasonable place in town at which to learn the basics of video production, editing, and CD-ROM development. Two- to three-week classes usually run in the $100–$200 range. Members also get access to the center's equipment as well as its archive of tapes of Chicago video artists.

Chicago Access Corporation, 322 S. Green, Chicago, IL 60607-3502
(312) 738-1400
Want to do a show on local access cable, one of those low-budget shows on Channels 19, 21, or 36 like *Drag Racing Weekly*, *Dyke TV*, or *Kiss My TV Show*? First you've got to take a class here. Basic small-group video production courses as well as editing workshops are required before you will be allowed to ready yourself for the small-time broadcast world. Most classes require about three meeting sessions and cost $150.

Chicago Filmmakers, 1543 W. Division, Chicago, IL 60622
(312) 384-5533
Founded in 1973 as the Filmgroup at N.A.M.E. Gallery by students of the School of the Art Institute, this center has long been a locale for premieres of local independent films as well as a training center for aspiring film and video artists. Classes offered in film production and screenwriting. Ten weeks of six-hour sessions in film production run in the neighborhood of $500.

Community Film Workshop, 1130 S. Wabash, Suite 302, Chicago, IL 60605 (312) 427-1245
This longtime training center for basics of filmmaking can get a bit pricey at times, but few others can compare with the intensive, rigorous training it gives in all aspects of film. An eleven-hour-a-week, nine-week introductory film production course resulting in the production of a short color film costs $1,350. A twelve-week, way-intensive film workshop meeting approximately thirty-five hours per week runs $3,500.

Major graduate and undergraduate institutions with highly reputed programs in the field

Columbia College, 600 S. Michigan, Chicago, IL 60605
(312) 663-1600

Northwestern University, 1905 Sheridan Rd., Evanston, IL 60302
(847) 491-7315

School of the Art Institute, 280 S. Columbus, Chicago, IL 60603
(312) 443-3733

Warning Signs

It's sad but true that the film industry here, as in L.A., is composed of equal parts of brilliant, hardworking artists and shameless bullshit artists. For every legitimate film producer here, there's another dreamer, goofball, or thief who promises far more than he or she can ever deliver. The unemployment lines are full of hopeless dorks who will tell you, even as they're being carted away by the authorities, that the next $100,000 is just around the corner. There's no good way to tell a con artist from an honest, by-the-books novice looking for his or her first break working on a feature. But speaking as a screenwriter who's been scammed, lied to, misled, and basically screwed, I can tell you with authority that when you're looking for a crew to film your project, a producer to back you, or a director to shoot your script, whenever you hear any of these ten phrases, get your track shoes and run. Do not stop. Get the hell out and do not turn back.

Ten Statements That Should Tip You Off to a Con Artist

1. "Well, right now we have $200,000, but I'm waiting for the other $100,000 to come into place."
2. "I just wanted to take your script home, make some changes, and show it to some people."
3. "Now, what kind of money do you personally have that you're willing to funnel into the project?"
4. "Can we work a car chase into the script somehow?"
5. "I wanted to give you a cassette of the theme song I wrote for your movie."
6. "Here, sign this."
7. "I think we need a big star attached to this project if we want to sell it. Do you know Heather Locklear?"
8. "Would you mind picking me up for our meeting? My car's in the shop."
9. "I'm flying down to South America to meet with some potential investors."
10. "I've been waiting for twenty-five years for a project like this to come along. This is going to turn my entire life around."

Publications and Other Resources

Chicago Film Office, 1 N. LaSalle, Suite 2165, Chicago, IL 60602
(312) 744-6415
Basically the place you need to go if you want to block off a street or blow up a building. Reputedly very cooperative, the office acts as a liaison between film production companies and city departments, like police, fire, and transportation. Also works diligently to attract major film productions to the Chicago area.

Community TV Network, 2035 W. Wabansia, Chicago, IL 60647
(312) 278-8500
Provides hands-on training for high school students in producing *Hardcover*, a local-access cable show dealing with typical teen issues: gangs, self-esteem, drugs, and more. The Network's Monday meetings are open to all interested students.

Illinois Film Office, 100 W. Randolph, Chicago, IL 60601
(312) 814-3600
You can't really argue with a resource that's free. Offers help in finding locations and a crew for your film. Also publishes a vital annual directory of film business in Chicago.

Illinois Film Office Casting Hotline, (312) 427-FILM
Provides information about casting for motion pictures in Chicago.

Illinois Film Office Production Hotline, (312) 427-WORK
Provides information about film crew jobs in and around Chicago.

Independent Feature Project Midwest, 116 W. Illinois, Chicago,
IL 60610 (312) 467-4437
Networking organization for people interested in getting feature film projects together.

Screen **Magazine**, 720 N. Wabash, Chicago, IL 60611 (312) 664-5236
Rather strident and gossipy trade magazine generally focusing on the commercial and industrial film and video world of Chicago. But for some reason, publisher Ruth Ratny is said to wield influence in this town, and industry folks have been known to try desperately to get on her good side. Go figger.

Women in Film: Chicago, 116 W. Illinois, Suite 2E, Chicago, IL 60610
(312) 467-0500
Networking organization for women in the business which hosts readings, screenings, and meet-and-greets.

Where You Can Get Your Work Seen, Heard, or Screened

Chicago Latino Cinema, c/o Columbia College, 600 S. Michigan, Chicago, IL 60605 (312) 431-1330
Host of the annual Chicago Latino Film Festival, which focuses on Latino film-makers, some of whom are locally based. In professionalism and quality, this festival is every bit the equal of the Chicago International Film Festival.

Cinema Chicago, 415 N. Dearborn, Chicago, IL 60610 (312) 644-3400
This quirky organization headed for years by Michael Kutza has hosted Chicago's fall international film festival for decades and has recently begun to organize screenings of classic films at Navy Pier. The festival, which still has yet to achieve much of a serious international reputation, has never been particularly kind to local filmmakers, though occasionally one or two find their way into the mix.

Copernicus Foundation, 5216 W. Lawrence, Chicago, IL 60630 (312) 777-8898
You'll have to work out your own deal to rent out this place for your film screening, and it won't be cheap. But this theater, formerly the Gateway Theater, is probably the coolest and hugest screening facility in town. Imagine a slightly dingier combination of the Music Box Theatre and Radio City Music Hall, complete with a balcony, pillars, and the phony night sky above.

Facets Multimedia, 1517 W. Fullerton, Chicago, IL 60614 (312) 281-9075
The largest video rental facility in Chicago and one of the city's major screening centers for classic and overlooked work, Facets also has been known to occasionally (but not often) screen the work of local filmmakers, most notably Robert Munic's *Pros and Cons of Breathing*. Also offers film study courses. It would be nice if they showed a few more local projects rather than hauling out F. W. Murnau's *Nosferatu* all the time. Just a thought.

Film Center of the Art Institute, 280 S. Columbus Drive, Chicago, IL 60603 (312) 443-3735
Attached to the School of the Art Institute, the center hosts screenings of and lectures on classic or foreign films. Once in a while, a local filmmaker crops up in the screenings as well.

Image Union, c/o WTTW, Channel 11, 5400 N. St. Louis, Chicago, IL 60625 (312) 583-5000
One of the only places in Chicago where video filmmakers can get their work screened on normal TV, this cornucopia of animation and short subjects is open to whoever feels like sending in his or her tape and fulfilling WTTW's rigorous aesthetic criteria.

WBEZ, 91.5 FM, 105 W. Adams, Chicago, IL 60603 (312) 460-9150
It's a long shot, but this eclectic local branch of National Public Radio has been known to air locally produced programs with some creativity behind them (most notably Ira Glass's *The Wild Room*) when they're not airing *Car Talk* or *All Things Considered.*

Women in the Director's Chair, 3445 N. Sheffield, Chicago, IL 60657 (312) 281-4988
Founded in 1980. Hosts an annual festival and screenings of films dealing with women's issues or by female directors.

The Brokered World of TV and Radio

The airwaves supposedly belong to the public, but since we've leased them to corporate giants who are more concerned with selling hemorrhoid creams and beer than putting on quality artistic projects, getting your work seen or heard might be something of a problem. The best luck you'll have in attracting anybody's attention is by offering to do something in the wee hours of the night, like at 4:00 A.M. on a Sunday, when all you can find on your dial are low hissing noises, reruns of old Sox games, fishing shows, and Jesus Gonna Gitcha broadcasts. The other thing you can try to do, if money's no particular object, is screw the station managers of the local media outlets and just go straight to the source: buy your own radio or television time, find your own advertisers if you must, and do it yourself. A handful of radio and TV stations in town will just sell you the time you need. Among these are:

WCBR-FM 92.7, 120 W. University, Arlington Heights, IL 60004 (847) 255-5800

WCIU-TV, Channel 26, 26 N. Halsted, Chicago, IL 60661 (312) 705-2600

WPWR-TV, Channel 50, 2151 N. Elston, Chicago, IL 60614 (312) 276-5050

WVVX-FM 103.1, 210 Skokie Valley, Highland Park, IL 60035 (847) 831-5250

Ten Companies Helping to Put Chicago on the Video and Film Maps

Blackball Films, (312) 235-9341
Founded in 1993, this Wicker Park–based company has produced videos for the likes of Soul Asylum, Reverend Horton Heat, Babes in Toyland, and The Jayhawks.

Chi-Boy Productions
A feature film production company too cool to have a phone number and headed up by Robert Munic. Chi-Boy brought Munic's *Pros and Cons of Breathing* to the silver screen.

Covert Creative Group, (708) 578-4492
A production company headed up by John Covert, this company has won unprecedented raves from the underground zine *Film Threat* for the feature films *The Blind Lead* and *Waiting for the Man*. Covert Creative has also coproduced Annoyance Theatre's first foray into film, *Fatty Drives the Bus*.

H-Gun, (312) 804-0134
Located in the Bathhouse District on the city's Near South Side, this outfit has become one of the country's hottest music video production companies, producing eye-popping work for hard-edged acts like Nine Inch Nails, Revolting Cocks, Ministry, Soundgarden, Pigface, Living Colour, and De La Soul.

Kartemquin Films, (312) 472-4366
For more than twenty-five years, this operation has been one of the country's foremost producers of documentary films. Received international acclaim for *Hoop Dreams*.

Koch-Marschall Productions, (312) 463-4010
This small film production company, which has worked on short films starring the likes of Joe Mantegna, has just begun to resurface with feature film projects after it released the well-received *Pink Nights* starring Kevin Anderson back in the eighties.

McNaughton-Jones Motion Pictures, (312) 384-6306
Became one of the true success stories of Chicago filmmaking when Steve Jones and John McNaughton, after scoring with *Henry: Portrait of a Serial Killer*, went on to make *The Borrower*, *Mad Dog and Glory*, and *Sex, Drugs, Rock & Roll*.

Menagerie Films, (312) 871-3944

Hot young film company of Columbia College grads George Tillman, director, and Robert Teitel and Jason Novak, producers. Hit it big the first time out with *Scenes for the Soul*, which was picked up by Hollywood-based Savoy Pictures for a cool million.

Montrose Pictures, (312) 275-8343

Feature film production company headed up by Mather High School grads Steve Diller and Michael Caplan. Years of working in the video and industrial world led to the production of their first dramatic feature *Peoria Babylon*, starring Ann Cusack and Obie Award-winner David Drake.

Runandgun! (312) 225-1211

Video and 3D-animation production company located in the Bathhouse District. Has produced the interactive 3-D video game *Dueling Firemen*, starring noted underground stars like The Jesus Lizard's David Yow, producer-musician Steve Albini, and the Church of the Subgenius's Reverend Ivan Stang.

You'll Need

Bagels

How anyone can expect to approach and impress a producer without a generous bagel brunch is beyond me. Buy them at *New York Bagels and Bialy, 4714 W. Touhy, Lincolnwood, IL 60646 (847) 677-9388*, the undisputed 24-hour-a-day, 365-day-a-week champion of bagel society since its opening in 1962.

Cigar

There's nothing like a little cure for an oral fixation during a heavy day of negotiating, particularly if you're a producer. Unless you're gonna buy Cubans on the black market like Harvey Keitel in *Smoke*, I'd recommend Chicago stalwart *Iwan Ries & Company, 19 S. Wabash, Chicago, IL 60603 (312) 372-1306*.

Director's chair

Once you know how to cross your legs, speak into a bullhorn, and sit in one of these without tipping it or yourself over, you're halfway to being a successful director. Buy one at *Roosevelt Chair and Supply Company, 1717 W. Belmont, Chicago, IL 60657 (312) 248-3700*.

Editing and production facilities

They say that the film is made as much in the cutting room as behind the camera. The most highly reputed editing operations and post-production houses in Chicago include *Swell Pictures, 455 N. Cityfront, 18th Floor, Chicago, IL 60611 (312) 464-8000; Optimus, 161 E. Grand, Chicago, IL 60616 (312) 321-0880;* and *IPA, the Editing House, 1208 W. Webster, Chicago, IL 60614 (312) 871-6033.*

Film processing

For processing your 35-millimeter film, folks in the film biz in town swear by *Astro Video Services, 61 W. Erie, Chicago, IL 60610 (312) 280-5500.*

Lighting equipment

The first thing you're gonna need to make your movie look cool is a lighting designer. The second thing you're gonna need is some lights. Buying them is absurd. Rent them at *Designlab Chicago, 806 N. Peoria, Chicago, IL 60622 (312) 738-3305,* or *Grand Stage Lighting Company, 630 W. Lake, Chicago, IL 60661 (312) 332-5611.*

Locations

There's no bigger pain in the ass in the film biz I know than cruising around all day looking for just the right sleazy tavern for your shootout scene only to find out that the toothless grunt behind the corner already cut a deal with John Hughes and now he wants ten grand a day for his "authentic location." Luckily there are people you can pay to wade through this muck for you. Try the *Illinois Film Office, 100 W. Randolph, Chicago, IL 60601 (312) 814-3600.* They'll be able to recommend any number of folks, and if they can't come through for you, try *Ochi Location, 2247 W. Chicago, Chicago, IL 60622 (312) 235-2594.*

Motion picture camera

Yeah, you'll need one of these. If you're looking for a top-of-the-line 35-millimeter job, rent it at *Helix, 1205 W. Jackson, Chicago, IL 60607 (312) 421-8080,* or *Victor Duncan, 2650 W. Bradley, Chicago, IL 60618 (312) 267-1500.* If you're more interested in a gritty, low-budget feel, you can find a beat-up old job for thirty bucks at *Ambers, 4036 W. Armitage, Chicago, IL 60639 (312) 252-2205.*

Pirate costume

For all those swashbuckling scenes in your period adventure flick or for any other kind of costume that might come in handy, pop into *Broadway Costumes, 954 W. Washington, Chicago, IL 60602 (312) 829-6400,* or *Fantasy Headquarters, 4065 N. Milwaukee, Chicago, IL 60641 (312) 777-0222*

Police protection

Unless you're a risk-taking, guerrilla hit-and-run filmmaker, you're gonna need to hire a couple of cops to *a)* secure the streets for you and *b)* keep you from being harassed by other cops. Do it through the *Chicago Film Office, 1 N. LaSalle, Chicago, IL 60602 (312) 744-6415.*

Professional sports team cap

When was the last time you saw a successful filmmaker without a hip baseball cap or jersey—whether it was the White Sox cap prominently displayed in *Go Fish* or the Kansas City Chiefs hat worn proudly by Chicago filmmaker George Tillman during the making of Menagerie Films' *Scenes for the Soul?* Buy one outside Wrigley Field during the baseball season.

Scuba suit

I've yet to see an underwater sea adventure filmed in Lake Michigan, which is why you should be the first to give it a shot. Rent your wet suit and flippers from *Vern's Scuba Center, 3917 N. Ashland, Chicago, IL 60613 (312) 935 -0855.* You might consider bringing a scrub brush as well.

Sound effects

Unfortunately, once you get your film back from the lab, it ain't gonna sound like much. You're gonna have to add in all the cool background ambiance and nifty sea sounds later. There are a couple places in town that still do a pretty good job at it. Best known among these is *Zenith Audio Services, 32 W. Randolph, Chicago, IL 60601 (312) 444-1101.* They've done the sound for everything from hippopotami on *Wild Kingdom* to the train crash in *The Fugitive.*

Sunglasses

You don't want people to look you in the eyes and realize you're laying a con job on them during your power lunch, do you? Keep them eyes hidden with a pair of specs. Screw the designer kind; you'll look hipper in a pair from the dime store.

Sashimi

To seal the deal, you're going to have to host the dinner. If you're in the film biz, raw fish hasn't been out of fashion in ages. Buy a dozen tuna at *Isaacson and Stein Fish Market, 800 W. Fulton, Chicago, IL 60607 (312) 421-2444.*

Trailer

For the complete star treatment, make sure everyone has one of these to act as an office, a dressing room, or a place for aspiring stars to entertain aspiring groupies. Rent one or a jillion from *Chicago Trailer, 9600 S. 76th, Hickory Hills, IL 60457 (708) 598-5398,* or *Movies in Motion, 5685 W. Goodman, Chicago, IL 60630 (708) 673-6027.*

Trained dogs or other animals

What's a good movie without a scene featuring a hungry attack dog licking his lips after leaping atop a hapless police officer? Sufficiently Pavloved pooches and Lord only knows what else are available at *Animal Kingdom, 2980 N. Milwaukee, Chicago, IL 60618 (312) 227-4444.*

Interview

Fred Marx on How to Succeed in the Chicago Film Community

Part of the explosion of Chicago independent film projects of late, the Kartemquin Films movie *Hoop Dreams* is one of the city's great artistic success stories. Working on the most minuscule of budgets for more than seven years, filmmakers and film producers Fred Marx, Peter Gilbert, and Steve James turned what was once a PBS short film project into the most critically acclaimed film of 1994. And don't say anything about *Forrest Gump*, please. Yuck.

AL: Do you perceive with the success of projects like *Go Fish*, *Scenes for the Soul*, and *Hoop Dreams* and the rise of independent projects like *Waiting for the Man* and so forth that there is a burgeoning film community here, or is it just people making their own opportunities and working on their own separate projects?

FM: That's a question that's been debated through the ages, and a lot of the response you'll get from people on that issue depends on their particular psychological state at the moment. If they're feeling particularly alienated, they'll probably say no, and if they're feeling particularly connected and successful, they'll say yes, there is. I guess the answer to that is, in a sense, there's as much film community here as anyone wants to make or discover for themselves. If you are very, very intent on integrating yourself into the community, then you can do that. There are places like Chicago Filmmakers and the Community Film Workshop and places like that that are great, where you can get hands-on experience and meet other young filmmakers. And then there's lots of production companies in town, though very few like Kartemquin are actually doing cutting edge work to a large extent. But there are a number of them that are open to various levels of interactions and not in the sense of seminars and open screenings. You can integrate yourself into those places and make contacts. I think it really depends on how much gumption and energy you have.

AL: You've worked in New York and been wined and dined in L.A. What's the difference in how filmmakers work here?

FM: I think one of the really nice things about Chicago and its filmmaking people is that you'll get less of a competitive kind of edge in terms of people's personalities. They won't be feeling that they better not share information with you because you're going to one-up them in your next project. And that's a real difference. There is an extreme openness. I just got a call a half hour ago from a first-time filmmaker who was asking me how to make a documentary film. Now, obviously I don't want to spend a lot of time talking to this guy, because I could spend weeks talking to five hundred people on the same subject, but at any rate, I was willing to give him a few resources, a little information to get him started, and I think you'll find that from a lot of people. So there's more of an openness and a willingness to share information.

AL: Is that because filmmaking is a lot more sporadic here?

FM: I think it's the nature of Midwesterners and their character. They're a little more open, a little more willing to share. I suppose if there were suddenly a huge, billion dollar influx in cash and the industry started supplanting New York and L.A. and all kinds of other people arrived on the scene, then it would really change the nature of that openness and make it far more competitive.

AL: Do you perceive any boom in filmmaking here? It seems that, if you're looking for it, you can find hundreds of projects going on, but unlike New York or L.A., if you're not looking, you'd barely even know it existed.

FM: That's exactly right. It's a matter of research and your willingness to find what's there. If you do look for what's there, you'll find a lot, but if you don't, if you just wait for it to come to you, it will seem like there's not that much.

AL: It seems like there's a lot more crossover between documentarians and narrative filmmakers these days with the success of Michael Moore and Errol Morris. Is it not as necessary anymore to choose one field of film in which to specialize?

FM: It happens more in Europe, and it's frustrating that it doesn't happen more in the States, because you tend to get pigeonholed more in the industry. People tend to think you're a documentary filmmaker and that's it. But in Europe, they recognize that Wim Wenders can make twenty narrative films and never do a documentary, but who cares? We'll give him a documentary to do on a Japanese fashion designer and he'll do it right. I wish there was more of that acceptance here in the States. I think it's coming, though, and I think it's coming partly through Errol Morris and Michael Moore and people like that. Now, the lines that seemed so rigid distinguishing the two are dissolving. In some ways, I think that's a good thing, because we need to alert audiences who are watching documentary films as well as narrative films to the potential for manipulation and how it is that the material does get shaped.

AL: How important is technical training to becoming a filmmaker if you have a strong vision of what you want to see on the screen? Is it overrated? Do you need a whole lot of classes to learn? Or is it just a matter of surrounding yourself with people who have the know-how.

FM: It depends on what your goal is. If your goal is to become a producer or a director or a writer, then the technical issues are going to be less important to you. On the other hand, if you're interested in being a person with a craft—a gaffer, a key grip, a camera person—then it absolutely will behoove you to get enmeshed in the technical details.

First, you have to make that decision of what your long-term goal is. I think some people do not need school, an official sort of education environment, to learn and learn effectively. Other people do, for whatever reason. It doesn't have to be a purely character reason. It could be money. In some ways, you can look at schools and colleges as very cheap production companies that can facilitate the production of your film for the cost of tuition. If you can't produce a film in any other way, you can always think about enrolling in a program and getting access to a lot of equipment and producing cheaply that way.

In general, philosophically, I don't think that, if you're your own maker, technical things are that important. You can always find people that are trained technically and astute to fill those roles for you on production, but you can't always find people with the vision, who have the real idea in their head of what a film should be, how it should look, what it should sound like, and what it's gonna be about. And that's what's the most special and most important thing.

I think *Hoop Dreams* proved that, that you don't need to have huge technical expertise in production or have huge amounts of money or have huge, expensive equipment. We began it with very little money—$2,500—and we wanted to shoot on film, but we couldn't afford it. So, we started shooting on videotape. And I always encourage people that it's the quality of their ideas. You can be shooting on 8-millimeter or VHS or home movie cameras; you can make something that can be seen in theaters if you have ideas and can produce it well enough.

AL: Another filmmaker in town has told me that, in order to proceed, you have to have a complete idea of your finished product before you begin filming, but *Hoop Dreams* kind of proves that wrong.

FM: I think you do need to start with that, but you need to know that it can change. Maybe that's paradoxical. But I think it's important to do all of the research you possibly can before you begin a project, to have a firm sense of what your goal is in terms of finished length, format, et cetera, including your audience and researching your audience a little bit to make sure that they will in fact be interested in your product. Film is a little bit different than the fine arts. We are talking about a medium that exists very much in a commercial sphere. You need to do all that legwork, but once done, you also have to realize that when you begin your film, it can totally change. What you end up with could be something totally different from what you initially envisioned.

AL: Another thing I've been told by Ron Falzone, a Chicago filmmaker who's been working on a film project for years and years and years, is that when you're starting out on a project, you need to be working on something that you would be happy spending ten years on, because sometimes that's how long it takes.

FM: I think there's some truth to that. If you're an independent filmmaker and you're trying to implement your own vision, I think it is important to have that vision be something that is very, very dear to you, that means a lot to you, that you would be comfortable working with for years, because the reality of independent filmmaking today is that it does take years to finish projects.

AL: But at the same time, when you were beginning *Hoop Dreams*, you had no idea it would take as long as it did.

FM: *Hoop Dreams* is a perfect case in point of how you have to be prepared for your project to change. Our original plan was to make a half-hour stay-in-school-oriented program about playground basketball. The project just changed enormously from that original conception, and we were open to those changes and willing to accommodate them.

AL: You've been quoted as saying you try to attain a voice in filmmaking that is down-to-earth, with no bullshit. How reflective is this of a Chicago school of filmmaking like the voice of Chicago literature?

FM: I'm not really sure. I like to think that Chicago filmmakers and viewers are ones who are less dazzled by the latest fashion trends by either L.A. or New York and are more commonsense, no BS makers, and are viewers who understand the solidity of a good story. And they also have more of an everyday social grounding. I think that people who make films in Chicago have more of a social conscience, that they take the social realities that we all live in to heart and are not willing to just abandon them in order to effectively masturbate on screen in whatever pyrotechnical ways happen to be in fashion.

AL: Let's say I'm a great vision guy. I've got a great idea for a film, but my technical knowledge is limited to, say, home movies. Where do I go first to start working on my project? Should I go to some networking seminar or Chicago Filmmakers?

FM: Sure, or the film schools—Columbia, Northwestern, the Art Institute. Those are the biggest and the most logical. I also think that it's important for people to start getting out of their heads as fast as possible and start getting into their hands and start using the materials. I'm a great believer in the notion that if you've got great ideas and even if you can't find anybody to help you, then just take your mom's home video camera and start doing what you can on your own. That's how Spielberg started, for God's sake, just making home movies.

FIVE

Literature

Some cities have literary scenes; some just have great writers. Chicago is in the latter category. But then again, there's something weird about the concept of a "literary scene" anyway. *Scene* implies some sort of collective, cooperative arrangement, but writing is a damn solitary activity, no matter what I happen to be listening to on the stereo at the moment, no matter who happens to be in my apartment as I write this. People speak of a New York literary scene, even on into the eighties, when the poseur posse of Brett Easton Ellis, Jay McInerney, and Tama Janowitz were the darlings of the Big Apple media. But this is to be expected, because of the fact that there are only about a gazillion publishing houses based in that city and twice that many would-be authors. One speaks of San Francisco and Greenwich Village literary scenes during the height of the Beat Generation in the fifties and sixties, but that's to be expected, too, because that's where all the grass was. But Chicago, with its dearth of publishing houses, mere handful of literary publications, and lack of public forums in which to air one's latest work, does not seem much of a ripe locale for the flowering of a new 1920s Paris with authors sipping cafés au lait, smoking unfiltered cigarettes, and cracking wise about what F. Scott and Zelda are up to now. Naturally, we have a ton of cafés here, this being the mocha Frapuccino era, but you can't sit down in half of them, and, in most of the rest of them, you might not want to.

There are writers here, to be sure, but they're an isolated bunch, holed up in South Loop lofts, scratching their pens on legal pads at Urbus Orbis in

Wicker Park, contemplating the sky and themselves on the rocks by Belmont Harbor. And, perhaps, it is this isolation that contributes to an unmistakable Chicago voice that shows up in the writing of our most illustrious authors. If I could use *brawny* in a sentence here without cringing at the cliché, I'd like to, but instead I will describe the voice as urban, street-smart, reeking of smoke-stacks and Maxwell Street grilled onions, and defined by an undeniable sense of citified independence. It is the sort of voice that links generations, that connects Theodore Dreiser (*Sister Carrie*), Carl Sandburg ("hog butcher of the world, stacker of wheat, blah, blah, blah"), Sherwood Anderson (*Winesburg, Ohio*), Frank Norris (*The Octopus*), and Upton Sinclair (*The Jungle*) to Studs Terkel (*Working*) and David Mamet (you know who he is; no reference is needed in these parentheses). Hmmm, perhaps it's a rather sexist voice, as well.

It is the tough-minded and hard-hearted world-weariness, savoir faire, and lack of pretension that has informed the works of the immigrant laborer and the disenfranchised minority and is visible in the poetry of Gwendolyn Brooks; the fiction of Willard Motley, Nelson Algren, and Meyer Levin; the scripts and essays of Ben Hecht; and even in the contemporary voices of authors like Sara Paretsky, Anchee Min, Stuart Dybek, and Robert Rodi. It is a style that some-times touches individuals who were only here for a relatively short time, like Edna Ferber, Ernest Hemingway, Richard Wright, and even John Dos Passos, who was just about out of here by the time he was able to walk upright.

True, you don't have to sound like you just smoked a pack of Pall Malls, threw on the rattiest undershirt you could find, and sat down with cigarette-yellowed fingers to tap out your latest fictional opus on the working man, the freight train hobos, and the construction site whistle to be a successful Chi-cago writer. You can eschew the salt-of-the-earth toughness of the traditional Chicago author's lifestyle for the frustration of life as a Hyde Park academic on your way to a Nobel Prize for literature like Saul Bellow. You could make a mint as the Steven King of the legal profession, Scott Turow. Or turn cloying, feel-good prose and Michael Jordan hagiography into a cottage industry like *Tribune* columnist and author Bob Greene. Or join the seminary and turn out bestsellers like Father Andrew Greeley. Or you could nuzzle your way to the top of the bestseller lists by invading the humor section of your local Barnes & Noble with your clever, gimmicky, and soon-to-be-obsolete (like *The Preppie Handbook* and *I'm OK, You're OK*) book, *Politically Correct Bedtime Stories.* Or you could write a guidebook. Somehow, some way, someone's gotta make a living. You can't turn yourself overnight into the next voice of Chicago with your Slats Grobnikified *deses*, *dems*, and *doses*. But if you don't start out lucky, about twenty years of rejection slips, bouts with the booze, and long walks between the lake and the transient hotel might just do it for you. And then you won't need this guide after all, nor will you have to write one like it.

Chicago Author Desert Island Reading List

Chicago: City on the Make, Nelson Algren

Herzog, Saul Bellow

A Street in Bronzeville, Gwendolyn Brooks

USA, John Dos Passos

An American Tragedy, Theodore Dreiser

The Coast of Chicago, Stuart Dybek

The Front Page, Ben Hecht

The Old Bunch, Meyer Levin

American Buffalo, David Mamet

Knock on Any Door, Willard Motley

V. I. Warshawski, Sara Paretsky

Boss, Mike Royko

Chicago Poems, Carl Sandburg

The Jungle, Upton Sinclair

Working, Studs Terkel

Getting Schooled (if you must)

I've always been suspicious as hell of writing schools, seminars, workshops, and the like. Too many of them are clogged up with folks in nowhere jobs looking for a way out. Grad school creative writing programs are filled with misguided individuals who say things like "Oh, no. No, I don't want to *write*. I want to *teach writing.*" You see these folks with copies of *The Writer's Guide* and *The Writer* under one arm and a copy of *The Writer's Marketplace* under the other. I stopped reading *The Writer's Guide* the moment I saw an article in it about how to write a script for *Diff'rent Strokes*. Keep in mind this: When I was still in college, I read an article in *The Writer's Guide* titled "How to Sell Your Articles." I followed the instructions clearly given to me therein and sent an article proposal to about ten magazines. I got at least a response from every magazine. Every magazine, that is, except *The Writer's Guide.*

Assuredly, there are some national and local writing programs that have turned out some worthy scribes, like the University of Illinois at Chicago, the Iowa Writers' Workshop, and the Organization of Black American Culture (OBAC) Writers' Workshop. But the most of what any seminar or workshop can offer a would-be writer is a kick in the ass. And if you need a kick in the ass, which a lot of people really do, then go for it. But the truth is, pen and paper are a lot cheaper.

Chicago Dramatists Workshop, 1105 W. Chicago, Chicago, IL 60622 (312) 633-0630
If writers' workshops were graded solely on the output of their students, CDW would be a decidedly mixed bag. Though this is one of the few places in town to receive instruction in the art of playwriting, the work turned out by workshop members in company productions and short play festivals is frequently spotty. Eight-week sessions in such topics as Playwriting Fundamentals and Advanced Screenwriting run in the neighborhood of $200.

The Compleat Gargoyle, University of Chicago Center for Continuing Studies, 5835 S. Kimbark, Chicago, IL 60637 (312) 702-1722
Fiction writing workshops and literature classes at the grad school I quit because parking was lousy. Nine weeks of four-hour, intensive workshops cost $325.

Major graduate and undergraduate institutions with highly reputed programs in the field

Columbia College, 600 S. Michigan, Chicago, IL 60605-1901 (312) 663-1600

Northwestern University, 1905 Sheridan, Evanston, IL 60302 (847) 491-7315

University of Illinois at Chicago, 400 S. Peoria, Chicago, IL 60607-7034 (312) 996-6114

The Best Places in and Around Chicago to Write

If you're serious about this writing thing, you'll need a place away from home where you can work, someplace quiet, someplace atmospheric, someplace that doesn't smell like a tavern—even if it is one—someplace where people won't be bugging you to buy crap all the time. Some places are too crowded. The Harold Washington Library Center is too damn bright. And in half of the city's cafés, they make the seats uncomfy so you won't sit there long. Here are, in my humble opinion, the best places to work and write in and around town.

Carter Woodson Library, 9525 S. Halsted, Chicago, IL 60628
(312) 747-6900
A very quiet research facility, especially before school lets out. Try to locate yourself at one of the desks by the African-American history research center.

Chicago Historical Society Library, 1601 N. Clark, Chicago, IL 60614
(312) 642-4600
It's free to get in if you ask for a pass downstairs. Not only is it the city's best research facility for Chicago history but also a remarkably quiet, friendly, and comfortable space with great wooden desks.

Comiskey Park Upper Deck, 333 W. 35th, Chicago, IL 60616
(312) 924-1000
Remote, far away from the action, a great view of the city. Occasional fireworks and irritating piped-in music, but aside from that, devoid of distractions.

Higher Ground Café, 2022 W. Roscoe, Chicago, IL 60618
(312) 868-0075
A quaint Roscoe Village coffee shop with highly reputed scones and classical tunes on the stereo. The kind of place where people give you a look if you have a conversation.

Indian Boundary Park Duck Pond, 2500 W. Lunt, Chicago, IL 60645
Relatively secluded park benches overlook the frolicking mallards as trees hang down over you. Don't mind the calls of the yaks from the nearby zoo.

The Rocks by Belmont Harbor
Not only is it a great, isolated part of the city with a view of the lake but also a perfect place to work on developing characters as skateboarding young toughs, horny slacker couples, and cruisers of all races and sexual orientations stroll up and down.

Skokie Public Library, 5215 W. Oakton, Skokie, IL 60076
(847) 673-7774
A crowded nightmare on weekends. During the weekdays, one of the quietest, most pristine, and well-equipped facilities around. Now if only they'd get rid of those horrific chairs.

Urbus Orbis Café, 1934 W. North, Chicago, IL 60622
(312) 252-4446
The ultimate bohemian café and one of the few places in town where they'll
let you sit for hours without harassing you to order stuff.

Getting Paid

The world of writing in Chicago is not a just one. There's something horribly,
horribly wrong with the fact that if you want to write serious fiction for any
publisher in town, you're probably going to make the most money writing for
Playboy. Contribute to a scholarly, literary journal and place your poem among
the works of those who have published in the *North Americana Review* and
The New Yorker, and you might get fifty bucks and a copy of the journal for
your troubles. Pen a saucy short story for placement beside a spread of Nancy
Sinatra photos and you can easily secure yourself a thousand bones.

Sure you can make a living in Chicago as a writer, but not solely by writing
for Chicago-based publications. The world of magazines and books with any
sort of literary merit has shrunk continually over the years. And the great
Chicago writers of our time rarely have any ties to any Chicago publisher.
Still, there are a fair number of opportunities in town where your fiction, poems, or literary journalism can find its way into print.

While you're doing it, however, do keep in mind the following mandates,
um, regulations, um, tips. Know the magazine you're sending your stuff to.
Speaking from personal experience, there's nothing lamer than working as
an editor of a journalism-based publication and having a thirty-page novella
wind up on your lap, even if it's good. In your proposal, make your piece something a magazine or a book publisher absolutely needs, positively must have.
The easiest thing and the safest thing for an editor to do is to say no to a project.
Most of them love doing it, too. Editors are petty people who once were aspiring young writers, and they enjoy saying no to you just like others said no to
them. It's sad but true. Anticipate every possible reason why an editor would
nix your project and work to address these problems or find another magazine or publishing house. Write a nice, cordial query letter and please don't
misspell anything. Even if your idea is great, you'll look like a moron, and God
knows they hate morons. Please, no fancy, fucked-up fonts. If you don't use a
typewriter, make it look like it came out of one. None of this Futura Con-
densed Bold crap. It makes you look like a rank amateur. Make follow-up
calls if you haven't heard, but don't be a schmuck about it. One call per week

is sufficient. Always remember to send a Self-Addressed, Stamped Envelope if you want to see what you wrote ever again. And never, ever, ever, ever wait by your mailbox for a positive reply about your work. Remember the following golden rule in the publishing world: good news comes over the phone; bad news comes through the mail.

Chicago-Area Publishers

Books

Have you ever thought about starting your own book publishing company? Well, maybe you should. The list of publishers who'll consider putting your work out is a short one. And if you're into fiction, well, short gets shorter fast. Even Maxine Chernoff and Paul Hoover's literary magazine *New American Writing* cruised town and went to the West Coast.

Academy Chicago, 363 W. Erie, Chicago, IL 60610 (312) 751-7300
First-rate, eclectic literary and trade publisher featuring both new works and reprints with no particular focus on Chicago authors. Recent titles include *Chicago by Gaslight: A History of Chicago's Underworld*, *Facets Non-Violent, Non Sexist Children's Video Guide*, and *Journey to Chernobyl: Encounters in a Radioactive Zone*.

Another Chicago Press, 230 W. Huron, Chicago, IL 60611
(312) 943-0947
Wow. A genuine, for-real literary press based in Chicago largely for Chicago writers. Poetry, fiction, and literary nonfiction from such fossils of the Chi-town literary landscape as Maxine Chernoff, Leon Forrest, and Sterling Plumpp. Recent titles include Jerome Sala's *Raw Deal*, Robert Pope's *Northern Fiction*, and Plumpp's *Home/Bass*.

Bonus Books, 160 E. Illinois, Chicago, IL 60611 (312) 467-0580
A rarity in the Chicago publishing scene: as an all-purpose, semi-major publishing house, Bonus will publish most anything, well, with rare exception, most anything except serious literature, it seems. Fiction appears to be a no-no. But, if you're a good poker player, if you know how to get out of parking tickets, if you know a lot about the Cubs and baseball card collecting, or if you can write a really good oncology text, this could be your ticket. Recent titles include *Stuck in the Seventies*, *Used Cars: Finding the Best Buy*, and *Second to Home: Ryne Sandberg Speaks Up*.

Chicago Plays, 2632 N. Lincoln, Chicago, IL 60614 (312) 348-4658
Located in the back of the Act One Bookstore, this tiny specialized publishing house's primary dedication is the production of plays by Chicago playwrights. Also publishes specialty books for actors. There are few blockbusters here, but Chicago Plays tends to lend an air of respectability to a writer's work. Examples of titles published are *Movie Queens*, by Claudia Allen; *Girls, Girls, Girls, Live Onstage Totally Rude*, by Sharon Evans; and *American Enterprise*, by Jeffrey Sweet.

Chicago Review Press, 814 N. Franklin, Chicago, IL 60610
(312) 337-0747
Nonfiction and trade books. Call me up; I'll tell you all about it.

Kidsbooks, Incorporated, 3535 W. Peterson, Chicago, IL 60659
(312) 509-0707
If you can't figure out what this company is up to from its name, maybe you need to read one of their books. Recent titles include *The Animals' Merry Christmas*; *Bible Stories from the Old Testament*, and *The Giraffe Numbers Book*. Very, very, very, very light on text (if your story can fit on a pillow, you're in great shape).

Third Side Press, Incorporated, 2250 W. Farragut, Chicago, IL 60625
(312) 271-3028
Relatively small publishing house dedicated to feminist authors. Genres are fiction, plays, self-help, mystery, health, lesbian literature, and short story collections. Recent titles include *She's Always Liked the Girls Best: Plays by Claudia Allen*; *The Country of Herself: Short Fiction by Chicago Women*, and *SomeBody to Love: A Guide to Loving the Body You Have*.

Third World Press, 7822 S. Dobson, Chicago, IL 60619
(312) 651-0700
Founded in 1967, publishes fiction, poetry, and social criticism regarding the African-American experience. Recent titles include Amiri Baraka's *Jesse Jackson and Black People*, Sterling Plumpp's *Hornman*, and Craig Hodges's *Beyond the Three-Point Line*.

Thorntree Press, 547 Hawthorne, Winnetka, IL 60093
(847) 446-8099
Publishing strictly poetry, this tiny outfit tends to go for the quiet, subtle, nature-loving genre rather than stuff that would go over well at the Green Mill. Those not ready to send manuscripts may send ten pages of unpublished po-

ems as well as a $4 reader's fee to be considered for inclusion in Thorntree's anthologies. "We are *not* a vanity press," Thorntree's editors insist.

Tia Chucha Press, PO Box 476969, Chicago, IL 60647
(312) 252-5321
A small, multicultural publishing house founded by poet and journalist Luis Rodriguez. Publishes a lot of poetry and fiction (in small publishing runs) from a wide array of Chicago voices that would not find a place at many mainstream houses. Recent titles include Andres Rodriquez's *Night Song*, Kyoko Mori's *Fallout*, and poetry slam champion Patricia Smith's *Life According to Motown*.

Periodicals

Unlike the meager skeleton of Chicago publishing houses, there has always been a large selection of interesting, eclectic magazines and journals in the town, and not just magazines about the concrete, debris, or food service industries (though if you're interested in selling out and contributing your, um, literature to those fields, such opportunities are always available). No, there are always magazines here willing to publish the work of young, up-and-comers and older, established scribes. The problem is that none of them seem to stick around very long. Every few months another character with a pile of money plunks down half of his or her net worth to start the one cool magazine that Chicago needs, only to find a year or so later that the publishing business is not as kind as he or she expected. Said individual usually closes up shop and returns, older and wiser and more in debt, to the profession that made him or her the huge pile of money in the first place. The scrapheap of Chicago periodical publishing history is stacked aplenty with such ill-fated titles as *Chicagoan, Inside Chicago, Chicago Times, Neon, The Seed, Metro, Pure*, and dozens of others. Only time will tell whether the cursed scrapheap awaits the magazines that currently exist in Chicago, but just between you and me, if you're writing for a magazine in Chicago, I'd just suggest you try to get paid in advance.

Another Chicago Magazine, 3709 N. Kenmore, Chicago, IL 60613
(312) 248-7665
Founded in 1977, this long-standing local literary magazine focuses on poetry, fiction, essays, and author interviews with a slight amount of criticism as well. Contains a good amount of Chicago authors. Payment is usually in the low- to mid-two-figure range.

Chicago Magazine, 414 N. Orleans, Chicago, IL 60611
(312) 222-8999
A general-interest magazine big into crime stories, personality profiles, restaurants, bars, and music with an above-average writing quality. Pays between $50 and $5,000, but more toward the lower end than the higher one.

Chicago Quarterly Review, 517 Sherman, Evanston, IL 60202
A somewhat hit-and-miss literary journal featuring the works of relatively young poets and fiction writers. Rather facile computer graphics detract from some of the stronger writers in here.

Chicago Reader, 11 E. Illinois, Chicago, IL 60610 (312) 828-0350
No fiction here, at least not intentionally, and even then, usually only in the letters section. This general interest alternative weekly focuses on music, politics, and Chicago issues that the mainstream media overlooks. Will publish articles on just about any topic as long as the writing quality is up there, but please, nothing on deep-dish pizza, the Chicago Cubs, or improv. Payment varies between $50–$1,500.

Chicago Review, University of Chicago, 5801 S. Kenwood, Chicago, IL 60037 (312) 702-0087
Quarterly highbrow publication featuring essays, poetry, and fiction. Has no particular emphasis on local authors.

Cinefantastique, PO Box 270, Oak Park, IL 60303 (708) 366-5566
A slightly cheesy cross between cinema criticism and fanzine, this $5.95 monthly is dedicated to behind-the-scenes looks at the makings of sci-fi, horror, and animated flicks, TV shows, and games. A place for comic book fans to hone and mature their tastes (if only a little bit).

Downbeat, Maher Publications, 102 N. Haven, Elmhurst, IL 60126-3379 (630) 941-2030
One of the preeminent jazz publications in the country, this $2.95 monthly is around 50 percent reviews (the best way to break in). The rest consists of short informational "riffs" and longer feature stories.

In These Times, 2040 N. Milwaukee, Chicago, IL 60647
(312) 772-0100
An intelligent, left-leaning newsprint political journal, which has a reputation for being both a little dry and a little lax in paying its writers on time. But what's $25 compared to the charge you'll get from supporting the cause?

Letter Ex, PO Box 476920, Chicago, IL 60647 (312) 247-6553
A rarity. A poetry magazine with hardly any poetry in it, this eight-page news-print freebie contains all the gossip you might want to chow down about your fellow starving artists in the poetry scene. Accepts book reviews and the occasional essay. Available in stacks at local discriminating bookstores (and perhaps at non-discriminating bookstores as well).

The Lumpen Times, 2558 W. Armitage, Chicago, IL 60647
(312) 227-2072
You won't make anything writing for these sometimes politically astute and often completely irresponsible folks, but you're liable to attract some attention. This highly opinionated and sometimes viciously funny monthly is the voice of the self-disenfranchised and a good place to get clips with your record reviews, political commentaries, humor columns, or confused rants.

New Art Examiner, 314 W. Institute, Chicago, IL 60610
(312) 649-9900
This monthly magazine provides insight into the national art scene. Usually publishes five to six feature stories and a slew of exhibit reviews.

Other Voices, Department of English, University of Illinois at Chicago, 400 S. Peoria, Chicago, IL 60607 (312) 413-2209
One of the strongest Chicago-based literary blends of established authors and ones with few to no credentials. Willing to take risks in both form and content in the short stories they publish. Regarding payment, you'll get a couple of the copies of the magazine, isn't that payment enough? Tips: send entries in the fall or the spring.

Playboy
I'm not printing their damn address; they make enough money as it is. If you want to find out how to get your work published here, follow the big bunny.

Poetry, 60 W. Walton, Chicago, IL 60610 (312) 280-4870
Publishes slim, elegant, and classy collections of poetry from some of the most renowned poets of our time. John Ashbery was one of the poets recently featured. Will consider but rarely publishes the work of those who have not been previously published in literary magazines or journals of some repute.

Poetry East, DePaul University Department of English, 802 W. Belden, Chicago, IL 60614 (312) 362-5114
Published twice a year and costing a healthy eight bucks a pop, this is a good collection of novice and well-traveled poets. Tips: try not to write anything that won't fit on a single page.

Primavera, PO Box 37-7547, Chicago, IL 60037 (312) 324-5920
Founded in 1977 and initiated as an offshoot of the women's feminist organization at the University of Chicago, it is now a solid annual collection of women's fiction, art, and poetry.

Strong Coffee, PO Box 1959, Evanston, IL 60204 (847) 864-3105
Publishes fiction, poetry, and book and café reviews in a free newsprint monthly. Though it struggles to maintain an image as a literary mag, it's still more than 50 percent ads. Still, with the ever-dwindling number of outlets for literature, beggars can't be choosers.

The Third Word, 1840 W. Hubbard, Chicago, IL 60622
(312) 666-3076
Following the demise of mom-and-pop hipster mag *Pure* and the extended hiatus of the late and lamented *Subnation*, this chunky, too-cool-by-half, four-color arts and culture magazine is equal parts slick poseur rag and intelligent literary journalism. Either way it's the only mag in town for which people under thirty don't have to write like they're over forty. And it's the only mainstream magazine where the work of poets and fiction writers won't come off on your hands.

Tomorrow Magazine, PO Box 14846, Chicago, IL 60644
This occasionally published journal/zine of decent poetry and spotty fiction is marred by a rather cheesy desktop publishing feel and a presumptuous $5 cover tag.

TriQuarterly, Northwestern University, 2020 Ridge, Evanston,
IL 60208 (847) 491-7614
There's no particular emphasis on Chicago writers in this three-times-a-year NU-based publication featuring a wide variety of high-credential authors of fiction and poetry. Although they do read whatever prose and poetry they receive, it's probably a good idea to have a rather impressive résumé and/or be a part of some Ph.D. program if you want to be taken seriously. Affiliated with TriQuarterly Publishers, a well-reputed publisher of fiction and poetry.

You'll Need

Aspirin
Oh yeah, a lot of it, particularly if you're spending all day in front of the computer screen or the typewriter. Your headache will allow you your one trip out of the house for the day, this time to one of those really cool old-fashioned

drugstores, like *Merz Apothecary*, a relic from the nineteenth century at *4716 N. Lincoln, Chicago, IL 60625 (312) 989-0900* where they just might recommend a homeopathic cure as well.

Booze
Not to drink, necessarily, just to have on hand so you can cultivate the image. A big bottle of bourbon will set the tone. Every soused aficionado can tell you about the selection at *Sam's Wine and Liquors, 1100 W. North, Chicago, IL 60622 (312) 664-4394; Zimmerman's Discount, 213 W. Grand, Chicago, IL 60610 (312) 332-0012*; or the venerable *House Of Glunz, 1206 N. Wells, Chicago, IL 60610 (312) 642-3000.*

Coffee
The stuff puts me to sleep, but then again, I'm odd. For most everyone else, it's enough to inject them with the creativity to blast through another page or three. If you can tell the difference between the blends at Starbucks, Gourmet Cup Coffee, Coffee Chicago, and Corby Coffee, be my guest. As for me, if I want to snooze, I buy a nice big Styrofoam cup from 7-Eleven.

Coffee beans
Or you could just make it yourself. Buy the beans at *Coffee & Tea Exchange, 3300 N. Broadway, Chicago, IL 60657 (312) 528-2241.*

Comfy desk chair
I'm frigging straining my neck as I write this. I wish I had one of those cool chairs that molds itself to your body. If I'd received a larger advance for this book, I would have bought one from *Order from Horder, 135 S. Clark, Chicago, IL 60603 (312) 648-7208.*

Computer (maybe)
I hate them. They're devil machines. You can have mine. Contact me through the publisher and make me an offer.

Dartboard
Nothing like a dartboard to work off the frustration of writer's block and kill some time. Buy one at *LaSalle Dart Supplies, 1134 W. Armitage, Chicago, IL 60614 (312) 871-4640.*

Paper
It's a fact: the cooler the paper you use, the better your writing will be. Well, maybe not, but somehow, a nice piece of thick, beautiful paper always makes me think that my words have that much more importance. Try *Paper Source, 232 W. Chicago, Chicago, IL 60610 (312) 337-0798.*

Pillow

Writers keep weird hours. You'll be working all night, and then, suddenly, you'll just need to crash. Don't bother walking to bed. Just throw the pillow down on the floor. Snag one from *Arrelle Fine Linens, 445 N. Wells, Chicago, IL 60610 (312) 321-3696.*

Pool cue

You've got to meet characters if you want to be a good writer, particularly one of those raw Chicago writers with a feel for gritty settings like pool halls. You can buy your cue and use it, too, at *Chris' Billiards, 4637 N. Milwaukee, Chicago, IL 60630 (312) 286-7414.*

Red pen

The masochistic streak in all of us requires us to be harsh on our own work. Scratch up your lame rough draft with abandon with a pen from *Jansco Incorporated, 4670 N. Elston, Chicago, IL 60630 (312) 283-8833.* They'll even put your name on it for you.

Table

Why is a raven like a writing desk? Because Edgar Allan Poe wrote on both of them. If he were around today (and able to free himself from the straitjacket), he'd probably be writing on a sturdy table or desk. Find a new cheap one at *The Great Ace, 1445 W. Webster, Chicago, IL 60614 (312) 348-0705,* or a nice old clunker from the *Chicago Recycle Shop, 5308 N. Clark, Chicago, IL 60640 (312) 878-8525.*

Typewriter

I don't care what Bill Gates says; there's nothing more satisfying than the clacking of typewriter keys against a fresh sheet of paper. I recommend a restored Royal or IBM Selectric from the old standard, *Russ Brown Office Machines, 3417 Church, Skokie, IL 60203 (847) 679-7330.*

Typewriter ribbon

Supplies for the Royal typewriter don't come easily anymore. Now it's a whole case of toner from some faceless Comp-USA. But you still can supply the old clunker with ribbon from *Ernie's Office Machines, 5343 W. Devon, Chicago, IL 60646 (312) 775-6266.*

Vintage bicycle

You want to cultivate an image, don't you? That starving artist with the pen and paper in hand. . . . Riding around from café to café on your '59 Schwinn will help you along. Try to find one or something newer at *Cycle Smithy, 2468*

N. Clark, Chicago, IL 60614 (312) 281-0444; Kozy's Cyclery, 3712 N. Halsted, Chicago, IL 60657 (312) 281-2263; or Edgebrook Cycle, 5404 W. Devon, Chicago, IL 60646 (312) 792-1669.

Poetry: or the Curse of the Poetry Slam

It all started at the Green Mill, that ultrarude, combative hybrid of performance poetry and Jell-O wrestling, where audiences may feel free to shout you off the stage, unless of course you're the poet-host for the evening. Remember, if you're going up to read poetry in front of a tanked crowd, that there are certain topics that work better on paper than in front of an audience. To succeed, here's a brief list of some things that a slam audience will appreciate and some things they won't.

Ten Topics That Might Work in a Poetry Slam

1. Hookers under the Wilson el
2. Sex
3. Drinking whiskey
4. Sex
5. Losing your virginity
6. Sex
7. How you hate other poets
8. Sex
9. An ode to the Maxwell Street pornographic video hawkers
10. Sex

Ten Topics That Probably Won't

1. Trees
2. Love
3. The moon
4. Love
5. Anything that rhymes
6. Love
7. The sunset
8. Love
9. The sea
10. Love

Slam and More Friendly Poetry Reading Opportunities

The Bop Shop, 1807 W. Division, Chicago, IL 60622 (312) 235-3232
Holds friendly but somewhat cliquey and often poorly attended poetry reading nights. This scene is refreshingly open to the whims of its poets, on one
occasion allowing two to recite different poems at the same time. Sometimes
too open-minded, eh?

Estelle's Cafe & Pub, 2013 W. North, Chicago, IL 60647 (312) 486-
8760
Audiences are much friendlier (and much smaller) than the ones at the Green
Mill. But then again, half of them seem comatose anyway. And, though there
is an appealingly grungy neighborhood feel to the place, grabbing the microphone behind the bar and gruffly shouting your beat rants to wasted
twenty-somethings and delinquent home escapees is a lot more fun to talk
about afterwards than to actually do.

Green Mill, 4802 N. Broadway, Chicago, IL 60640 (312) 878-5552
It's the slam that started it all and the one place where you'll have to arrive
early if you want to get on the program. In this venue, flashy delivery and
stage presence count just as much as the content of your work. Buy a funky
hat, adopt a gruff voice, maybe swear a little bit, and control your audience
and you might just walk away with a prize in the low- to mid-two-figure range.

No Exit, 6970 N. Glenwood, Chicago, IL 60626 (312) 743-3355
If you want to feel what it was like to be a beatnik poet back in the fifties, this
sure is the place to do it. The crowd here is supportive but sometimes just a
little too absorbed in the hummus. Poem title idea: "Post-Hummus"?

O Bar, 3343 N. Clark, Chicago, IL 60657 (312) 665-7300
Holds open-mike poetry readings geared toward lesbian and gay themes. At-
tendance is sporadic and so is the schedule.

Weeds, 1555 N. Dayton, Chicago, IL 60622 (312) 943-7815
Seemingly male-dominated evenings of poetry readings on weeknights in this
once-hip-but-now-fading neighborhood bar tend to get a little sleazy and obnoxious. Not for the easily offended or those with sensitive lungs.

Interviews

Michael Collins on Developing an Image on the American Literary Scene

Born in 1965, the Irish-born graduate of the UIC English Ph.D. program Michael Collins has already published three books, including the highly praised collection of short stories, *The Man Who Dreamt of Lobsters*. Since then, his latest two books, *The Life of a Tea Boy* and *The Feminists Go Swimming*, have been released in the United Kingdom, but not yet stateside.

Location: Coffee Chicago, 3323 N. Clark

AL: Are there any generalizations you can make about the differences between the American and British literary scenes?

MC: I think reviewers in Britain have a definitive kind of agenda which they kind of fit you into. They concentrate on who else is in your school. They try to situate you in a school of modern writing. So instead of just being an individual, they'll put you in with four other British or Irish writers and fit you in there and then develop a cosmology or sociology of what your writing is trying to do.

The British don't seem to be as concerned with recouping their losses. They seem more willing to take chances. There's some kind of old-time glory where they still like to have the front page in the *Times* and they just want the publishing house to be out there as a recognized entity, as a purveyor of culture, whereas here they tell you your book sold this much and where you have to go from there. Everything's much more centered around the dollar. When you're over in Britain and you have a British publisher, you're caressed a lot more and they'll talk a lot more about the writing and the stories. Or they'll tell you about a development you've made.

AL: And that doesn't exist here.

MC: No. From my experience, most of the people in New York who are editors, a lot of them are in their late twenties, a lot of them are women out of those East Coast colleges. I don't know where Amherst is. Is that on the East Coast? Out of good liberal arts colleges, but they seem to do it for about three years and then they're gone into another career, whether it's advertising or out of the field altogether. You just have this transitory quality here, so you're never fully sure that you're with one house and that you have a commitment from them. That's a major strain, really. In Britain, once you're taken into their stable, you're there until you're completely lost.

AL: Is there also pressure here to write things that are commercial?

MC: Well, with one of my recent books, I went to Doubleday. And the fellow said he liked it but he couldn't publish it. Nonfiction is the commodity they want. There was a book two years ago where some Harvard graduate wrote about women's experiences in Ireland, and he wanted the same type of thing. He wanted an Irish person to talk about the Irish who come and scuttle around in America. Once they see that you can write, they ask if you can change it into something that's marketable. The subject matter doesn't really matter. Once they see the quality of writing is there, they try to tack on different subject matter to it. Just write at the same level, but write about things that people would want to read about, as though you the writer are kind of interchangeable, that your writing style can become chameleon-like.

AL: That's getting away from literature as any sort of an art form.

MC: Oh, it is. In the last few years, so many publishing houses in New York have closed down or consolidated. If you actually look, there are only five or six who own all the subsidiaries.

AL: How do you find your voice?

MC: I think you have to go through sketches. Like a painter doing flowers and abstract kinds of things, so you can figure what kind of characters are interesting to you. They surface very slowly. Your main interest in life, what really captures you, isn't always apparent. I don't think people do enough of that. They're much more plot oriented. They just want to write a story with a beginning, middle, and end. What constitutes plot is character, setting, all that. It's really like a jigsaw, and plot is sometimes the most subordinate of all those. If you can just get characters moving around, the plot will come in. A lot of people try to put plot before character and setting.

I was teaching Hemingway, *In Our Time*, and it's centered around fishing and long journeys and that's one of his earliest books. And then you look at *Old Man and the Sea*. He's still writing the same story. Your world is tiny as a writer. Your whole cosmology is small. He's writing about a fucking fish at the end of his life, as he was at the beginning. Now, he might have more maturity at the end, but conflicts are still settled in a kind of ritualistic manner around fishing, around bullfighting.

So once you get a handle on that, the next step is how to get it out there and recognized by someone. My attitude is to get it out through the universities. It seems to be so closed that if you're not associated with academia, to try and get an agent is difficult. You can buy books like *The Writer's Guide*, and they'll have places that say they'll read your manuscript for ten dollars or whatever. Any of those agents will think anybody who follows that path is kind of a loser. They won't read half of the things. They're not reputable agents. They're not agents who really deal with publishers. Sending out blindly or going through one of those writer's books and picking out an agent that way is not going to lead to anything. Nine out of ten times it will lead only to frustration and no response. At a school, you can just audit a course and that puts you into the thing. It gives you access to a teacher who will have access to agents.

AL: How much does one have to be a self-promoter to be a writer these days?

MC: It's a huge part of the thing. I was listening to Martin Amis and his new novel is about two loser writers, one of whom's pretty bad and the other one who sucks too but is also pretty successful. He made some comment that, as a writer, you must pick out one particular trait that you want to be known for, because the public can only keep one thing in mind, one attribute. And if you want to get somewhere, you have to develop some type of uniqueness and exploit that, whether you're short, whether you're fat. There's such a limited audience and such a small time to catch people's attention that any time you do get into the public eye, you have to push that. You can't be one way to someone and another way to someone else. You're giving out different messages. You definitely have to be the fat guy or the curser or this or that.

AL: Is there something you've tried to be known for?

MC: No. For people who interview me or whatever, the virtue of being Irish, that kind of sets you up as being different, just the nature of being from Ireland. Everyone's obliged to say "in the wake of James Joyce" or "in the wake of Samuel Beckett." I think you need a resiliency as well, like when you go to do readings at shops or things like that. There might not be tons of people there and you have to go on with it. I had to call up my publisher and ask if I could do a couple of readings in Boston. They were involved in something else, so I had to phone up all these Irish bars and say, "Listen, I know it probably sounds ridiculous, but how about if I read for half an hour in a bar on a Thursday night?"

Even if you do get published, you have to come up with the schemes of how you get to people. You can't really step back and hope that some publicity person will make you a star—they don't. They leave it up to you. If you're too nice about your book, it becomes old news very quickly. I think you have to have that in mind.

The first time around before I got an agent, I started my own book publishing company. In 1990, I was at Notre Dame and I had eight stories that basically constituted *The Man Who Dreamt of Lobsters.* I didn't know how to get it published. I asked the teachers and they gave me no solid advice. So I formed a company in the Isle of Man, an off-the-shelf company called Batavia Incorporated, because I know desktop publishing. I had my sister take it over to the newspapers over there to try and get it reviewed. I dropped a couple thousand dollars into that venture, because I didn't know how to break into the literary scene. I ended up being on the front cover of the *International Herald Tribune,* "Young Writer Pulls Scam on Publishing World." That's what interested America in me, and I had to wrangle out of my own fake contract to get published here.

AL: Do you feel at any disadvantage having located in Chicago?

MC: My agent said it would be better to be in New York, that by being there and going to parties you might develop a rapport, and that can get you to do articles in things like *Esquire* and *Harper's.* Down here you wouldn't run across that kind of influence. Nobody has the power to publish this or influence that. But if you're around New York too long with aspirations that you're going to go to parties and meet up with people, there's going to be a lot of clash where you see a lot of yourself out there, a lot of people out at parties just like you, trying to schmooze and get places. And that could become a total preoccupation in your life and you could become completely self-conscious and defeat yourself.

Stuart Dybek on the Chicago Voice

Born in Pilsen, author and poet Stuart Dybek has been roundly hailed as the heir apparent to legendary Chicago authors Nelson Algren and Theodore Dreiser and their ilk. He's been published in the *Atlantic Monthly, The New Yorker,* and everywhere else you could possibly imagine. Several of his stories have appeared in O. Henry prize story collections, and he's the author of *Childhood and Other Neighborhoods, Brass Knuckles,* and the collection of short stories and sketches *The Coast of Chicago.*

AL: A lot of people talk about the so-called Chicago voice from Algren to Sandburg, and your name comes up quite frequently as well. Do you think there is such a thing as a Chicago voice?

SD: Yeah, to a certain extent. There've been so many writers whose subject matter has crossed similar paths, and the different takes that the different writers have had have nonetheless added up into some constant.

AL: What characterizes that constant?

SD: The influence of neighborhood or 'hood. It isn't that writers in other places haven't explored it. But I'm not sure that I can think of any other place other than New York City that rivals the obsession Chicago writers have with it, thinking of Algren here. Not to mention my name in that company, but it is also a huge concern of mine. And nonfiction writers as well. It's the heart and soul of Mike Royko when he used to be a good writer in that book *Boss*, and I'm sure that given the time to think it over, I could come up with other examples. Brashler, for instance, and Studs Terkel. Bellow is a great investigator of neighborhoods. On both sides of the line, it's become not just a matter of setting, but an actual way of structuring material.

AL: In what sense?

SD: Well, *Division Street* is a clear example where the sense of neighborhood actually becomes a structural characteristic of the book.

AL: What is it about Chicago that triggers the obsession?

SD: I think people who grew up in the city undergo a similar experience, which is that as much as they live in the city, they live all the more in their own neighborhood. And so it almost creates in one two contrasting but interconnected feelings. One is the very insular sense of the world so that the writer looks inward to the neighborhood rather than outward to the world. The other is that it creates the possibility for the character to move from the neighborhood into the greater world of the city so that the city comes to represent a kind of cosmopolitan growth. In that way, within this one place called Chicago, what is actually going on is a kind of move from village to city, the nineteenth-century novel move from hamlet to London.

For writers who are associated with Chicago but are outside the city like Sherwood Anderson or Dreiser, there you also have the immigration story, which takes place in the kind of geography that we usually associate with the kind of move I'm talking about rather than the move from neighborhood to city at large. You've got the move from foreign country to Chicago.

AL: Is this sense of neighborhood and outside cosmopolitan area something that still exists in Chicago?

SD: Very strongly. Where you first see it is with the ethnic groups like the Irish and the Jews and the Slavs. But then that whole new wave of immigration actually very strongly repeats it, so you can feel it in Sandra Cisneros's Mexican population. When I was a caseworker on the South Side, no matter how street-smart and hip the kids wanted to think themselves, what impressed me over and over and over again was how insular their world really was, how the 'hood really dominated their existence, and how huge a foray it was for them to go downtown, as it was for me growing up.

AL: You grew up in Pilsen.

SD: We moved from Pilsen to Little Village and considered it a huge move. It was a move of about a few blocks, and it was like this enormous migration to the promised land. Little Village had more trees than Pilsen, and we suddenly had a backyard that was mud and clumps of grass, rather than concrete and a sandpile. I still remember that perspective very clearly, and it's certainly something that I write about.

AL: When you were growing up in Chicago, did you perceive any kind of literary scene?

SD: None whatsoever, no. But then, I didn't perceive any literary scene almost anywhere. So you have to put that statement into context. I didn't grow up in an environment that promoted awareness of literary scenes. My father was an immigrant. My mother was first generation, and I still grew up in a partly Polish-speaking household. Literary scenes were not even on the horizon of what we thought about, and that was pretty much reflected in schools. When I began to have the kind of intellectual breakthroughs that accompany this migration out of the neighborhood, I started to become aware of notions of literary scenes. It happened to be that there was a very highly publicized one, the beatniks. And that was really my first inkling that such a thing existed and that there could be a literary scene equivalent to what I was already very interested in, which was a music scene.

AL: Do you remember your first piece of writing?

SD: Clearly. How far back are you talking about?

AL: Well, how far back does your memory go?

SD: My memory goes back to fourth grade. I was a grade ahead back then. That was really the first time I felt a kind of surge of energy, the engagement of the endocrines, where thought suddenly translates into emotion that comes from writing. From that point on, on some level I always felt this special relationship with language, although I would not have been able to articulate that until much later, but it was something that would get reinforced every so often by my teachers. Each time it got reinforced, I became more sure that what I was feeling inside when I wrote it also had some outside effect on people who read it.

AL: Was it nonfiction you were writing?

SD: I wouldn't even grace it with genre. In fourth grade, for some reason I had become a bad boy and remained one. I don't even really know why I became not a mean kid but a mischievous kid who wound up sitting outside the classroom. I was a comedian, a fool, a joker. And part of that was that in fourth grade I was in the Slap-a-Face club. The nun would take all of us who had not done our homework out of class, and the worst part of it was waiting to get the slap in the face. It's like the worst part of getting a shot when you're a kid is waiting for the injection. But I found out that actually getting a slap in the face for not doing my work was worth not having to screw around with it at night. We had this esprit de corps between us. We wouldn't do our homework, goddamn it; we'd take the slap in the face. And we'd come in class smiling, with the nun's fingerprints imprinted on our cheeks.

We had an assignment for geography to write about Africa, which of course we all knew incredible amounts about. I woke up that morning and my mother was sick with the flu. My father was already at work. So he had made me some Cream of Wheat and left it in the bowl, and I never really liked Cream of Wheat anyway. It just coagulated into this hideous white gum. So I happily flushed it down the toilet, and with this extra time I thought I'd actually do my homework. So I sat down and wrote on a loose-leaf sheet of paper this one-page thing about Africa.

I got to the point where I was trying to describe how tall the trees were in Africa, and in looking for a way to describe how tall the trees were, I tried to think of the tallest things I knew. And the tallest things I knew were skyscrapers, and so I wrote this thing about the trees scraping the skies. And this bolt came. All I'd done was made a metaphor, but when I did it, the notion I'd been trying to describe was how tall trees were. And when I combined it into skyscrapers, I could feel the scrape of the green against the blue, and this bolt went through me, and I jumped up and ran into my mother's bedroom where she was in bed with the flu with a bucket beside her bed. She was too weak to even get up and make it to the toilet to throw up. And I asked her if I could read this to her, which pretty much amazed her, and as I was reading it, she got the heaves. So she never really said anything about it and I kind of just forgot about it and I went to school and handed it in.

It was really important to me, I must say, that this nun then made a big deal out of the piece. The fact that I felt this jolt and received this outside confirmation totally encapsulated the writing process. One is always creating in isolation and trying to evoke or be blessed with these inner jolts and transmit them and give them to somebody else. I couldn't certainly have articulated this at the time, but I do remember that process. And that happened repeatedly through grade school and on into high school, and it didn't just happen with nuns. My buddies reacted in the same way, and what that did was it made me feel that writing was not an academic subject.

AL: When you were talking about the reactions of your friends to the stories you read to them, was it cool in a tough crowd to be a writer?

SD: No, it had nothing to do with being a writer; it had more to do with being a comedian. The first literary piece I remember was when I was in high school at St. Rita, which I detested, and I mean, if one needed something to rebel against, that place was like going to the orchard in full bloom. There was so much to define yourself against it was an embarrassment of riches. So in a way, this was a piece that was a turning point for me just like that Africa piece in fourth grade was. I sat down and I wrote this piece called "Opus Turd." It was a story told by a piece of shit flushed right down the drainage canal, which flowed right through my neighborhood, and I handed it out to my buddies and they laughed as if I'd told a really good dirty joke. The fact that they liked it, though, gave me some kind of status in the group.

AL: Now, when did this knack for entertaining your friends turn into a conscious career choice?

SD: It became serious as I began to read more and learn more and more about what being serious meant in writing. I began realizing that there was more to it than pulling the nose of the bourgeois and began to understand on some rudimentary level about notions of craft, which I understood much more clearly in music.

Sadly for me at the time, although I'd been playing the saxophone and been in and out of some pretty sad-ass bands, which was what they'd have had to be to have me in them, it became clear to me that I wasn't able to play what was in mind. It wasn't that I didn't have ideas. I really did have genuine musical ideas, but I didn't have the skill to express them, and my reverence for music was so great that I didn't feel like I could keep offending this stuff that was so important to me with my own shabby playing. And I knew on some level that I was not going to progress enough, that I hadn't progressed fast enough so that I could ever catch up to where I wanted to be.

But in writing, partly because you didn't make so much damn noise doing it and you weren't constantly offending a live audience and partly because I felt I was making progress, I was able to translate what I was thinking into something more concrete, it started to seem like an avenue for which I was better suited. So, finally I took all my personal investment in music and put it into writing. I've always tried to do in writing what I wanted to do in music, to treat language as musically as I could.

AL: How do you write? Pen and ink? Computer?

SD: I jot in a notebook a lot. Then, if something clicks for me in a notebook, which is kind of the scrapyard—sometimes I'll visit the scrapyard and pick stuff out of it that looks good a year later—I'll turn on some music and try to bash out a rough draft based on these notions, which generally come to seem like other people's ideas by this point.

AL: Does the music fit the mood of the story you're writing?

SD: Not specifically. But I'll put on something that puts me in a writing frame of mind, almost always instrumental.

AL: How do you deal with writer's block?

SD: I don't know. I constantly have it.

SIX

Music

There is, of course, no one history of Chicago music; each form has its own separate history. If Paris was Hemingway's moveable feast, Chicago, naturally, would be his musical one. And, frighteningly enough, the feast is enough to make a poor, innocent soul gorge. There was a time in Chicago when the only music you could hear was that of the Indian tom-tom. Then there was a time when all you could hear were string ensembles in the salons of tuxedo-clad movers and shakers. Much later, there was a time in Chicago when everyone had a Sears guitar and a set of Archie drums in their basement. I wouldn't know. I grew up in the time when everyone had a black light poster in their basement, strings of beads, and a bong that they pretended was Obi-Wan-Kenobi's light saber whenever the parents or the police came by. The history of Chicago music is huge. Too huge. It deserves a book of its own. And, who knows, once I get a new pair of glasses, maybe I'll write it. As for now, since there is no way to adequately write local music history in the space available, we'll try to make it as brief as possible, by telling the entire story of more than a century's worth of music in *a thousand words or less.* Here goes.

The Entire History of Chicago Music . . . Briefly

No more Indian tom-toms. Settlers make quick work of that, make room for rich real estate moguls fond of classical music. String ensembles, chamber groups. 1891, the Chicago Symphony Orchestra founded by Theodore Thomas. One hundred years later, still kicking. 1910–20: The Great Migration. Black families ride rails bringing north Delta Blues sound. 1928, Tampa Red's Hokum Jug Band featuring Big Bill Broonzy record raunchy "It's Tight Like That." Sells 100,000 copies. 1917: Storeyville district of New Orleans shuts down, comes north to 35th and State, doorway to Black Metropolis. More nightclubs than you can shake a stick at: The Elite Cafe, Dreamland, Royal Gardens hosting Louis Armstrong, King Oliver and his Creole Jazz Band, etc. Sound influences 1920s West Side white boys, clarinetist Benny Goodman, Gene Krupa, et al. Austin High Gang (Jimmy McPartland, Budd Freeman, etc.) founds 1920s Chicago Jazz sound. Art Hodes, Barrett Deems emerge on hopping jazz scene.

More black migration. Post-war onslaught of South and West Side clubs Breathtaking talent. Willie Dixon, Arthur "Big Boy" Cruddup, and Muddy Waters rock Sylvio's on Lake and Kinzie. WOPA hypes the sound. 1950, Chess Records founded, and later WVON, too. Chuck Berry, Bo Diddley, Howlin' Wolf, Muddy Waters. South Michigan Avenue becomes city's music row. Blues morphs into doo-wop and R & B. Gene Chandler does "Duke of Earl" with the DuKays. Jerry Butler explodes ("For Your Precious Love," "He Will Break Your Heart") with and without The Impressions and pioneer genius Curtis Mayfield. Junior Wells, Buddy Guy arrive. Ken Nordine invents *word jazz*. Fritz Reiner leads CSO with iron fist, electrified baton.

Borrowing from Muddy Waters—Blues has a baby, names it rock and roll. White boys get into the act. *American Bandstand* on everybody's telly. Loud-mouthed deejays (Dick Biondi, Dex Card, Ron Britain) boost scene. Can't play Them's "Gloria" on radio—too dirty. The Shadows of Knight, serious borrowers from South and West Side blues artists, do own version, skyrocket national top ten. Make way for bubblegum popsters The American Breed ("Bend Me, Shape Me"), The Cryan' Shames ("Sugar and Spice"), Ronnie Rice and The New Colony Six ("I Will Always Think About You"), and The Buckinghams, who top charts with "Kind of a Drag." Chicago Democratic convention. Psychedelic San Francisco rock movement leaves local bubblegummers eating dust. Most done by early seventies. Heavily jazz-influenced Chicago Transit Authority forms, becomes Chicago, soft rock monster band. Georg Solti takes helm of CSO. Formation of American Alliance for Creative Musicians (AACM), seminal, avant-garde South Side jazz collective.

Soul music emerges. The Dells ("Oh What a Night") and the Chi-Lites ("Oh Girl," "Have You Seen Her?") play Regal Theater at 47th and King with every other big name in black music. Flared bell bottoms, wild fashions, long

Cadillacs. Curtis Mayfield does soundtracks to *Superfly*, *Short Eyes*, and *Let's Do It Again*.

1970s. Bad times for everyone. Most everyone. Soul music industry crashes. Chess closes doors. Local entrepreneurs start up cheap blues labels, Earwig, Alligator, etc. American Breed members join Rufus. Jim Peterik and The Ides of March hit number two on national rock charts with "Vehicle." Folk music scene. Rogers Park and Old Town bars. Sandals. Jeans with ripped pockets. Ed Holstein, Bob Gibson, Hamilton Camp, John Prine. Steve Goodman writes "City of New Orleans." Aliota, Haynes, and Jeremiah write druggie folk ballad "Lake Shore Drive." Disco days. Big hair. Plastic pants. Flashing lights at Faces on Rush Street. Late seventies, early eighties, nothing too cool happening. Chicagofest. (Honkeyfest.) Hard rock. "Disco Sucks." Black "Loop" T-shirts. One-hit wonder Off Broadway singing "Stay in Time." Local cheese-rockers hit it big with suburbs nationwide. Cheap Trick rocks Budokan. Styx tops charts with "Babe" and concept albums (e.g., *Pieces of Eight*). REO Speedwagon and Chicago write back-seat-of-the-car-make-out soundtrack classics "Keep on Loving You," "Hard to Say I'm Sorry." Jim Peterik's Survivor best part of lame *Rocky III* ("Eye of the Tiger"). Blues moving north.

Underground movement kicks in edgily. Punk rock rebellion, Mohawks, leftie politics in combat boots. The Effigies rock North Side clubs, Steve Albini's Shellac. Industrial apocalyptic sounds energize strobe-lit Thunderdome dance clubs. WaxTrax! leads Ministry to unprecedented mainstream success in Bud Dry commercial. Rock and roll scene emerges. No longer heavy metal clubs. Bands rock Metro, Lounge Ax, Czar Bar, Phyllis's. The Insiders sign to Epic, get unceremoniously dumped. Eleventh Dream Day sign to Atlantic, get eventually unceremoniously dumped; Material Issue sign to Mercury, don't get dumped. Chicago invents house music. Smash in Europe. Local press essentially ignores. Solti gives up reins of CSO after unprecedented Grammy run to Daniel Barenboim.

Lounge lizards Urge Overkill go national; Smashing Pumpkins release indie *Gish*, release *Siamese Dream* goes platinum. Producer Steve Albini signs on for Nirvana's *In Utero*, won't take more than ten grand. Potty-mouthed rocker Liz Phair does demo *girlysound*, signs to Matador, releases *Exile in Guyville*, appears on cover of every frigging magazine in the universe. Chicago soulster R. Kelly goes platinum with *12-Play*.

Chicago next major musical scene, next Athens, Georgia, next Seattle. Industry types sign everything that moves. Veruca Salt, on strength of demo and couple shows, becomes buzz band. *American Thighs* released on Geffen, quintessential modern "grrl" rock. The Drovers do soundtrack for Michael

Apted's *Blink*; Red Red Meat signs to TVT, Giant nets Certain Distant Suns, TVT snaps up Catherine, Imago gobbles Wickerman, Capitol signs Triple Fast Action, Smoking Popes, RCA signs Lupins, bands you've never heard of wind up with five-record contracts. Aggressive underground scene persists—The Jesus Lizard, Shellac.

No signs of letting up on any front. Vultures continue circling around Metro, Double Door, et al. Jazz scene alive and well—Kurt Elling signs to Blue Note. Hip-hop national phenomenon, starts rolling here, starts cooking with Common Sense. Jazz experimentation AACM alumni Ernest Dawkins, Edward Wilkerson Jr. and 8 Bold Souls. Buddy Guy finally getting long-deserved national attention. Alligator celebrates twenty-fifth anniversary. Urge Overkill, Smashing Pumpkins, Liz Phair, Veruca Salt, etc. continue rising. Somehow blues, jazz, classical, rock music scene all thriving in 1996. (One thousand words exactly. Check them, buddy.)

The Ultimate Made-in-Chicago Cruising Tape

"Snatch It Back and Hold It," Junior Wells

"A Little Encouragement," 8 Bold Souls

"Stratford-on-Guy," Liz Phair

"Midnight Ride," The Kinsey Report

"Messin' with the Kid," Buddy Guy and Junior Wells

"Geek USA," Smashing Pumpkins

"Hoochie Coochie Man," Muddy Waters

"Bend Me, Shape Me," The American Breed

"Kind of a Drag," The Buckinghams

"High or Low," The Insiders

"Roll Over, Beethoven," Chuck Berry

"Feelin' Handsome," Lava Sutra

"Seether," Veruca Salt

"Mr. Roboto," Styx

"25 or 6 to 4," Chicago

"Dennis DuPree from Danville," The Cryan' Shames

"Gloria," The Shadows of Knight

"Nickel and a Nail," Otis Clay

"Wang Dang Doodle," Koko Taylor

"Wound up Tight," Lonnie Brooks

"Back on Me," Urge Overkill

"Every Day is Halloween," Ministry

"Kim the Waitress," Material Issue

"I Like the Crotch on You," R. Kelly

Getting Schooled

American Conservatory of Music, 16 N. Wabash, Chicago, IL 60602
(312) 263-4161
Founded in 1886. A serious, academic institution offering undergraduate and graduate degrees in all areas of musical study. Well-rounded faculty boasts members of the Chicago Symphony Orchestra and countless other professionals with impressive credentials. Undergraduate tuition tends to run in the neighborhood of ten grand (scholarships and financial aid are available). The conservatory also offers adult education programs, as well as private instruction. Depending on the experience, desires, and overall greediness of the instructor you choose, private lessons run $40–$100 per hour.

American Music World, 333 S. State, Chicago, IL 60604
(312) 786-9600
Private piano and organ classes are taught here for $10–$13 per half hour lesson.

Bloom School of Jazz, 100 E. Ohio, Chicago, IL 60622
(312) 280-8298
The only institution of its kind in the city, offering serious group instruction in jazz instrumentation, keyboards, ear training, music theory, and blues guitar, piano, drums, and bass. Classes are taught by well-respected professionals in the Chicago music industry. Eight-week classes (once a week for two hours) generally run $200–$300.

Jack Cecchini School of Music, 1552 N. Milwaukee, Chicago, IL 60622 (312) 489-9900
Private or group instruction in pop and classical guitar is offered from the man who founded the DePaul classic guitar degree program and who's played alongside the likes of Frank Sinatra, Peggy Lee, Judy Garland, and Carol Channing, and even for Was-He-Really-President Gerald Ford. The school also offers classes in drums, bass, and piano. Prices are $25 (if you want to study with Cecchini himself) to $17 (if you want to study with one of his underlings) per half hour.

Center for Voice, 410 S. Michigan, Chicago, IL 60605   (312) 360-1111
As you might expect from its name, this nonprofit institution is dedicated to
every aspect necessary to becoming a singer, from beginning voice classes to
stage presence to music theory to approaching the business end of being a
vocal star. Eight-week classes tend to run in the $200–$300 range.

Old Town School of Folk Music, 909 W. Armitage, Chicago,
IL 60614   (312) 525-7793
It's like something out of a forgotten era, 1963–1974, to be more precise. It's
the folkie school and performance center to end all folkie schools and performance centers. Founded in 1957 by folk musician Win Stracke and others,
this has long been both a performance and training center. Even Roger
McGuinn of The Byrds took classes here (we'll forgive them for that). Classes
are offered in everything you could possibly imagine, from banjo to fiddle to
harmonica to tin whistle. Blues and jazz schools here also offer the opportunity to learn how to play with an ensemble. Grateful Dead and Bob Dylan
ensembles are also offered. All classes generally run eight weeks and cost $100.

Sherwood Conservatory of Music, 1014 S. Michigan, Chicago,
IL 60605   (312) 427-6267
Longtime downtown music center offering individual and group instruction
in voice, piano, jazz, and theory as well as opportunities for younger students
to join ensembles. Classes rarely run more than $10 per weekly hour-long
session.

Major graduate and undergraduate institutions with highly reputed programs in the field

Chicago State University, 9501 S. Martin Luther King, Chicago,
IL 60628   (312) 995-2000

Northwestern University, 1905 Sheridan, Evanston, IL 60302
(847) 491-7315

Roosevelt University, 430 S. Michigan, Chicago, IL 60605
(312) 341-3500

Getting Paid

The ultimate goal is, of course, to play with the Chicago Symphony—or at
least to start out with their training orchestra, the Civic Orchestra. Vocalists
worldwide would kill to be part of the ever-popular Lyric Opera of Chicago, or

at least part of their apprentice program. But these are not the only highly reputed classical music outfits in the city or in the burbs. If you play a mean harp or you've got that coloratura working, we've compiled a short list of some of the better ones around town.

Outlets for the classically trained musician

Chicago Chamber Orchestra, 410 S. Michigan, Suite 631, Chicago, IL 60605 (312) 922-5570

Chicago Sinfonietta, 105 W. Adams, Chicago, IL 60603 (312) 857-1062

Chicago String Ensemble, 3524 W. Belmont, Chicago, IL 60618 (312) 332-0567

Chicago Symphony Orchestra, Orchestra Hall, 220 S. Michigan, Chicago, IL 60604 (312) 435-8122

Civic Orchestra, Orchestra Hall, 220 S. Michigan, Chicago, IL 60604 (312) 435-8122

For vocalists

Apollo Chorus of Chicago, 410 S. Michigan, Chicago, IL 60604 (312) 427-5620

Halevi Choral Society, 3480 N. Lake Shore, Chicago, IL 60657 (312) 868-6700

Light Opera Works, 927 Noyes, Evanston, IL 60201 (847) 869-6300

Lyric Opera of Chicago, 20 N. Wacker, Chicago, IL 60606 (312) 332-2244

Windy City Performing Arts, 3171 N. Halsted, Chicago, IL 60657 (312) 404-9242

Other classical gigs

If you're not ready to make it into the CSO or you're more of a chamber group or solo performer sort of person, there are other options. Classical musicians frequently are required to do background music for radio and television commercials. You can find out about these through the Musicians Union newsletter or from other musicians. Or you might want to snag a gig at one of the city's classier or snootier restaurants and hotels. A few favor classical entertainment—or just have pianos, which you can jump on after a few snifters of brandy to show your stuff and prove why you should be hired.

Fondue Stube, 2717 W. Peterson, Chicago, IL 60659 (312) 784-2200

Gentry of Chicago, 712 N. Rush, Chicago, IL 60611 (312) 664-1033

Pump Room, 1301 N. State, Chicago, IL 60610 (312) 266-0360

Toulouse, 2140 N. Lincoln Park West, Chicago, IL 60614
(312) 665-9071

Yvette, 1206 N. State, Chicago, IL 60610 (312) 280-1700

The Open Mike and Open Jam Session Scene

Let's be honest—nobody ever gets launched into the big time on the basis of playing acoustic guitar on an open mike night or tinkling the ivories in a sing-along piano bar (unless he or she is incredibly good-looking or his or her mother owns the bar). That's not why you're here. But you're not here to just play James Taylor tunes and impress your friends, either. The open mikes are the safe place to experiment, to perfect (well, practice) your act, to get a few free Cokes, and to overcome your stage jitters before you start approaching major venues (venues that pay). It will be tempting to do a lot of cover tunes to please the crowd (you know, the dorks waving their lighters mockingly and wailing "Free Bird"). Screw that. Your ability to play R.E.M.'s "Losing My Religion" for the Lakeview faithful tells you nothing. Do your own stuff. Ignore the advice Jack Weston gave to Dustin Hoffman and Warren Beatty in *Ishtar*, "Sing songs people know. That way if your act stinks, at least they'll have *something* to applaud."

While you're open-miking, you'll meet a diverse group. Hopefully, since these are usually held on off nights, you'll meet a number of professional musicians trying to keep their chops up. If you can impress them with your talent, maybe they'll help you get a gig somewhere down the line. But you'll also meet a strange posse of folks who've been open-mike regulars for years. They go every Wednesday to the Gallery Cabaret, every Thursday to No Exit, and so on down the line. This is an interesting crew. They tell good stories about their experiences on the street trying to bum a couple dollars here and a couple dollars there, but they're never going to go beyond the open mikes.

Most of them don't even want to. Buy them a couple of drinks. Listen to them. But don't wind up like them. And, if it's two years later and you desperately want to but still haven't moved beyond the open mike scene, give yourself a good look in the mirror and ask yourself why.

Carol's Pub, 4659 N. Clark, Chicago, IL 60640 (312) 334-2402
Like something out of another time and on the other side of the Mason-Dixon line, this country and western bar lets you pick 'n' grin 'n' barbecue your way into the hearts of an always receptive and friendly if somewhat shnockered crowd. They have hardly an elaborate sound system, but the fact that the regulars know how to two-step almost makes up for it.

Charleston, 2076 N. Hoyne, Chicago, IL 60647 (312) 489-4757
The poorly lit area stage situated smack dab in the middle of the young, up-and-coming crowd here is possibly not the best place to win over your audience (you might have better acoustics in the subway), but the folks are friendly and you might get a few tips, especially if you know R.E.M.'s "Losing My Religion."

Coq D'or, Drake Hotel, 140 E. Walton, Chicago, IL 60611
(312) 787-2200
The folks at the Drake will probably be pissed off at me for calling their tony piano bar an open-mike venue. But if you get in good with the something-out-of-a-weird-movie-from-the-1940s crooner Buddy Charles, he'll let you take the mike for a few tunes, preferably to do something from*Guys and Dolls*. Best experienced after a couple of the Drake's signature martinis.

Cotton Club, 1710 S. Michigan, Chicago, IL 60616 (312) 341-9787
This slick, upscale Near South Side jazz club has weekly open jam sessions.

Gallery Cabaret, 2020 N. Oakley, Chicago, IL 60647 (312) 489-5471
Sometimes it's a pretty scuzzy crowd, but if you can carry a tune and drown out the conversations of the other, often unreceptive acoustic musicians who want to play here, you'll have a step up on your competition.

Gentry of Chicago, 712 N. Rush, Chicago, IL 60611 (312) 664-1033
Brush up on your showtunes. Start quoting them now. Midweek this predominantly gay bar is a great place to work on audition pieces for musicals or just to belt out that *Sunday in the Park with George* tune you've been playing on your Casio for years to see how a generally receptive audience reacts.

Inner Town Pub, 1935 W. Thomas, Chicago, IL 60622
(312) 235-9795
Acoustic tunes only in friendly neighborhood bar on Thursday nights.

Joann, A Piano Bar, 751 N. Clark, Chicago, IL 60610 (312) 337-1005
Not an open-mike venue in the traditional sense, but the showtune sing-alongs that go most nights here allow you the opportunity to belt them out with the best of them.

Kav's Korner, 5600 N. Milwaukee, Chicago, IL 60646
(312) 774-8787
Acoustic music nights on Thursdays in a tavern in a Northwest Side neighborhood not known for musical entertainment, or, come to think of it, not known for much of anything at all. "Play anything you want," says the owner.

Kerrigan's, 5355 N. Clark, Chicago, IL 60640 (312) 784-0700
You might have to contend with the wails of a couple neighborhood hounds who tend to hang out here, and if you want to drown out the pool players, you'll have to bring your own sound equipment. Hell, if it's a slow night, you might want to bring your own audience, too.

No Exit, 6970 N. Glenwood, Chicago, IL 60626 (312) 743-3355
The ultimate throwback café/restaurant in the ultimate throwback neighborhood. All forms of acoustic music are welcomed here in this cramped, seventies hippie hangout, but you might have the best luck if you start your set out with "Michael, Row the Boat Ashore." Hallelujah.

Red's Lounge, 3479 S. Archer, Chicago, IL 60608 (312) 376-0517
Has a slightly seedy but mostly cool scene on Wednesday nights, when blues musicians of all shapes and sizes come to strut their stuff.

Townhall Pub, 3340 N. Halsted, Chicago, IL 60657 (312) 472-4405
Slightly seedy locale smack dab in the middle of Boys' Town, catering to old-school folkies with acoustic guitars.

U.S. Beer Company, 1801 N. Clybourn, Chicago, IL 60614
(312) 871-7799
Because the crowds are light at this tavern in a once-hot neighborhood strip, the owners are not particularly choosy about the kind of music they want to hear. Acoustic? Electric? "Play whatever you want," snaps the bartender.

Six Ways to Find the Right Name for Your Band

Every great band needs a great name. Here are some ways to choose or not to choose a name. None of these are copyrighted; they're all yours if you want them.

1. Something easy to remember, like a name—like *your* name, but only if you have a cool one. And please, use only the first or the last name, never both. Beth is a good name for a band, but not Beth Johnson. Rodriguez is an all right band name, but not Steve Rodriguez. And please, none of this The Dave Mulejuice Band. This ain't the seventies. This ain't the suburbs. That's cheesy.

2. Something cryptic and political sounding that does not betray any particular political significance. Bad idea: Richard Nixon's an Asshole. Better: Nixon Quandry. Ideas: Lone Gunman Theory, King's English, Rich Be Damned.

3. Any eccentric combination of an adjective and a noun, but nothing trite or expected. Try not to make too much sense. Bad idea: Deadly Warning (hackneyed and sounds like a metal band). Better: Cautionary Dreamphase. Ideas: Amphibious Motion, Liturgical Quiver, Borborygmic Squirrel.

4. A noun without an article, preferably a peculiar one. No plural nouns. For some reason, those went out around the seventies. Bad idea: The Wayfarers. Better: Wayfarer. Ideas: Juice, Detriment, Rump, Hick.

5. A reference to a TV show. With all the seventies nostalgia in the air, any in-joke will attract those scary folks who align themselves with Generation X and say they like "alternative rock." The more obscure and in-jokey, the better. Bad idea: The Laura Petrie Dancers. Better: Rob's Ottoman. Ideas: Samantha's Twin, The Regal Beagle, Orson from Ork, Whatcha Talkin' 'Bout Willis.

6. Oblique reference to a fictional character, preferably someone from a cool movie or book. No dork movies, please, and nothing trite. Bad ideas: Chewbacca. The Caulfields. Better: Rick Blaine. Ideas: Liberty Valance, Arquette's Scar, Plaster of Paris Bagel, Corleone's Horse, X's Game, Belle's Day Off, Split Coweye.

Recording Studios and Rehearsal Spaces

So you've got this band, and you want to get booked, and you want to record your demo tape. You'll need a place to do it that can turn out a professional product. This city has a ton of them, but don't go if you don't have your act together. They charge by the hour, and if you don't watch out, you might wind up paying a ton. There are also a lot of people in the recording business who shouldn't be there. One of the biggest decisions for a band starting out is whether to use an old-style analog recording system or a digital one. There are schools of thought that say ADAT, a cheap form of digital recording, is a lousy way to go about business and doesn't give as pure and authentic a sound as vintage gear. Largely, it's a matter of taste.

When you're ready to record your demo or an album's worth of material, realize that the equipment a studio has is only part of the ball game. What's most important is the dude or dudette running it. After all, what good's a Ferrari Testerosa if you've got a moron driving it? Try to find a studio with an engineer and producer who dig your stuff and have produced stuff you like. Also, keep in mind the vibe of the studio. If it's not comfortable for you and you think the studio operator's a schmuck, then there's no way in hell you're going to want to spend twelve hours a day there refining your songs. Here's a look at the lucky twenty-one places to record and rehearse in and around the Chicago area.

Acme Recording Company, 1708 W. Belmont, Chicago, IL 60657 (312) 477-7333
Founded in 1974 as ZZZZZZ, Incorporated. It has 24-track, 16-track, and 2-track recording studios with rates of $55–$75 per hour. The company also offers high-speed tape duplication services on-site. Star sightings: The Coctails, Oo Oo Wa, Maggie Brown.

Airwave Recording Studios, 2108 W. Roscoe, Chicago, IL 60618 (312) 404-0453
A 24-track studio that tends to lean toward more classical- or jazz-oriented projects. Star sightings: Brad Goode, Ira Sullivan, Northwest Indiana Symphony.

American Creative Entertainment Company, 16 N. Wabash, Chicago, IL 60653 (312) 548-4600
Does mostly radio theater and hip-hop music production. Produced radio soap operas *Grand Boulevard* and *East 47th Street*. It's not the most elaborate studio you've ever seen, but certainly one of the only ones doing this sort of work.

Battery Recording Studios, 700 N. Green, Chicago, IL 60622 (312) 942-9000
A 24-track studio with the ability to handle all-over-the-map clientele. Star sightings: Michael Jackson, R. Kelly, The Jesus Lizard, Reverend Horton Heat, Poi Dog Pondering.

Chicago Recording Company, 232 E. Ohio, Chicago, IL 60611
(312) 822-9333
Founded in 1979. All-purpose, professional recording center has three 24-track analog studios, digital editing capability, and more. A graduated rate scale is based on your ability to pay. Star sightings: Pearl Jam, Michael Jackson, Smashing Pumpkins, Steve Albini, Robert Plant, Jimmy Page, Al Jourgenson, Nine Inch Nails, The Jesus Lizard, Buddy Guy, The Smithereens.

Chicago Trax Recording, 3347 N. Halsted, Chicago, IL 60657
(312) 525-6565
Three 24-track studios are available. Depending on the sophistication of the studio you choose and the time you want to record (after midnight is cheaper), rates run $40–$110 per hour. A special package deal is available for unsigned artists: $1,400 for twenty hours of studio time, reel, master, and ten cassettes. Has a huge staff and client list. Star sightings: Ministry, Red Hot Chili Peppers, Michelle Shocked, Dizzy Gillespie, R. Kelly, Buddy Miles.

Dress Rehearsals Limited, 1840 W. Hubbard, Chicago, IL 60622
(312) 829-2213
Founded in 1980. Has three rehearsal spaces ($12–$15 per hour), 24-track recording ($40 per hour), and live sound. Star sightings: Liz Phair, Smashing Pumpkins, Veruca Salt, Poi Dog Pondering. Tips: Book two to three weeks in advance.

Flat Iron Recording/Loose Booty Studios, 2631 W. Division, Chicago, IL 60622 (312) 243-0167
Flat iron is a 24-track studio that recently merged with Loose Booty to form a company designed to service the alternative rock community. Rates are $35 per hour. Star sightings: Vandermark Quartet, Tarpit, Fix Your Wagon.

Gravity Studios, 2250 W. North, Chicago, IL 60647 (312) 862-1880
A 16-track, automated digital recording studio specializing in the local alternative rock scene. Rates are in the neighborhood of $500 per day. Star sightings: Smashing Pumpkins, Veruca Salt, Red Red Meat, Loud Lucy, Figdish, Punch.

Idful Music Corporation, 1520A N. Damen, Chicago, IL 60622
(312) 772-1000
By-now-legendary local, cool, 24-track studio boasting a minimal, basic sound pioneered by Liz Phair, Veruca Salt producer Brad Wood, and former Phair sideman Casey Rice. Star sightings: Gastr del Sol, Tortoise, Liz Phair, Red Red Meat.

Mainline Studios, 2211 N. Elston, Chicago, IL 60614
(312) 862-4545
A 24-track digital recording studio charging $40 an hour. Mostly deals with alternative rock, R & B, and rap. Dim star sightings: Drag, Daughter, The Hipnotics.

Odyssey Sound Studio, 1820 S. Michigan, Chicago, IL 60616
(312) 842-1371
A 36-track recording studio. Rates are on a graduated scale, $55 per hour and up. Star sightings: Willie Dixon, Howlin' Wolf, The Chi-Lites. It's very choosy about clients and works mostly with major label artists.

Off World Studios, 5219 N. Clark, Chicago, IL 60640
(312) 728-1078
Works with heavy rock artists. Uses vintage equipment, tube gear. Owner-producer Dane Roewade offers this advice: "Stay away from recordings that will make you 'sound good for a local band.' There's no such thing as 'good for a local sound.' A record you make now should sound as good as an old Aerosmith record or whatever sounded good way back when." Star sightings: D.O.P.E., Teen Alien, The Hushdrops.

Paragon Studios, 820 W. Fulton, Chicago, IL 60607 (312) 942-0075
Has 2-track to 24-track equipment. Star sightings: Ohio Players, Junior Wells.

Playroom Recording Studio, 520 N. Michigan, Chicago, IL 60611
(708) 626-8873
Everything from dance music to blues to ad jingles is recorded here. Has 16-track digital and 24-track analog. Rates are on a graduated price scale, $65–$150 an hour. Star sightings: The Out Here Brothers, Cicero Blake, AYA. Reserve at least one week in advance.

Pumpkin Recording, 8453 Rob Roy, Orland Park, IL 60462
(708) 349-1845
And you wondered what happened to Chicago rock legends once they fell out of the limelight. A 24-track suburban rock studio run by former American Breed ("Bend Me, Shape Me") founder-member Gary Loizzo. Star sightings: Dennis DeYoung, Styx.

Soto Sound Studio, 838 W. Grand, Chicago, IL 60622
(312) 738-0771
A 16-track recording studio with experience in basically all forms of pop music, yet leans toward rap and dance. Studio time runs $40 per hour. For the

novice, Soto also offers to write the music for your song or rap for a minimum of $125. Star sightings: GT Posse, 4PM, Buddy Guy, Barking Bill, Walter Payton, William Perry, Peter Tork, The Luvabulls (!).

Soundworks, 3126 N. Greenview, Chicago, IL 60657
(312) 296-4820
A 24-track studio dedicated to album-ready rock artists. Graduated rates are available. Star sightings: Smashing Pumpkins, The Drovers, Triple Fast Action, Green, 77 Luscious Babes.

Streeterville Studios, 161 E. Grand Ave., Chicago, IL 60611
(312) 644-1666
Not really affordable for the average Joe off the streets with a demo to hawk, this top-of-the line 24-track joint is the place where you aspire to wind up when the record company's footing the bill. Cool, professional atmosphere makes this a place you'd want to laze around for hours on end, even though it costs a minimum of $250 an hour to do a 24-track recording here. Star sightings: Eric Clapton, Collective Soul, Robert Plant, Madonna, Neil Diamond, Donny Osmond.

Trackwork Orange, Incorporated, 520 N. Michigan, Chicago, IL 60611 (312) 644-4304
Priding itself as much on its cool city view as its cushy atmosphere, this 24-track studio offers graduated rates for its eclectic selection of pop and alternative rock clients. Star Sightings: Adamjack, Crucifix.

Warzone Recorders, 865 N. Larrabee, Chicago, IL 60610
(312) 751-1131
Founded by members of industrio-politico-dance-noise outfit Die Warzau, this 24-track studio at the edge of Cabrini prides itself on its motto: "No Hype—Just Loud Noise." Star sightings: Bjork, Liz Phair, Poi Dog Pondering, Pigface, and of course, Die Warzau.

Gigs and Where to Get Them (and ones you might want to avoid)

The first thing you're gonna need if you want to play any of the local clubs is a promo kit: basically, a list of some places you've played, a demo of your music, and a picture if you can afford one. Most of the times these wind up in the trash, so you're going to have to expect to deliver about three of them to a club before it responds. Offices in bars are notoriously disgusting, dirty, dank, musty places where things get lost. Make sure to deliver your kit in person so that you can have some kind of personal contact and they can't say, "We never got that; send us another one." No one is going to seek you out; you have to be the one making the calls. There is an art to calling a club's booking agent often without being a pain in the ass. Learn it.

When you're first starting out, it's obvious that you should just play whatever gigs you can. Even if it's in the back of some gas station out on River Road, at least you're getting established and developing a following. That's the most important thing to clubs before anyone's heard of you. Can you fill a club? Can you sell drinks? That's what you're there for at the beginning, not for the music. One of the first things people are going to ask you is "How big is your mailing list?" Make sure you have one consisting of all your friends, family, et cetera, and make sure you add to it every time you play by passing out cards or having a friend go around with a clipboard. Also, when you're starting out, you're going to be on a bill with two other bands. Try to get on a bill with bands that are complementary to you, so that if you're a power pop trio, you don't have to spend your time winning over the heavy metal crowd that came to see the other band. Try to be the middle act on a bill. No one ever gets there to see the warm-up act, and by time the last show starts up, people have already started to leave.

Once you have a few gigs under your belt and you've completed the promo kit, you're going to need to be a little more selective about the clubs you choose and the days you play there. Be wary if some club is all eager to book you on weekends that are notoriously shitty for business (Christmas Eve, Labor Day, Memorial Day). You're better off taking a weeknight sometimes, especially if it's Halloween or St. Patrick's Day. There are some places you can play in town and actually damage your reputation. Not only will it hurt you if you happen to play some repulsive metal bar that sandwiches you in between Van Halen tribute bands, but it might start giving people the idea that you're just another Journey rip-off band from Westmont, and then the cool folks will think twice about signing you to that hip independent label. Please keep in mind your hair, too. No short in the front, long in the back cuts for you men out there (and no droopy mustaches), and no feathered hair and go-go boots for you ladies, either.

There are prestige gigs and there are money gigs. Sometimes you make only $50 playing Lounge Ax on a weekday night or some summer night, but it's worth it for your exposure and your reputation. Then again, you might also make $500 playing a sports bar, but no one else will hire you on the basis of your having played one of these. Some of the highest profile and best paying gigs are the city's neighborhood festivals (e.g., Sheffield Garden Walk, Oz Park Festival), but these are often hard to get booked into and are chosen way, way, way in advance. You can get a list of festivals from the Mayor's Office of Special Events, (312) 744-3315.

There are hidden costs in the music business, too. Once you get booked into a club, you'll frequently have a sound person who gets paid out of your take of the door. Don't be a dick about it and say "We can do our own sound." The sound guy can make you sound good or lousy and he or she can give you a recommendation to the boss if you're cool.

There's no possible way to chronicle all the bars in Chicago that showcase music. Blues clubs alone would have to be an entire book to include everything from Lee's Unleaded Blues to the Cuddle Inn to the New Zodiac to Koko Taylor's. Jazz is a nightmare as well, pulling in the crowds everywhere from the downtown Underground Wonder Bar to the Celebrity Club. Of course, there's Joe Segal's legendary Jazz Showcase, undoubtedly the best jazz room in the city, but it is rare that any local jazz musician can get work here except as an occasional sideman. And then there's that exploding rock scene with Czar Bar, Sweet Alice, dozens of high-profile locations in the city, and a smattering in the suburbs. What I've done is provide a cross-section of forty or so city clubs to give you an idea of the kinds of things that different clubs look for and what some are willing to pay.

To further expedite your decision-making process in choosing the gigs where *you* want to play, I have included a handy Suburb-O-Meter (copyright pending). Remember, if you're the next big band out of Chicago, the higher up you go on the Suburb-O-Meter, the less you want to play there.

Key to the Suburb-O-Meter

0/5: Cool place, great atmosphere, groovy people in the audience, great bands. Any one in their right mind would hire you after you played here, 'cause it's just that cool.

1/5: Slightly more conservative atmosphere, better dressed crowd, pleasant vibe, but lacking just a little bit in grit and urban flavor.

2/5: Only good bands play here, so you're in good company, but why do all the boys and girls have such cool haircuts and why do they all look like they go to DePaul?

3/5: While you're on stage, are you getting the feeling that everybody in the crowd's part of some accounting firm and drives a Nissan? Somehow, you get the impression that people want to eat fried mozzarella and buffalo wings more than listen to your music.

4/5: You're in Chicago, or at least you're near it. So what's with all these guys with cut-off motorcycle jackets and ladies with feathered hair? And why's the guy in the band that's up before you singing "Open Arms" by Journey?

5/5: You feel out of place. Lots of leather pants, go-go boots and short in the front, long in the back haircuts. Time to leave, you think, but for some reason, you think you'd better not for fear of getting your ass kicked by that blonde guy with the lazy eye and the tire iron in his jacket pocket.

Abbey Pub, 3420 W. Grace, Chicago, IL 60618 (312) 478-4408
Has a neighborhood pub atmosphere for neighborhood pub music. Be mellow, no hard rock, no blues, either, even if it is mellow. Leans toward acoustic and Irish folk. Your best chance is if you've got an Irish guy in your band. Bands negotiate their own deal, usually a cut (sometimes a major one) of the door. Suburb-O-Meter: 1/5.

After Shock, 5405 W. Addison, Chicago, IL 60641 (312) 202-9209
Tough crowd. Plus, they like cover bands, though you can do originals here, too, if the audience will let you get away with it. Very high MQ (Mustache Quotient). Bands negotiate their own deals with the manager. No rap ("What's that new stuff? What do they call it? Is that rap?"), no heavy metal, either, though sometimes the crowd might fool you. Suburb-O-Meter: 3/5.

Alexander's Steak House, 3010 E. 79th, Chicago, IL 60617
(312) 768-6555
A South Shore standby since 1917 booking mainly jazz with the occasional blues or comedy night. Looking for acts with a following—it's best if you can guarantee a house of about one hundred a night, then you get a cut of it. Bookings are mainly done through agents or if you send a video of your performance, though sometimes sitting in for an open jam session works, too. Suburb-O-Meter: 1/5.

Andy's, 11 E. Hubbard, Chicago, IL 60611 (312) 642-6805
Ninety-eight percent jazz, two percent late night blues. One of the top jazz places in the city and peopled by aficionados, lunching businessmen, and the occasional flock of German tourists. It helps if you know musicians who play here. Bookers require a small bio with your demo (best if it's a CD). Your best chance of breaking in is on late night sets on weeknights. Bands make a flat rate, but the rate you get—well, that depends on who you are. Suburb-O-Meter: 2/5.

Arena, 5859 S. Harlem, Chicago, IL 60638 (312) 586-0906
Oldies groups, tribute bands (e.g., Santana) play here, mostly rock and roll, no heavy metal. Your band gets a flat rate, which gets boosted if you go over real well, and then you may be asked to perform on a monthly basis. Suburb-O-Meter: 3.5/5.

Augenblick, 3907 N. Damen, Chicago, IL 60618 (312) 929-0994
Not exactly a location to get you famous (more neighborhood artists and Arthur Andersen employees than hungry A & R execs looking for the next Veruca Salt come here). Nor will it earn you any more than gas money. But there's a very cool Bohemian vibe here, if you can allow yourself to be heard among the rude swingers trying to talk up their dates and the pinball players. Books acoustic musicians only with an emphasis on Irish folk. Suburb-O-Meter: .5/5.

J. D. Batt's, 12237 S. Western, Blue Island, IL 60406 (708) 389-7910
Big-ass, somewhat cheesy sports bar with big-screen sports events and/or karaoke during the weeknights and original or tribute bands on the weekends. All booking is done by United Talent Coordinators, (708) 620-1154. Send your tape, promo kit, and maybe even a list of your best tunes, including cover versions. Send them a pseudonym for your band as well if you don't want the bigshots in the industry to know you played here. First criterion is how much audience you can draw. Second criterion is whether you are any good. After all, "even if you have a great fan base, there's at least a modicum of taste involved." Suburb-O-Meter: 4.5/5.

Beat Kitchen, 2100 W. Belmont, Chicago, IL 60618 (312) 281-4444
The club owner has a reputation for being very fair with bands. Books 95 percent rock here and rarely seeks out bands, relying on tapes coming in through the door or band recommendations. Professionalism is a must. During the week, bands starting out get the door. If you hand out free passes, you'll get a buck for each of them. Weekend bands get $100–$150 plus percentage; more prestigious ones can get a $1,500 guarantee. That's rare, though. Bands must remember, says owner, that "it takes a certain amount of effort to get your people out for a show and hold up your end of the bargain. If you can draw a hundred people, you can usually get a weekend gig." But, though this is a very friendly bar in a cool, relatively untraveled location, one band member who plays here gripes that the managers are too worried about volume and "force you to turn it down past all reason." Suburb-O-Meter: 1/5.

*B.L.U.E.S., 2519 N. Halsted, Chicago, IL 60614, and **B.L.U.E.S. Etc.**, 1124 W. Belmont, Chicago, IL 60657 (312) 525-8371
Top-of-the-line Chicago blues clubs booking top-of-the-line Chicago bands. They'll listen to tapes, but unless you're established, it's really difficult to get in here. Besides, they don't really trust tapes. Sometimes if you've got a Grammy, it's still difficult to get in here. You can play the open jam sessions, but those are usually packed, and it's difficult to shine when you're trying to intersperse your licks with a trader from Oswego who's trying to sound like Howlin' Wolf. Advice: Know how to construct three sets with beginnings, middles, and ends. If you're "Joe Hotlicks from Schaumburg" and you know some Clapton tunes, good for you, but don't bother coming here. Best way to get booked is to have a big shot in the Chi-town blues scene recommend you. Pay for the Halsted location ranges from $250 to the semisignificant four-figures. For Belmont, it's $250 to the very significant four-figures. Halsted Location Suburb-O-Meter: 1/5; Belmont location Suburb-O-Meter: 2/5.

Bop Shop, 1807 W. Division, Chicago, IL 60614 (312) 235-3232
Groovy, eclectic neighborhood venue that's around 90 percent jazz, 5 percent rockabilly, and 5 percent God knows what else, sometimes even theater. "Anything but hip-hop," says the manager. Send a picture along with your promo kit and expect to hear back in about two to three weeks. Bands cut their own deals. Suburb-O-Meter: .5/5.

Brother Jimmy's BBQ, 2909 N. Sheffield, Chicago, IL 60657 (312) 528-0888
Trying-too-hard-to-be-authentic, down-home, too-cute, pseudo-Southern roadhouse atmosphere detracts from usually high-quality bands booked here. Emphasis is on roots-rock, blues, R & B, most anything hip, which can draw from the college circuit. No alternative rock, no metal. Bookers frequently consult *Pollstar Magazine* to get a feel for bands to book. Feel free to send or drop off a disk, but booking is rarely done solely on this basis. "Disks can be deceiving." Advice: Be persistent and aggressive. Contact Yoel at Gulf Coast, (312) 929-4777. Suburb-O-Meter: 2/5.

Bub City, 901 W. Weed, Chicago, IL 60622 (312) 266-1200
For years, this was not so much the groovy Western bar it pretended to be. After all, you could always find many a suburban Sweet Sixteen party. But lately, the restaurant/bar has tried to establish a reputation as a roadhouse featuring blues acts, jump bands, and zydeco. Regular local bands tend to make $500–$1,000. Advice: They'll listen to anything, but it's best if you're

recommended by a band that's played here. Bands that have played include Rosa Bailey and Southern Exposure, Guy Lawrence & Chideco-Zydeco, Pistol Pete & The Professionals. Suburb-O-Meter: 2.5/5.

Buddy Guy's Legends of Chicago, 754 S. Wabash, Chicago, IL 60605
(312) 427-0333
One of the most musically solid, commercial clubs on the Chicago scene (emphasis on blues) which, unfortunately for musical purists and fortunately for musicians, has become a major feeding area for tourists from all of the Loop area and Michigan Avenue hotels. Musicians cut their own deals based upon reputation and drawing power. Advice: The poor booker is swamped with tapes he won't listen to unless someone of note on the music scene recommends them. Band Suburb-O-Meter: .5/5; audience Suburb-O-Meter: 4/5.

The Bulls, 1916 N. Lincoln Park West, Chicago, IL 60614
(312) 337-3000
This claustrophobic, basement cavern has been an outpost for jazz since 1965. Though through the eighties and nineties, it was known more for NewAge-y, contemporary jazz outfits, lately The Bulls has been trying to move more toward straight-ahead bebop during the week with some funk and R & B touches on the weekends. You need not be a seasoned pro who's been around the block a zillion times to play here. Local up-and-coming artists are frequently booked early in the week. Advice: Send a promo kit and get a booking somewhere else so the folks here can see you in action first. Suburb-O-Meter: 1.5/5.

Cafe Continental, 5515 N. Lincoln, Chicago, IL 60625
(312) 878-7077
Sometimes it's a bar mitzvah. Sometimes it's a wedding. And it's probably the only place where you can play klezmer music during the dinner hour and get paid for it. Maxwell Street Klezmer Ensemble occasionally invites well-trained musicians with talent to sit in. Weird-O-Meter: 5/5.

Checker Board Lounge, 423 E. 43rd, Chicago, IL 60653
(312) 624-3240
Though lately it is home to more U of C students than neighborhood blues aficionados, this is still the legendary home of the blues where the Rolling Stones came to jam with Junior Wells. Has a very mellow booking policy. Call up, chat with the manager. If he likes how you sound over the phone, he'll ask for a tape. If he likes that, you're in. Pay is variable, anywhere from a couple hundred to a couple thousand bones. Performers' Suburb-O-Meter: 0/5; audience Suburb-O-Meter: 1/5.

Connolly's, 8434 S. Kedzie, Chicago, IL 60652 (312) 476-3646
Books tribute bands, jam sessions, and assorted sleaze on the weekends. You'll find people just getting wasted during the week. Booking is done by United Talent Coordinators. See J. D. Batt's. Suburb-O-Meter: 5/5.

Cotton Club, 1710 S. Michigan, Chicago, IL 60616 (312) 341-9787
Club requires a tape, a bio, and a video. If you're in Chicago, they'll ask you where you're currently playing and will dispatch one of their managers. Primarily, they want to make sure you're crowd pleasing with good stage presence and that you know how to dress. Attitude and appearance is key. Books 75 percent jazz, 25 percent blues. Does showcases for "exceptional talent" on Fridays. Acts generally make $400–$500. Suburb-O-Meter: 1/5.

Cubby Bear, 1059 W. Addison, Chicago, IL 60613 (312) 327-1662
Has a great sound system. It's a great place to see a show. This tightly run bar begins shows promptly as announced. Suffers a little bit from its Wrigley Field sports bar vibe (occasionally you have to try to drown out the well-coifed hordes playing drinking games and chanting "Drink beer! Drink beer, motherfucker! Drink beer! If you can't drink like a man, get that beer out your hand! Drink beer!"). Has two soundmen on the premises who work the room for audio (stage and house sound). They leave the sports events playing on TV while you play. If a game goes to double overtime, you're screwed. All booking is done through Conroy Productions. Suburb-O-Meter: 2.5/5.

Culture Club, 1351 S. Michigan, Chicago, IL 60605
(312) 922-6414
Weird place but cool. Bookings are often done through agents. Local musicians get booked after playing Tuesday night jam sessions, if they're good. Some of these jam sessions, however, can get really rough. Genres include jazz, reggae, salsa, calypso, blues. Payment works on straight percentage. "If you got more pull, you get more of the door. It makes sense, don't it?" Suburb-O-Meter: 0/5.

The Dalmatian Lounge, 2683 N. Halsted, Chicago, IL 60614
(312) 348-9800
Wicker Park–style music lounge in Lincoln Park yuppie stronghold. Prides itself on its rudimentary sound system and the way it treats musicians (a couple of local musicians run the place). Bands get 100 percent of the door (wow). Tapes and promo kits are OK but not required to get a gig here. Says one of the coproprietors, "We're not buttheads; we talk to people." Notable acts include Dick Justice, Tart. Suburb-O-Meter: 1.5/5.

Double Door, 1572 N. Milwaukee, Chicago, IL 60622
(312) 489-3160
Despite an occasionally annoying suburban vibe, this club maintains a gritty, urban, underground feel. Like the long-standing Metro, it's a classy, professional place to rock. All booking is done through Metro, (312) 549-4140; see them for advice on getting booked here. Suburb-O-Meter: 2/5.

Elbo Room, 2871 N. Lincoln, Chicago, IL 60657 (312) 549-5549
If you can deal with the sometimes stifling DQ (Dork Quotient) here, this is a cozy basement inner sanctum with great acoustics on a stretch of Lincoln Avenue that looks like it's right off a 1940s movie set. Warning: Getting booked and getting back in isn't always a given here, even if you do well. Notable acts who've performed here include Barrett Deems and his big band and acid jazz outfit Liquid Soul. Suburb-O-Meter: 2/5.

The Empty Bottle, 1035 N. Western, Chicago, IL 60622
(312) 276-3600
One of the top rock venues in the city. You have to be persistent in order to get in to play. One band member reports that they always say they didn't get your tape. Be prepared to give your tape to them about three or four times. Suburb-O-Meter: 1/5.

Fireside Bowl, 2646 W. Fullerton, Chicago, IL 60647
(312) 486-2700
The epicenter of the teen punk movement (and you thought it died along with The Clash back in 1984). Not a big moneymaker, but a wild, hip, fun place to play, despite the questionable acoustics. Suburb-O-Meter: 1.5/5.

Fitzgerald's, 6615 Roosevelt, Berwyn, IL 60402 (708) 788-6670
The rowdy roadhouse atmosphere attracts top talent in this surprisingly up-and-coming artsy enclave. Does everything from blues to rock to zydeco, but mostly name acts. Call Bill Fitzgerald for booking information. Suburb-O-Meter: 2/5.

Gold Star Sardine Bar, 680 N. Lake Shore, Chicago, IL 60610
(312) 664-4215
It'll help your getting booked here if you can fake a New York accent. Most of the acts come from the East Coast. Here's why: "I'm old enough to know all the talent," says booker Bill Allen. "Bennett, Bobby Short. I know them, from New York from years ago. It's a different mindset over there. A lot of people all fight for a job and they're working their butt off. This city isn't as competi-

tive. This is a Midwest town. New York's got the best talent. They're exposed to more music, more art." Still, you might be able to sweet-talk your way into an audition. But it's not bloody likely. Upper-West-Side-O-Meter: 5/5.

Green Mill, 4802 N. Broadway, Chicago, IL 60640 (312) 878-5552
The oldest, coolest jazz club in the city. Founded in 1907 and rumored to be a hangout for both Al Capone and Essanay's silent movie stars. Not particularly respectful to the musician, but if you can tolerate shnockered customers talking over your act, you'll be all right. All booking is done through Green Mill Booking, (312) 665-8400. There's no set way to approach this place. Tapes and CDs tend to wind up at the bottom of piles for years. There are no auditions, either. Dedication helps. Sometimes it takes two years of haranguing to get a gig here. Being cool helps, too. "Even if you're great, if you're a nitwit, I probably won't be hiring you," says Dave Jemilo who owns and books here and at the Vu. Best advice: "Kick ass in the jam sessions" and impress the other musicians. Try Friday night and Saturday night jam sessions to attract attention. "Unless you're a real hacker, they'll let you play." Suburb-O-Meter: 0/5.

Gulf Coast, 2251 N. Lincoln, Chicago, IL 60614 (312) 929-4777
Yet another in the ongoing trend of pseudo-Louisiana crab houses, but still a major booker of roots-rock, blues, funk, zydeco, rock and roll, hip-hop, and reggae. No alternative, no metal. See Brother Jimmy's for advice. Suburb-O-Meter: 3.5/5.

Hidden Shamrock, 2723 N. Lincoln, Chicago, IL 60657
(312) 883-0304
Does mostly rock in a college drinking atmosphere. Looks for music that "will bring people in and keep them in." It's more a money gig than a prestige gig. Prefers mostly cover tunes, anything from Johnny Cash to Meat Loaf, but they'll let you stick in a couple originals if you're keeping the crowd happy. Has an excellent payment arrangement. Beginners get 75 percent of the door. Bands usually take home $400–$1,200. More established acts take 80 to 100 percent of the door. Rarely picks bands based on tapes. Once in a while, will give newcomers a chance. Advice: Pester the owner over the phone. Frat-O-Meter: 3.5/5.

Hog Head McDunna's, 1505 W. Fullerton, Chicago, IL 60614
(312) 929-0944
Most important criterion: "Is your mailing list big enough?" Usually looks for a list of about 500. Second criterion: "Do you play decent?" Books mostly rock music here. Not a highly respected, high-profile gig, but bands can make tall cash if they have a lot of friends and get a good percentage of the door, which,

depending on your pull, can be anywhere from 20 to 100 percent. Suburb-O-Meter: 2/5.

Kopi, A Travelers Café, 5317 N. Clark, Chicago, IL 60640
(312) 989-5674
Even though you can get booked to play here, it still feels like open-mike night. Has no stage space to speak of; they just clear away a couple of the tables and there you are sandwiched somewhere in between the young groovers snacking on raspberry brownies, snooping through the cases of travel books, or browsing through the clothes section. Suburb-O-Meter: N/A; Wannabe-Hippie-Meter: 4/5.

Lounge Ax, 2438 N. Lincoln, Chicago, IL 60614 (312) 525-6620
Only deals with "what we hear and what we like" even if it's been recorded on a boom box. Send a letter, copies of press clippings, and they'll get to you. Management has a gut-wrenching listen once a week. Call Tuesday and Thursday 3:00–7:00 P.M. "When we're moving like a machine it takes three weeks." Does mostly rock, but still does singer-songwriter and jazz stuff. "We treat people like people. We give a case of beer. We won't hold it against them if they don't draw." Starting-out bands get a percentage of the door. Payment is anywhere from $50 on up into the four-figure range. "If they fill the room, they're going to get paid that way, but either way, you can't let bands leave without gas money." Reputed for treating its musicians well, but sometimes more interested in the national indie scene than the locals. Does soundchecks always. Says one Lounge Ax veteran player, "Nobody should be bummed to come see you here." Suburb-O-Meter: 1/5.

Lunar Cabaret and Full Moon Cafe, 2827 N. Lincoln, Chicago,
IL 60657 (312) 327-6666
A cool folk and jazz place strong on acoustic tunes and veggie cuisine, which somehow, despite what you'd think, has a decidedly nineties twist. Interested in unusual, good sounding music. Quite a bit of avant-garde jazz. Started by members of Maestro Subgum and The Whole and the Curious Theater Branch. Artistic strength is a criterion, not how well you draw. Acts who've played here include Vandermark Quartet, Erwin Helfer, and Ferron. "If you've got regular gigs at Lounge Ax and Elbo Room, we're probably not interested." Is skittish about offering guarantees. Offers 70 to 80 percent of the door. Suburb-O-Meter: .5/5.

Metro, 3730 N. Clark, Chicago, IL 60613 (312) 549-0203
One of the best places for rock bands to play in Chicago. Has a top-of-the line
sound system (it's not that common, believe me). "They give you the total
rock star treatment here," says one Metro veteran. Always treats musicians
and their guests well. Always will give you a soundcheck. Gives you a decent
dressing room and sometimes will even put a case of beer on ice for you. Even
has people here to help haul in your gear. Frequently deals with booking agencies, but will listen and respond to everything sent to them within a month.
Best advice: If you're friends with a bigger band that has drawing power, try
to coordinate a show with them. Suburb-O-Meter: 1.5/5.

Phyllis's Musical Inn, 1800 W. Division, Chicago, IL 60622
(312) 486-9862
Everybody starts here. Call Clem after 7:00 P.M. to try to get a booking. An
excellent place for bands just starting to hit the scene. Has a very cool vibe,
but sound system virtually nonexistent. Bring your own PA system and your
own parts. Suburb-O-Meter: 1.5/5.

River West, 1860 N. Elston, Chicago, IL 60622 (312) 276-4846
A very roomy, immaculate bar with just a tiny dose of suburbia in it. The
booking policy is all over the map, including everything from blues to tribute
bands. Your best chance for breaking in is to come to the club's open blues or
rock and roll jams. Suburb-O-Meter: 2/5.

Rosa's, 3420 W. Armitage, Chicago, IL 60647 (312) 342-0452
One of the more daring, experimental blues clubs in town. That experimen-
talism is the product of owner-booker-musician Tony, who emigrated from
Italy in 1978 to discover and educate himself about the blues. Books all sorts
of blues artists from old traditional folk musicians to more sophisticated, contemporary bands. Willing to take risks. Suburb-O-Meter: 0/5.

Schuba's Tavern, 3159 N. Southport, Chicago, IL 60657
(312) 525-2508
It's very difficult to get into this casual, yuppie-vibed bar, which has a reputation for booking acoustic acts, but does everything from rock to folk to country
to big band jazz. Very few slots are available for local acts, and those are usually on Wednesday and Thursday nights. The majority of local acts get a
straight, high percentage of the door (80 to 90). Often does not accept demos.
Call booking hotline to see if they do today, (312) 327-0552. Suburb-O-Meter:
2/5.

Thirsty Whale, 8800 W. Grand, River Grove, IL 60171
(708) 456-2414
The ultimate heavy metal nightmare venue, which is a great place to work out for bands with a sense of humor who survive the ordeal. Features groups which occasionally have been known to identify themselves as kill-your-mother-type bands. Spotty on soundchecks, and the word on the street is that sometimes you've got to pay the right guy to get one. If you want to get booked here, show up on Tuesday between 6:00 and 9:00 P.M. and talk to the booking agent. Acts booked include Malevolent Creation, Suffocation, Mudface, and Technicolor Yawn. Suburb-O-Meter: 4.5/5.

Thurston's, 1248 W. George, Chicago, IL 60657 (312) 472-6900
Slightly cramped performance space nicely sequestered from the downstairs pool players listening to Bush on the jukebox and thinking they're major. You always need to send a tape and some kind of bio. Books a lot of bands just off tape, rarely books off of just plain recommendation. Does 80 percent rock, but some funk and hip-hop, too. Mail tapes. The booker says, "Bands drop a lot of tapes off at night at the bar and they think that by handing it to someone it's better. They get left behind the bar and I never get them." Bands get percentage of the door, anywhere from 20 to 100 percent. On three-band nights, bands split the door. Suburb-O-Meter: 2.5/5.

The Vu, 2624 N. Lincoln, Chicago, IL 60614 (312) 871-0205
A great neighborhood jazz bar. All booking done through Green Mill Booking, (312) 665-8400. See Green Mill for its booking policy. Advice: Try to sit in on Sunday night jam sessions. Suburb-O-Meter: 1/5.

Wild Hare, 3530 N. Clark, Chicago, IL 60657 (312) 327-4273
The reigning preeminent reggae bar in the city still is the best place to play your hot, spleef-tokin tunes, even if the audience looks ready for a frat party. Call Ashi after 10:00 P.M. if you want to try to get booked here. Suburb-O-Meter: 2/5.

The Wrigleyside, 3527 N. Clark, Chicago, IL 60657 (312) 525-5909
Not all that hard to get into, this sometimes obnoxious, sometimes fun (depending on your mood) venue usually offers a good percentage of the door and, if there's a Cubs night game that night, you might clean up. Has a nice sound system, but won't draw many of the city's more prestigious bands. Young-Dan-and-Marilyn-Quayle-O-Meter: 4/5.

More Than 40 (well, 41) Labels and How to Approach Them

Alligator Records, PO Box 60234, Chicago, IL 60660
(312) 973-7736
Founded in 1971. The premier Chicago blues label began as founder-producer Bruce Iglauer's dream to record Hound Dog Taylor and has released over a hundred traditional and contemporary blues titles. Acts produced: Koko Taylor, Son Seals, Albert Collins, The Kinsey Report, A. C. Reed. Advice: Start out by being an established blues star. That'll help.

Bee Hive Records, 1139 Colfax, Evanston, IL 60201 (847) 328-5593
Small jazz label dedicated to producing less-exposed talent. Acts produced: Von Freeman, Johnny Hartman, Clifford Jordan.

Black Top Records, 1480 W. Grace, Chicago, IL 60613
(312) 477-9224
Multipurpose label producing relatively well-known acts in blues, soul, rockabilly, and zydeco. Acts produced: Maria Muldaur, Anson Funderburgh. Advice: Call first to see if they're accepting demos.

Black Vinyl Records, 2269 Sheridan, Zion, IL 60099 (847) 746-3767
Begun as a sort of offshoot to Zion-based alternative rockers Shoes (who were alternative before alternative was cool), this label has been branching out to tackling other lesser-known alternative pop acts. Acts produced: Shoes, The Spongetones, The Critics.

Blind Pig Records, 3022 N. Allen, Chicago, IL 60618
(312) 772-0043
Another small label dedicated to preserving this city's blues roots tradition. Acts produced: Otis Rush, Pinetop Perkins, Magic Slim, Junior Wells.

Bloodshot Records, 912 W. Addison, Chicago, IL 60613
(312) 248-4709
If you got stuck in Chicago and, for some reason, you're still playing country, you're in luck. Bloodshot's probably one of the only places where you can get your country tunes produced. Not if it's straight country, though. Bloodshot's far more interested in the hard-edged, underground country sounds. Acts produced: The Waco Brothers, Moonshine Willy, compilation album *For a Life of Sin*.

Buzz Records, 2048 N. Damen, Chicago, IL 60647 (312) 489-8800
An alternative, indie label, which seems to produce a lot of talent that plays local clubs like the Double Door. Acts produced: Throw, Peat Moss, Starbilly.

Cargo Records, 3058 N. Clybourn, Chicago, IL 60618 (312) 935-5663
Aggressive, alternative, indie rock pop label. Acts produced: Coral, Pitchblend, 7 Seconds, Smudge.

Carrot Top Records, 2438 N. Lincoln, Chicago, IL 60613
(312) 929-9117
Founded in 1992. Advice: This is a company with limited resources. You've got to be lucky and/or original to attract their attention. Acts produced: Drunken Fish, The Coctails, Poi Dog Pondering.

Delmark Records, 4121 N. Rockwell, Chicago, IL 60618
(312) 539-5001
Founded in 1953. It's the oldest active label still run by its founder, who is Chicago's foremost jazz and blues authority, Bob Koester. Produces top-of-the-line jazz and blues. No amateurs. No vocalists, really. Keep in mind the idiosyncratic tastes of the label by looking at the type of acts they've recorded. They passed on local emerging star Kurt Elling before Blue Note picked him up. Acts produced: Junior Wells, Magic Sam, Jimmy Dawkins, Ira Sullivan, Lin Halliday, Malachi Thompson.

D.J. International, 727 W. Randolph, Chicago, IL 60606
(312) 559-1845
One of the labels that have continued to push the house music scene, D.J. has made Chicago an international center for dance music. Acts produced: Joe Smooth, Julian "Jumpin'" Perez.

Drag City, PO Box 476867, Chicago, IL 60647 (312) 455-1015
One of the major indies in town, Drag City has produced a number of alternative rock bands as well as dabbling in more experimental and/or hip-hop bands. Acts produced: Pavement, The Silver Jews, King Kong, Gastr del Sol.

Earwig Music Company, 2046 W. Lunt, Chicago, IL 60645
(312) 262-0278
Founded in 1979. Dedicated to preserving the blues tradition by recording infrequently produced Chicago and Delta blues artists. Advice: start a long, unheralded career and contact label prez Michael Frank sometime in the twenty-first century. Acts produced: The Jelly Roll Kings, Honeyboy Edwards, Jimmy Dawkins, Lester Davenport, Homesick James.

Firebrick Records Incorporated, PO Box 93, Evanston, IL 60204-0093
(312) 509-5182
Founded in 1994. A do-it-yourself label that requires bands to do most of their own work, like helping out with mailings, phone calls, and developing contacts. Firebrick is more interested in getting music "out there" than acquiring big money contracts. Leans toward the alternative rock side of things with a decidedly low-fi sound. Acts produced: Marble, Kal-Ri, X-Parrot, Infraction.

Fuse Records, PO Box 578497, Chicago, IL 60657 (312) 549-6410
Don't let me tell you. They say it themselves. "The best shitty little label in the world" is the motto here. Produces hard-edged alternative rock with an attitude. Acts produced: Buster Soundcheck, Shat, and Wicker Park legend Wesley Willis.

Gold Karat Records, 5501 N. Broadway, Chicago, IL 60640
(312) 989-4140
This North Side label has all-over-the-map interests. Has done everything from blues to R & B to country and gospel. Acts produced: Linda Clifford, Timothy Onumonu, Nanette Frank.

Goose Island Records, 5004 N. Cicero, Chicago, IL 60630
(312) 283-2704
Small, mellow label dedicated to country-folk, or is it folk-country? Acts produced: Chuck Koster, Ron Hines.

Heart & Soul Productions, 6050 W. Touhy, Chicago, IL 60646
(312) 775-9797
Founded in 1986. A small label attached to a 24-track recording studio, the Acoustic Cafe. Emphasis is on hard rock, hard alternative, and metal. Send your tape and/or promo kit. Acts produced: Sphinx, Squadron, Hugo.

Hit It Recordings, 232 E. Ohio, Chicago, IL 60611 (312) 440-9012
Founded in 1994. Runs the gamut from punk rock to ambient. Advice: research the company—no bad bar bands, metal bands, or other misguided folks. Acts produced: Butterfly Child, Global Communication, and 'O' Rang, featuring members of Talk Talk.

Invisible Records, PO Box 16008, Chicago, IL 60616
(312) 808-0222
Produces alternative music that leans toward the heavy and/or industrial. Acts produced: Pigface, Murder Inc., Bizarre Sex Trio.

Jive Records, 700 N. Green, Chicago, IL 60622 (312) 942-9700
It's the local arm of a vital, powerful hip-hop and R & B label. Acts produced: DJ Jazzy Jeff and the Fresh Prince, R. Kelly.

Johnann's Face Records, PO Box 479164, Chicago, IL 60647 (312) 226-0957
Emphasizes post-punk rock with an aggressive pop edge. Acts produced: The Smoothies, Chia Pet, Smoking Popes.

Lion's Lair Records, PO Box 264, Rolling Prarie, IN 46371 (312) 561-9652
Founded in 1995. Does jazz and avant-garde, new music, as well as improvisation. Advice: Only contact if you work in jazz or in the tradition of Laurie Anderson, Philip Glass, Steve Reich, and so forth. No rap, no metal, obviously. Acts produced: Gwynne Winsberg, Tim Tobias.

March Records, PO Box 578396 Chicago, IL 60657 (312) 296-4321
Aggressive promotion is offered by this relatively new label, headed by consummate scenester, former Thurston's booker, and sales pro John "Skippy" McFadden, who is said to have quite an eye for discovering talent. He says so, too. Acts produced: Loud Lucy, Catherine, Outrageous Cherry, Holiday, Bunnygrunt.

Minty Fresh, PO Box 577400, Chicago, IL 60657 (312) 665-0289
The indie brainchild of a local music aficionado, most notable for having signed up Veruca Salt. Acts produced: Veruca Salt, Papas Fritas.

MonsterDisc, 1333 N. Kingsbury, Chicago, IL 60622 (312) 266-5770
Fast becoming a major force for the local bar band set, this label leans toward accessible pop. Acts produced: The Insiders, Spies Who Surf, Texas Rubies, Nicholas Tremulis.

Organico, 858 W. Armitage, Chicago, IL 60614 (312) 227-1474
Dance, techno, house, and ambient music label started up by former WaxTrax! talent scout Matt Adell. Attempts to release experimental and entertaining electronic music. Listens for musicians capable of channeling the voice of God or the other side of existence. Acts produced: Derrick Carter, Dubtribe, Octarine, Squishy.

Pravda, 3823 N. Southport, Chicago, IL 60613 (312) 549-3776
The label that everybody with a buzz cut, a razor necklace, and a Dead Kennedys T-shirt always thought was cool. Produces trash pop, alternative

weirdness, and psychopathic hard core. If you haven't heard of this label, you shouldn't want to be on it. Acts produced: The Service, The New Duncan Imperials, Boom Hank, Susan Voelz, Green.

Quarterstick, PO Box 25342, Chicago, IL 60625 (312) 463-4446
Hard-driving, influential, aggressive rock label. Acts produced: Henry Rollins, Mule, Pegboy, Mekons.

Scratchie Records, 1914 N. Milwaukee, Chicago, IL 60647
(312) 342-6196
A new, artist-based label started in January 1995, founded by members of Smashing Pumpkins, members of Catherine, a dancehall music producer, and publicist Jeremy Freeman. Promises "not to work with weasels or fuck anyone over." Combines everything including dance hall, "jungle music," dub music, and rock. Acts produced: Chainsaw Kittens, Full Fledj, Pancho Kryztal and Hitmen, Lenky.

Skin Graft Records, PO Box 257546, Chicago, IL 60625
(312) 989-9202
New post-punk label that dabbles in electronic weirdness and aggressive rock. Acts produced: UFO or Die, Mount Shasta, and The Jesus Lizard offshoot project Denison/Kimball Trio.

Sonic Records, 1820 S. Michigan, Chicago, IL 60616
(312) 842-1371
Founded in 1977. Has an emphasis on soul, Latin, pop, and R & B. Acts produced: Smoke City, The Fifth Dimension.

Southport/Northport Records, 3501 N. Southport, Chicago, IL 60657
(312) 281-2510
Founded in 1979 by then Checker Cab driver Bradley Parker Sparrow, Southport has become one of the city's premier jazz labels. If you're a jazz performer, send your demo or promo kit to Sparrow at Southport. If you're cool and do Latin, world music, or maybe a little alternative rock, send it to Northport, Sparrow's label for anything he likes that's not traditional jazz. Acts produced: Bradley Parker-Sparrow, Joanie Pallatto, Von Freeman.

Tantrum Records, 4611 N. Seeley, Chicago, IL 60626
(312) 878-9988
Founded in 1993. Acts produced: The Drovers. Tantrum's emphasis: The Drovers. Advice: Call or send a demo—they've worked with Suede Chain,

Crabdaddy, and Fauna in the past and they'd like to do someone else besides The Drovers sometime soon.

Thermometer Records, PO Box 31731, Chicago, IL 60631-0731
(708) 545-2221
A subsidiary of Feedback Music Distribution, an import distributor, Thermometer's difficult to pin down to a specific genre, producing mellow contemporary stuff to metal to Joe Satriani–style guitar riffers. Acts produced: The Millions, The Morganfields, The Drovers, Aftermath, Michael Angelo.

Thrill Jockey Records, PO Box 476794, Chicago, IL 60647
Incredibly eclectic label with a well-known eye for spotting talent in all different genres of pop music, ranging from punk-flavored country to jazz-pop. Has a distribution deal through Touch & Go. Advice: They have an unlisted number, so drop a line first to see if demos are being accepted. Acts produced: Tortoise, The Sea and Cake, Freakwater.

Touch & Go Records, PO Box 25520, Chicago, IL 60625
(312) 463-6316
One of the major labels out of this town, which has made a name for itself through its promotion of uncompromisingly rough and aggressive rock and punk acts. Advice: No unsolicited demos. Acts produced: The Jesus Lizard, Tar, Seam, Shellac.

Waterbug Records, PO Box 6605, Evanston, IL 60204
(847) 332-1583
Founded in 1992. Mellow, poetic folk music label founded by longtime Chicago folk scenester Andrew Calhoun, which helps coffeehouse artists to finance their own releases (lucky you). Advice: Be prepared to help defray the costs, partner. Acts produced: Andrew Calhoun, Julie Henigan, Hugh Blumenfeld, Chuck Pyle, American Impressionist Songwriters (compilation).

WaxTrax! Records, 1659 N. Damen, Chicago, IL 60647
(312) 252-1000
Even after some widely publicized financial troubles, WaxTrax! remains the king of industrial record outfits through its association with New York-based TVT records. Founded in 1980, the label and its president, Jim Nash, steamrolled the way for the twentieth-century industrial revolution, turning smoky, pseudosuicidal black-clad nightclub goers and Bud Dry commercial watchers nationwide on to the thumpable Intellechno sounds of such groups as Ministry, Revolting Cocks, Front 242, and Skinny Puppy.

Whitehouse Records, PO Box 34363, Chicago, IL 60634
(312) 583-7499
The fact that Jay Whitehouse's label was founded after he created Waterdog, an exclusive label for suburban bar stalwarts The Bad Examples, is instructive. This is a label in search of pop tunes, catchy riffs, and sing-along rock. Guitar crunch is all right, just not too crunchy. Acts produced: Lava Sutra, Eric Lugosch, Soul Vitamins.

Widely Distributed Records, 1412 W. Touhy, Chicago,
IL 60626-2622 (312) 465-2558
Founded in 1988. Emphasizes "overly intellectual guitar pop bands." Advice: Call or send a demo. Be prepared to wait at least six months for a response. No metal. No singer/songwriters without bands. Acts produced: Green, The Lilacs, Algebra Suicide, The Joy Poppers.

Playing the Streets

The streets are the great equalizer. Nobody's going to stop for you unless they want to. And, if you're lousy, you might just get a steel-toed boot implanted in your guitar case. If you can make a decent living playing the streets, you must be good. Either that or you look really pathetic. The street definitely has its advantages. There's no middleman, no booking cretin losing your tapes, no one asking you if you can finish off your set with "Sweet Home Chicago." All you need is a couple of hours to haggle with officials at City Hall to get a street musician's license. Still, there is an art to playing outside, and that art mainly consists of finding the right location. Play the corner of 18th and Halsted and you'll be lucky if you get ten people walking by you and handing you spare change all day. Play the subway and, well, you can make fifty bucks in an hour. If you're going to want to play The Good Spots, one of those prime locations where people with ready cash and artistic ears pass by all day, you're going to have to get there way early in the morning, because it's squatter's rights and every man for himself in the street musicians' world. Also, research your spot before getting to one of The Good Spots, because there're some places where people have been playing for twenty-five years—and they won't take too kindly to your busting in on their space.

The Good Spots

The subway—preferably by the Randolph Street stop

Outside Wrigley Field, if you can compete with the two-zillion-piece Dixieland band

State and Washington, particularly during the lunch hour or on a heavy shopping day

Any underpass with great echoing acoustics leading out to the lake, the closer to Lincoln Park the better

North Michigan Avenue (you know, what the tourist council calls the Magnificent Mile) after 5:00 p.m. when you get the tourists, the shoppers, and the workers going home

State Street near Division, if you can deal with the unspeakable sleaze quotient and avoid the vomit spewing out of the mouths of revelers on route to Mother's (eew!)

Radio Stations That Might Play Your Stuff

A friend of mine who shall remain nameless advised sticking a joint into any package sent to a Chicago deejay. I neither suggest nor condone this, but his single got significant airplay. Coincidence? You be the judge.

WABT, 103.9 FM, 231 W. Main, Aurora IL 60005 (630) 551-3450
The Wabbit's *Homegrown Music Show* Sundays at 7:00 P.M. plays blues most often but will put anything the producers like on the air.

WCBR, 92.7 FM, 120 W. University, Arlington Heights, IL 60004 (847) 255-5800
One of the only "real" alternative rock stations in Chicago (even though they also broadcast the International Hockey League's Chicago Wolves games), which boosts both local and national product that doesn't normally get excessive airplay. Features *Chicago Songwriters Showcase* on Friday nights.

WFMT, 98.7 FM, 303 E. Wacker, Chicago, IL 60601 (312) 565-5000
Plays 91 percent classical music, 5 percent news, 2 percent radio theater, 1 percent spoken word, and 1 percent other. Your odds aren't great, but if you're a folkie you've at least got a chance. The still-kicking *Midnight Special* (Saturdays at 10:30) has long been one of the only radio outlets for local folk talent (e.g., Bob Gibson, The Holsteins). Your chances of getting on are probably even slimmer than they were in the seventies, but no one ever said the chances of becoming a successful artist were good.

WHPK, 88.5 FM, 5706 S. University, Chicago, IL 60637 (312) 702-8424
An arm of the University of Chicago, which is perhaps most noted for its excellent blues shows. But the station still, like any college station, experiments

with just about anything you send. Try the *Pure Hype* show, which has featured Tart and Number One Cup in the studio in the past.

WKQX, 101 FM, Merchandise Mart, Suite 1700, Chicago IL 60654
(312) 527-8348
Ultrahip, alternative pop-40 station (at least if you work for an accounting firm), playing the likes of Matthew Sweet, Courtney Love, and The Offspring. Features a Local Music Showcase, 9:00 P.M. Sundays, as well as *Chicago Sun Times* and *Chicago Reader* critics Jim DeRogatis and Bill Wyman's rock scene talk show "Sound Opinions," which sometimes will feature local bands in the studio. And, if they don't invite you to the studio, maybe they'll just talk about you at length.

WLUP-FM, 97.9 FM, 875 N. Michigan, Chicago, IL 60611
(312) 440-5270
Once the monster of all Chicago rock stations, like back in the eighties, when guys and gals in cut-off black Loop shirts would stalk Chicagofest at Navy Pier while grabbing each other's rumps. Now, mainly a talk-comedy station, which features talk and music from the local scene on *Rock Tonight*, Sundays at 7:00 P.M. hosted by *Illinois Entertainer* editor Michael Harris and *Chicago Tribune* rock critic Greg Kot.

WLUW, 88.7 FM, 6525 N. Sheridan, Chicago, IL 60626
(312) 915-6558
Loyola University's station, which for years has been geared mostly toward thumpety-thump dance music, but lately has been doing some more eclectic pop music programming.

WNUR, 89.3 FM, 1906 Sheridan, Evanston, IL 60208
(847) 491-7101
The mother of all college radio stations—the most organized, most eclectic, and best-run college station in town—from the campus of Northwestern University.

WXRT, 93.1 FM, 4949 W. Belmont, Chicago, IL 60641
(312) 777-8881
For years, XRT has been the station of choice for all left-leaning, rock-and-roll-listening, blue-jean-wearing folks. Though they tend toward mainstream AOR and singer-songwriter stuff during the day, shows like *The Big Beat* and *Local Anesthetic* give local bands an opportunity for airplay.

WZRD-FM, 88.3 FM, 5500 N. St. Louis, Chicago, IL 60626
(312) 794-2881

The weirdest radio station in Chicago, known to aficionados as The Wizard. Loosely associated with the Northeastern Illinois University, but you need to take only one credit here to get a show. Consequently, a lot of night school students have been taking one course a semester just to get on the radio and have been here for decades. I wouldn't send anything there if I were you. It's better to find someone you know who has a show and likes your stuff and then let them play the hell out of it. Or call one of the deejays and harass him or her about your music. Believe me, they don't get that many calls.

Cool Record Stores That Might Stock Your Stuff

Getting a recording deal isn't the only way to get your music out there. You could always press it yourself and hustle from radio station to radio station and record store to record store in hopes that someone will play or stock your material. It's not always the most successful method, but if you've got enough moxie, here are a few places that try to help out local musicians. You can bring your tunes here and hope that they might take them and sell on consignment.

The Quaker Goes Deaf, 1937 W. North, Chicago, IL 60622
(312) 252-9334

Reckless Records, 3157 N. Broadway, Chicago, IL 60657
(312) 404-5080

Tower Records, 2301 N. Clark, Chicago, IL 60614 (312) 477-5994

WaxTrax!, 1653 N. Damen, Chicago, IL 60647 (312) 862-2121

Ten Clichés to Avoid Using in Your Songs

1. "The wheel keeps on turning"

2. "Temperature's rising"

3. Punctuating verses with "babe," "baby," "yeah," or "heh!"

4. Yelling something cocky before a cheesy guitar solo, as in "Watch me now, baby!"

5. Beginning a song with a disingenuous dedication: "This one goes out to all you lovers out there."

6. Ending a song with a dedication to a litany of code names: "To all the brothers in the house, to Ray Ray on the mike, to Big Boy Mel Rosenberg, our manager . . ."

7. "You keep me hanging on"

8. "It's in your eyes"

9. Anything about mirrors and your reflection looking back at you

10. Anything whispered to give erections to teenage boys: "Hey big boy, you think you're big enough for me?"

Most Overdone Cover Tunes at Weddings

Joy to the World

Bad, Bad Leroy Brown

Open Arms

Theme from Batman

Feelings

Gloria

Sweet Home Chicago

Wang Dang Doodle

Yesterday

Celebration

Publications and Other Resources

Chicago Music Alliance, 410 S. Michigan, Chicago, IL 60605-1402 (312) 987-9296
Founded in 1984. A coalition of thirty-eight nonprofit institutions sponsors concerts, provides job referral and counseling service and access to health insurance, puts out a dry-but-informative newsletter with job listings, and offers workshops on fundraising techniques. Publications the Alliance produces include *Building a Successful Music Education Program* and *Sponsoring a Successful Live Performance.*

Downbeat, Maher Publications, 102 N. Haven, Elmhurst, IL 60126-3379 (630) 941-2030
Excellent resource material. One of the premier national sources on the jazz scene, and it's based out of Elmhurst. Go figure.

Illinois Entertainer, 124 W. Polk, Suite 103, Chicago, IL 60605-2069 (312) 922-9333
It's kind of a rag, but if you're looking for a guitarist for your band or a band for your guitar, the want ads are pretty good. Plus, they'll review just about

anything, and if you drop off or mail them a letter telling them about your band, there's a good chance they'll print it.

Jazz Institute of Chicago, 410 S. Michigan, Suite 716, Chicago, IL 60605 (312) 427-1676

An organization dedicated to the preservation of jazz, the institute sponsors concerts, an annual jazz fair, jazz club tours, and of course the annual Chicago Jazz Festival. The $30 annual membership entitles you to the monthly newsletter and discounts on jazz records, books, and events.

Showcase Chicago, PO Box 2428, Glen Ellyn, IL 60638 (630) 627-3757

Another free weekly, it's reminiscent of the *Illinois Entertainer*, only smaller, with far less comprehensive listings and far fewer reviews of local and national releases. Has some funny pictures of metalheads and ads for sleazy suburban clubs and roller hockey games, though.

Tailspins, PO Box 5467, Evanston, IL 60204

An occasionally sophomoric music zine, but seems to review whatever demo they get. So send one their way.

You'll Need

A musical instrument, for one thing. Here are some prime sources where you can get your hands on:

An accordion

Biasco Music, 5535 W. Belmont, Chicago, IL 60641 (312) 286-5900; Walles Music, 6846 W. North, Chicago, IL 60635 (312) 622-3446. These also tend to show up in pawnshops a lot.

A banjo

Different Strummer, 909 W. Armitage, Chicago, IL 60614 (312) 525-6165.

Drums

The Percussion Shop, 802 Custer, Evanston, IL 60201 (847) 864-2997.

A guitar

Flynn Guitars & Music, 821 Noyes, Evanston, IL 60201 (847) 491-0500; Bob Gorny's Custom Guitar Works, 6340 W. Belmont, Chicago, IL 60634 (312) 725-4225; Guitar Center, 3228 N. Clark, Chicago, IL 60657 (312) 327-5687; Sound Post, 3640 W. Dempster, Skokie, IL 60076 (847) 679-6070.

A piano
American Music World, 333 S. State, Chicago, IL 60604 (312) 786-9600; Kurt Saphir Pianos, 123 Green Bay, Wilmette, IL 60091 (847) 256-5225 and 310-22 W. Chicago, Chicago, IL 60610 (312)440-1164.

A synthesizer
Gand Music, 780 Frontage, Northfield, IL 60093 (847) 446-4263; Biasco, 5535 W. Belmont, Chicago, IL 60641 (312) 286-5900.

A violin
Carl Becker & Son, 1416 W. Belmont, Chicago, IL 60647 (312) 348-5698; Bein and Fushi Rare Violins Incorporated, 410 S. Michigan, Suite 1014, Chicago, IL 60605 (312) 663-0150; Sherry-Brenner Limited, 224 S. Michigan, Chicago, IL 60604 (312) 427-5611; Fritz Reuter & Sons, 3917 W. Touhy, Lincolnwood, IL 60645 (847) 677-7255; and Kenneth Warren & Son, 407 S. Dearborn, Chicago, IL 60645 (312) 427-7475.

You Might Also Need

Italian dictionary
All the better to tell *a cappella* from *un cappello*. Available at all bookstores but also at the best foreign bookstores around, including *Europa Bookstore, 832 N. State, Chicago, IL 60610 (312) 335-9677.*

Lemon
The vocalist's throat needs soothing. Squirt one from somewhere known for fresh produce, like *Fresh Fields, 2484 N. Elston, Chicago, IL 60647 (312) 862-5300.*

Music stand
You don't want a crick in your back as you play, do you? Get a stand at *Gand Music, 700 Frontage, Northfield, IL 60093 (847) 446-4263.*

PA system
A lot of the smaller venues make you bring your own. Get one from *Snukst Music, 6611 S. Pulaski, Chicago, IL 60629 (312) 585-7923.*

Sheet music
The best source for this has always been *Carl Fischer, 312 S. Wabash, Chicago, IL 60604 (312) 427-6652.*

And if you're playing a bar mitzvah, don't forget your spangly dress, your tuxedo, and how to play "Bad, Bad Leroy Brown."

Interviews

Bill Buchman on How to Audition for the Chicago Symphony

After having joined the Chicago Symphony Orchestra in 1992 at the age of twenty-six, second bassoonist Bill Buchman still remains one of CSO's youngest members. A 1988 graduate of Brown University, his undergraduate degree is in physics. He studied music at the graduate level at Yale University and USC and played second bassoon with the Dallas Symphony Orchestra before joining the CSO.

Location: Coffee Chicago, 828 N. State

AL: Although you've chosen classical music as your career, your academic background is in physics. Is there any correlation between these fields?

BB: People talk about that. You always have people saying that Bach is a very mathematical composer. But my own experience is that these fields are very different. I take perhaps an analytical approach to the music in that I try to be aware of the physical aspects of playing. But music has always been an emotional thing for me. I do it because I love doing it. And I never did it because of the neat little mathematical relationships between notes.

AL: When did you realize that you were going to head for a musical career instead of a scientific one?

BB: In college. I had a roommate my junior year who was a physics major. He was a very intense, competitive person, and he would come home and just study everything three or four times over, attacking the homework and picking it apart, trying to do his labs perfectly. I saw his enthusiasm for physics and I realized that I didn't have that, whereas I was playing chamber music, doing stuff outside Brown University, and I saw that I was more interested in that than in physics.

AL: What's expected in an audition for a symphony? Does everyone ask you to play the same thing?

BB: They pretty much ask everybody to play the same piece, and for the bassoon, it's very easy, because there's really only one piece that's worth hearing and that's the Mozart bassoon concerto and it's still not the best thing he wrote, as opposed to a violin audition where you have a million études and Paganini caprices. And you do a couple of orchestral excerpts which are pretty standard. They give you a big list of things you have to learn, but the most important thing is the Mozart concerto.

AL: So you start practicing your audition piece at the beginning of time?

BB: Yeah, even back in high school you start learning the Mozart bassoon concerto. It's not technically difficult, or at least it doesn't seem that way. It's only about twenty minutes long, and it's technically within the reach of intermediate bassoon players.

AL: Is the audition a frightening process, when you don't have the orchestra to protect you?

BB: Yes. Bassoon kind of blends into the orchestra, and you're not used to sitting by yourself except when you're with your teacher. So you try to extend that environment to not being self-conscious in front of strangers.

AL: Do you have any audition ritual?

BB: My best ritual is to start preparing way in advance and go through all the repertoire over and over and over and over, six or eight hours a day, so that the mechanical aspect becomes so automatic that you don't need to think about which fingers have to move, where you have to breathe. So that even if you lose your concentration, you can still keep playing without a break.

AL: No lucky key chains?

BB: No. No lucky shirt. A lot of people have things they do. A lot of people will take beta-blockers to reduce their adrenaline.

AL: Do they give you a lot of feedback, or is it a stony-faced person with hands folded?

BB: Very often it's a stony-faced person who would maybe say "Good" or "OK" or "Thank you very much." The feedback is from the kind of letter you get afterward.

AL: It must be a very palpably tense atmosphere while you're waiting to hear if you've made it or not.

BB: It is very tense. It's like that at every audition. When I auditioned for the Dallas Symphony, you had a whole range of people from students like me who didn't really care if they made it or not to forty-year-olds doing their fiftieth audition who've never had a good job and have a wife and three kids to support. And in Dallas, this was a $52,000-a-year job and this was a life and death situation for some people, so it's very awkward, very uncomfortable. You really can feel an acute sense of competition. Even if you're there with friends of yours, you're still competing for the $52,000 prize. You try to support other people, but at the same time you want to come out on top, but you only have five minutes to prove yourself.

You go out on the stage and the audition committee's behind a screen. You're sitting on stage in this empty hall alone in this place where you've never been before, playing your bassoon all by yourself. It's very tense and awkward to get your fingers moving right even though your heart's racing and remember all the little nuances you wanted to play. You have to be able to concentrate on playing the music and not think about the job or the committee or anything else but playing the music.

AL: What's the transition like from playing in a university orchestra or a summer festival orchestra to playing with a major symphony like Dallas or Chicago?

BB: It's amazing. People in Dallas, 90 percent of them don't have any other work. Many of them have been in the orchestra for twenty years or longer. I had to learn to play softer than I ever played before in my life, because I was sticking out too much and to play exactly in tune and in time with everybody else and perform to a level of precision that I'd never been asked for before. It was very frustrating. I felt I had been stamped into this mold and wasn't able to play expressively, and with Dallas, it was a very analytical, rote kind of thing, just play what was on the page and nothing else. I couldn't do anything emotive. I was an automaton.

AL: How does that compare to Chicago?

BB: Well, the principal here, Willard Elliot, lets everybody play and fend for themselves. People know how to play interestingly without detracting from the sound of the section.

AL: How did you come to take the audition for the CSO?

BB: In America, there are five orchestras which are generally looked upon as being the top; those are Boston, New York, Philadelphia, Cleveland, and Chicago. And right after I joined the Dallas orchestra I read in the musicians' union newsletter that there were openings for bassoon players in Philadelphia and here. It's a prestige thing. Everyone wants to see if they can make it into the big five.

AL: You didn't make it right away here, though.

BB: I sent a tape; they sent me an encouraging letter. You show up in the morning, you wait around for a while, they take you into a warm-up room where you go through stuff at the last minute, then they call you out on the stage and you go and you play for five or ten minutes. I made it into the finals. I was one of two finalists out of eighty-three people auditioning.

I came back to audition for Daniel Barenboim and he heard the two of us do the exact same things. Sometimes they ask you to do rhythm things and you'll see the conductor tapping out the rhythm and you try to keep right with them. I stared right at Barenboim to see how he was reacting. It turns out he didn't like either one of us and told us, "I very much enjoy your playing, but there are certain things that you did not do, and you both had trouble playing sharp in the low register and I'm looking for a player who plays more musically." He invited us back for the final round of the next audition, though. In the meantime, the position became vacant at the beginning of Ravinia, and they gave both of us the opportunity to play four weeks at Ravinia. We got to hear how the orchestra played and they got to hear how we played.

AL: And it was vastly different from Dallas?

BB: Night and day. In Dallas, what they try to do in the woodwinds section is to achieve a blend, so you do everything you can to prevent yourself from sticking out, play down the dynamics and play exactly in tune. You try to hide. In Chicago, it's every man for himself and very expressive, exciting playing. If you think there's something interesting in your part that ought to be heard, you play it out and nevermind if it sticks out. Willard Elliot never even suggested how to play something and let me decide how soft or loud to play. I felt for the first time that I was able to play freely and enjoy myself and make a tangible impression rather than just filling in the holes.

AL: And then on the second time auditioning for Chicago, you succeeded.

BB: Yes, I played very differently. The first time I played reservedly and quiet. The next time I played this really interesting and expressive audition and was hired.

AL: Can you talk about the atmosphere and rapport that exists in the CSO?

BB: It's very much a family. You know everybody on a first-name basis. I think musicians and artists generally associate themselves much more strongly with their work than someone who works retail or on the stock exchange because it is such an emotional and creative process. Because of our emotional ties to the music, we get really emotionally tied to the people we work with. It's a very wide age spread. The youngest person we have is twenty-six and we have people well into their seventies, while I'm pushing thirty, but we still get along. All the thirty-year-olds in the symphony get together and do things outside the symphony.

AL: What do the thirty-year-olds do outside the symphony?

BB: Parties. After a concert, we'll get together on weekends and go to the movies or go sailing. Nothing specifically music oriented. No jam sessions. Typical thirty-something after-hours stuff. Go out to the clubs.

AL: What's the hip, CSO club?

BB: The only place I know where you can definitely find CSO musicians after a concert is at the Exchequer. It's about the only place open after a concert, so you'll see half a dozen of us there.

Von Freeman on the Mysterious Art of Jazz

While his son Chico has found fame and fortune in New York, the world-renowned septuagenarian tenor saxophonist Von Freeman has remained in Chicago, playing high-profile gigs around town and stopping by every Tuesday to jam at the New Apartment Lounge on 75th Street. Freeman has recorded many albums, among them *Walkin' Tuff* on Southport Records.

Location: New Apartment Lounge, 504 E. 75th

AL: What does it take to succeed in jazz?

VF: Dedication. No commercialism whatsoever, and that's funny because if you're really into it, there are things that you do that are actually entertaining but they're certainly not meant to be, because you're thinking about the music and only the music and improving the music. It doesn't have much to do with self or self-aggrandizement. It's like sculpture or any of the arts where people are serious. It's strictly for the muse.

AL: What does dedication mean to you?

VF: Dedication to getting the music to as many people as possible and getting the music right. There are several ways to do this music wrong: for instance, not preparing. Music takes a lot of preparation and people I see walk in this door, especially if they watch me on the bandstand, they might think everything I do is extemporaneous, but it sure isn't. I've been thinking about what I'm going to play all day long, thinking about how I was going to play it, different tunes. If I can hear something a little different, make it sound a little fresher, and this takes a lot of thought and a lot of time. Of course, the whole idea is to get up on the bandstand and make it look extemporaneous, but it's really not. I've been around a lot of the better players and they practice all the time, mentally. There's always something to take the music a little higher.

AL: How do you get yourself in the mindset to practice mentally?

VF: It's no different from anything else. The only difference is that with this music, the feelings are right here, right here on your sleeve. When you play, you're exposed. I can listen to anybody play and tell what kind of person they are. That's how identifiable the music is—because it's personal. It's impossible for a cat to be the wrong kind of cat and play good jazz and fool me. I can see right through it by certain things he or she does while playing jazz. It's like fortune-telling music, it really is.

AL: Who's the right kind of cat to play jazz?

VF: Somebody who's giving would be ideal. If you're not, generally you don't play jazz that long and you go out and try to go into some other field. You generally end up playing contemporary music, where the money is. This music has very little money in it. A few guys make it big, a few ladies. But the majority are stuck off in these clubs somewhere, and that's all around the world. You can't be grandstanding or drinking whiskey or chasing the chicks.

AL: What has led you to continue to pursue your art rather than to try to commercialize your work and be more contemporary?

VF: There's enough people doing that, and it doesn't advance this music. If anything, it closes it down, which is bad. It's unfortunate that so many of the great guys are gone and most of them just kept it to themselves. After having played for years and years and luckily outlived a lot of them, I can see why it's like it is. If you look at it with a full view and see that there's got to be some guys like me, a bunch of them, that's what keeps the music going. I'm not bragging; it's just that everybody can't sell out, because the music is too powerful for that. When it comes time for the music to make some kind of jump, there's always some great jazz musician that does it.

AL: What has led you to remain in Chicago?

VF: I just think it's happenstance. I've had many opportunities to leave and I've traveled with my son Chico, and he's just the opposite of me. He left here in '72 and he never came back. He went to New York, paid his dues, and now he's well established there. In fact, he was so well established that he sent for me and we traveled some, back in '78 or '79. And I was never really happy, because traveling and fame mean nothing to me.

AL: Do you still play here on 75th Street to kind of keep the South Side music scene alive?

VF: I can do whatever I want here. I can play whatever I want to play, whenever I want to play, all I want to play, as long or as short as I want to play, and that's something you can hardly ever get. But I'm lucky. It took years and years for me to be able to get away with that. People used to hire me and tell me what they wanted. Now, as long as you please the cash register, it doesn't matter. I know when it's time to go, because the cash register stops ringing.

AL: How does anyone who hasn't been around as long as you have in the business start approaching it here in Chicago?

VF: You've got to pay your dues. You've got to play a lot for nothing. I've done it. I still do it. You've got to go around to the clubs. Take your group around and say, "Hey, we'll play here tonight for nothing." Because you're really not worth anything yet. You don't have a following. You're not going to draw anyone to a club, but you've got to start somewhere and that's the way you get instituted. You have to give a lot when you're young, unless you're lucky enough to go into a studio and cut a hit record, but I wouldn't depend on that. A hit just comes out of the air. Where it comes from, I don't know. Like I have no idea how I'm going to sound tonight. Sometimes I sound pretty good to myself and sometimes I sound real bad to myself. I have no idea. I try to keep a certain level that I try not to get under, but I've fallen beneath it sometimes.

AL: How would you define the music you play?

VF: I really wonder a lot, because I've seen guys who haven't been around half as long and they've got the answers, but I really do not. I have no idea what jazz is. I have no idea where it comes from. All I know is that I'm on the train and I can't seem to get off. I don't have any books to sell or any words of wisdom. You just gotta keep your nose as clean as you can and go with the music, because the music is going on. If there wasn't Von Freeman, the music would go on. Bird left and the music went on. That's just the way it is. This music seems to me to be a mystery. If you look way, way back at classical music, which is the forerunner of this music, all those famous guys were all destitute, known as weirdos, just like in jazz. The music itself is sort of mysterious. Of course not for the people who make it commercial and break it down to a level where everyone can understand it and make a lot of money at it. But they don't improve the music.

The music is something that's out there. It's like time. Either you get with time or time walks right over you. You're not going to really get in front of time and you can't walk behind it. Whatever this thing is that's going on, it attracts people like me and I don't even know why. It makes me feel good. When I write, it's a beautiful thing; it sure moves me. I'm seventy-three years old and I've been playing so long I don't even remember where I started.

AL: What inspires you to write?

VF: It just comes to me. Music is just a continuation of what's out there. There's so much music out there; it's all over the world.

AL: Do you listen to a lot to inspire you?

VF: My radio and TV never go off. I can't even sleep without a radio going, and I keep it right next to my ear.

AL: Has the music always been a mystery or has the mystery lessened over time?

VF: As I get older, it gets more mysterious. I saw a guy twelve years old, little bitty guy, playing all these Bird numbers. He could play. Now where did he learn that? It's mystifying. But, that's the way it goes. The music is out there. It doesn't belong to anybody. You just try to get the little bit of it that you can. This music here is supposed to be a product of Africa, but I've been to Africa and I've seen a lot of Africans who can't play jazz. I've been all over the world and I've seen lots of people who cannot play jazz, even lots of Americans. Where the music comes from, I do not know. Where it's going, I do not know. But it's incredible music, that I know.

AL: So when you write a piece of music, it's almost as if you're taking something that's out there, that's not inside you.

VF: I look up to the ceiling like I'm looking up to heaven. It's a music that you have to be in a certain mood and have a certain feel to play. You've got to listen as much as possible and play as much as possible. It could be a penny whistle. It doesn't matter. If you're an inspirationalist, it's gonna come out. It could be a harmonica—it could be anything.

Everybody says I know a lot about jazz; I don't know what they're talking about. I have learned a few things and that's you can't hate and play this music. You can't be angry and play this music. Whatever Lady Creativity digs, she doesn't dig those two things. You can't fight and play this music. You could play marching music if you're angry, but you can't play anything soulful. It's a very hip, meaningful type of thing that you have to find. And if I can't find it, I try to drink and find it, but that's bad, because then you can't play. You try to be nice to people, sweet, truthful, honest, and all that comes out in your music. It's never been about money. Maybe if I had a million dollars, I wouldn't be able to play the way I play.

AL: Do people who become rich forget how to play?

VF: It seems like money and this music, for some strange reason, don't go together. I've seen people win the lottery and they get a million dollars and run into all kind of problems.

AL: How often do you practice?

VF: I rarely do. I practiced so much in the preceding years, ten to twelve hours a day in my formative years. But that's just for skill. If it's not up here, it's not gonna come out no matter how much you practice. It'll come out sounding like you practiced.

AL: Did you ever become frustrated with the instrument and feel that you couldn't take it any further?

VF: No, I like the challenge. It takes a lot of studying and I love studying. I sit around and I write things on the wall all the time, different progressions. I hear these things and the kick I get is trying to play what I hear. Ninety percent of the time I fall flat on my face trying to play it, but every now and then I do it and it knocks me out.

D'Arcy on the Manic-Depressive Rock and Roll Lifestyle

As bass player for Smashing Pumpkins, the Michigan-born D'Arcy has been part of one of the quickest rises to international prominence ever for a Chicago band. Formed in Chicago, the Pumpkins, led by moody, psychedelic visionary Billy Corgan, topped national charts with their lush, swirly, angst-ridden *Siamese Dream* and the double album extravaganza *Melon Collie and the Infinite Sadness*. D'Arcy has recently become copartner in an indie label venture in Chicago, Scratchie Records.

Location: Offices of Scratchie Records, 1914 N. Milwaukee

AL: One thing I'm trying to figure out is how you can achieve a work of art, which is so often just a product of individual expression, in a group context like a band? Can you still be an artist in a group?

D: Well, when we're working as a group, I tend to just work on my bass lines. When I'm in the band, I'm in the band mindset. Within a band it's hard though, because we'll be jamming on stuff together, and I'll be like "Oh, this is really good," and then everybody else will be like "No, that's really bad. That's crap." That's really hard for me. And lately, the kind of things I like are what nobody else does. So some day I'll have to strike out on my own. I've written a lot on my own, but we haven't used anything of mine yet. I don't really show anybody anymore. I'm too sensitive.

AL: How rigorous is the rehearsal process?

D: We rehearse six days a week, twelve hours a day.

AL: How do you keep up the same inspiration when you've been playing for eleven hours?

D: Sometimes it's hard, sure. But then, you can get really inspired by it and you can be jamming on something that's really good and that keeps you going. Sometimes the hard part is when you leave. Sort of like, what do you do then?

AL: Being in a major rock band is rather a manic-depressive lifestyle.

D: Yeah, definitely, definitely. It's really hard to go from touring, such a strange and insane world, to just being at home in the quiet of your house and trying to have a normal life. But I've learned to try to switch it on and off. I try really hard to just take care of myself. It's really hard to take care of yourself when you're touring. If you can do that, you'll be okay. What you have to realize is that the band is only really a temporary thing. It wasn't there before and it might not be around after.

AL: A lot of people talk about the Chicago voice of literature or the Chicago school of music. Is there any influence of Chicago in your work?

D: No, I always thought when we were starting out there wasn't really much support in the press for the kind of music we were playing. It was a sports town and the people were really into the blues and the theater and stuff, but as far as rock music was concerned, the media wasn't very supportive of it. That's changed, because everyone's focusing on the "Chicago scene," but we always felt we were very separate from that. It always seemed to us that, when we were first starting out, there were a lot of cover bands or bands imitating what others were doing.

AL: So is the idea of a Chicago scene or a Chicago sound kind of a joke to you?

D: Chicago sound? It doesn't make sense to me. Every band that comes out of Chicago is so different. You couldn't compare us to any other of the bands. Liz Phair sounds like Liz Phair. Veruca Salt sounds like Veruca Salt.

AL: You just mentioned Liz Phair. Do you think with her success and yours and Veruca Salt that we're getting away from the era of rock being just a prepubescent boys' club?

D: Right now you get a lot of attention if you're a girl band. People make such a big deal about the fact that you're a woman and playing in a band. It's crazy to me. It just seems better to me to ignore it. I don't know why people make such a big deal out of it. I think people should just do whatever they want to do. I never felt when I was starting out that it was any kind of hindrance. People just wanted me because I played bass and there aren't a lot of people who play bass. Everyone wants to play guitar. No, it definitely wasn't an issue.

AL: Do you think people's personalities are reflected by the instruments they play?

D: Yeah, all drummers are insane.

AL: What inspires you to write?

D: When I write lyrics or poetry or whatever, whenever I come across or think of something that I think is a really basic truth that I've never thought of before or something that makes me think with a little more clarity, I always want to write it down, and I try to write it down in a way that I'd be able to utilize some day in the framework of a song.

As far as music is concerned, I don't know, I haven't been writing any music of my own lately. I don't know why. I'll come up with a few little things and then I'll be like, "Oh, no. No, don't bother to keep it." For me lately, the only way I've been able to write something is if I'm very depressed, which is not the best way to go. The best way to come up with something is through a dream, but that doesn't work all that well. You wake up in the middle of the night and try to write it down and you're like "Damn! I've got to write it down," because if you don't, by the next morning it's gone. Sometimes you wake up and you're like "What the hell did I write there?" The worst thing is when you work really, really hard on something and then you listen to it or you read it, you realize that it sounds exactly like something else.

AL: And do you care if the public ever gets to hear these thoughts of yours?

D: I haven't decided that. That's what I admire so much about Billy [Corgan], that he can just take everything inside of him and put it out in front of people. I don't know. I don't know if I could do that. I think that it could maybe really help a lot of people, because it's helped me a lot. But I don't know if I will want to go through all this stuff again.

AL: One of the things Billy Corgan said in an interview was that he really feels the music you play has a power to change people's lives and their attitudes. Do you think that your music can have that power?

D: Sure. There are just a million letters we get all the time from kids who say, "I was really so depressed, and your music really cheered me up and made me think about things in a different way." I don't really listen to our music, because I know what it's about and it really bums me out. I find it very depressing, frankly. But I pretty much know more about Billy's life, where the lyrics are concerned, than a person should, and so I would just rather not know so I can play the music and not get bummed out.

AL: What do you listen to to keep from getting bummed out? Was there any music that changed you?

D: The Flaming Lips; their music is brilliant, and their singer has a lot of really interesting ideas. Disney music. I like to listen to Sergio Mendes and The Kingston Trio. And The Beatles. It pretty much starts and ends with The Beatles.

SEVEN

Theater

Part I: Theater . . . With a Script

So, you want to be an actor, huh? Better you than me. I don't know how many more auditions I could have lived through, dragging those glossy eight by tens from theater to theater; memorizing that same damned Lanford Wilson monologue; boasting I was 5'9" when I was really only 5'8"; hanging around in those roundups all day, waiting for some mope to look me up and down and say, "Yeah, you look all right. Come back tomorrow with this side memorized"; checking the answering machine every day, looking for that blinking light only to find that solid red dot staring up at me, mocking me, making my self-image a ghastly cosmic joke.

But you've already decided to run away and join the theater anyway, and there's nothing your parents or I could possibly say to dissuade you. You've got big dreams of Broadway and Hollywood in that pulsating bean of yours, and you're all set to take the city by storm. Well, you picked a pretty good place for it. Chicago may not have the stockyards anymore, but we sure have cattle calls. Plays, plays, and more plays—there are over two hundred theater companies in the city, all struggling, all striving to become the next Steppenwolf Theatre, and they're almost all pretty open to newcomers. In fact, the less familiar you are, the better, because everyone wants to be the one who discovered you.

For years, Chicago was a second-rate theater town, a tryout town. If a play went well here, it cruised on to Broadway, and if a play did well on Broadway, well, it might come back here in some sort of traveling road show. Sure, there was always the Goodman Theatre; there were the old Yiddish theaters on the Jewish West Side where Paul Muni began his rise to Hollywood stardom, and on the South Side, there was the Pekin, where music director Joe Jordan began en route to working in New York with Orson Welles and the Federal Theater Project. True, this city was the first to vault Tennessee Williams to Broadway stardom with legendary acid-tongued critic Claudia Cassidy's dogged endorsement of *The Glass Menagerie*. But, for the most part, every show in town was on its way in or on its way out.

The city's downtown theaters did a booming business in musicals and hit shows. You could go to the Studebaker or the Shubert to see *Godspell* or *Pajama Game*, but once you were outside the Loop, you were pretty much stuck. The best you could do was to go to one of the hotels for some summer stock theater (Groucho Marx once appeared in a show at the Edgewater Beach Hotel) or a Hawaiian Tiki show or worse, head out to the burbs (what burbs there were back then) for some godawful musical comedy revue with scantily clad showgirls and guys in the audience with halitosis and bad toupees.

Then, some time around the late sixties, something strange happened. The children of hippiedom soon realized that theater didn't have to be stodgy entertainment for the overlords of production (i.e., their parents). Theater could be something fun and dirty and gritty and somewhat revolutionary. Storefront theaters and basement café playing spaces became home to experimental works by writers like Israel Horovitz, David Rabe, and Terrence McNally. There was a time when it was difficult to walk into a show in Chicago without seeing some brooding, long-haired, naked guy with a wee gut waxing philosophical about the state of the earth and the environment.

The storefront revolution exploded in the seventies, when highly educated theatrical goofs began to organize themselves into deeply committed theater companies with meaningful social, political, and artistic agendas. David Mamet, along with the now-fabled St. Nicholas Theater Company, turned the storefronts of Halsted Street into platforms for a new brand of intense and wonderfully profane drama. Granted, Mamet began with crap like *Squirrels* and *The Duck Variations*, but his missteps allowed him the education to springboard from minimalist drivel to magnificent success with *Sexual Perversity in Chicago*, *American Buffalo*, and the rest of his famed oeuvre. John Malkovich (*Places in the Heart, In the Line of Fire*), Tom Hanks's sideman Gary Sinise (*Forrest Gump* [aack], *Apollo 13*), Laurie Metcalf (*Roseanne, Internal Affairs*), and the rest of the Steppenwolf clan moved from one of hoity-toity Highland Park's church basements to the North Side of Chicago and turned the practice of standing around looking moody and pissing on picket fences into an entire school of acting, exemplified by the works of seventies theater pioneers like Sam Shepard and Lanford Wilson. Remains Theater and Wisdom Bridge Theatre helped launch the careers of Hollywood regulars William Petersen and creepy Ted Levine. Organic Theatre, founded in 1969 by some crazy UW-Madison students including Stuart Gordon (*Re-Animator*), brought an idiosyncratic sci-fi style to the stage with the pre–*Star Wars* saga *Warp!*, while the Body Politic fused high art with storefront basics, ushering dramatic works by Beckett and Stoppard into this blue-jean-wearing, folding-chair-sitting society.

The eighties and the nineties saw the institutionalization of Chicago as a national theater capital. Some theater companies, such as the Practical Theater, which saw 75 percent of its company join the cast of *Saturday Night Live*, shot to the forefront of civic attention and shriveled up just as quickly. Meanwhile, Steppenwolf, Body Politic, and Victory Gardens found their way onto Broadway and won themselves plum grants and yuppie-comfy theater spaces on the North Side of the city. Even the staid old Goodman got into the hip act, premiering works by David Mamet, David Rabe, Shel Silverstein, Elaine May, and others on a special, experimental studio stage, which also introduced Chicago to new and major artists like Spaulding Gray, David Cale, and new vaudevillians like the Flying Karamazov Brothers. Brash new theater companies started nudging their ways into the old, beat-up theater spaces that their now-illustrious predecessors had abandoned. Lookingglass Theater forged a new, acrobatic style strong on athleticism and rigorous theatrical and performance art training. Annoyance Theatre made national headlines with its foul-mouthed improv musicals and deconstructivist takes on pop culture icons like the Brady Bunch.

Today, you can hardly sneeze without having some of your spittle plop on the door of a theater company. In the back of bars, next door to bookstores, in the basements of our new rash of coffeehouses, drama continues to metastasize. Even in the dead of winter or in the blazing heat of summer, there are more than a hundred performances going down on any given night. High drama, low comedy, exciting experimentation, overdone classics, underdone obscurities, cheesy murder mystery, gooey romance, icky dinner theater— it's all happening. So, to paraphrase Burgess Meredith in *Rocky II*, what the hell are you waiting for?

Getting Schooled

Act One Studios, 640 N. LaSalle, Suite 535, Chicago, IL 60610
(312) 787-9384
Gets good reviews for the experienced eighteen-member faculty of this all-purpose training center. Gets mixed reviews for the wide variety of courses, which range from TV and film coaching to Meisner-based emotional commitment labs and "How This Business Really Works" self-marketing programs. Three-hour sessions lasting nine weeks run upwards from $200.

Actors Center, 3047 N. Lincoln, Suite 390, Chicago, IL 60657
(312) 549-3303
This highly praised (at least by the people I know) training center has an emphasis on the method school of acting. Classes are offered for both beginners and seasoned thespians. Warning: Things get a little tense here. I knew one guy who was supposed to do an improv scene about suicide here. He spent most of my dinner with him at a nearby Italian restaurant scraping away at his wrist with a butter knife. Beginning classes start at $185 for an eight-week scene study class.

Audition Studio, 20 W. Hubbard, Suite 2E, Chicago, IL 60610
(312) 527-4566
Founded in 1981 by Chicago casting director Jane Brody. Offers instruction consisting largely of audition skills with instruction based on the book *Audition* by Michael Shurtleff. Eight-week classes cost $295–$315. Private coaching runs $50 per hour.

Chicago Actors Studio, 833 W. Chicago Ave., Suite 600, Chicago,
IL 60622 (312) 275-7954
This reputedly cheesy, Stanislavski-influenced center for private acting coaching, monologue and Shakespeare workshops, and "Audition Power" is unusual for the on-the-job training it offers by casting its students in showcase evenings of one-acts open to the public. Lengths of classes vary; figure on spending $20–$30 a week for a two-hour class session.

ETA Creative Arts Foundation, 7558 S. South Chicago, Chicago,
IL 60619 (312) 752-3955
One of the city's best African-American theaters, ETA offers training in playwriting, sound techniques, lighting, video, and auditioning, and also offers internships in stage management.

Steven Ivcich Studio, 1836 W. North, Chicago, IL 60622
(312) 235-9131
There are very mixed reviews on this eccentric, idiosyncratic school founded
by maverick Chicago theater director and instructor Steven Ivcich. Some swear
by it; others swear at it; still others swear about it. The school focuses on actor's
"personal development" as opposed to a specific style, preparing actors in
small class sessions for forty weeks to perfect sixteen different roles. Classes
are about $6 a pop, and students always have access to the studio, even when
class isn't in session.

Judith Jacobs, 33 E. Cedar, Chicago, IL 60611 (312) 649-9585
Emphasis is on on-camera coaching and audition preparation from a former
independent New York casting director. Five-week small-group courses cover
pictures and résumés, marketing, on-camera videotape work, et cetera and
cost $250. Private coaching costs $50–$75.

Piven Theatre Workshop, 927 Noyes, Evanston, IL 60201
(847) 866-6597
Although most noted for jump-starting the Hollywood careers of gangly and
precocious North Suburban teens (not all of whose last names are Piven or
Cusack), the Evanston-based workshop led by Byrne and Joyce Piven has also
carved out a reputation for itself as a training center for adults and a producer
of story theater on Chicago stages. Granted, the workshop can sometimes in-
still an at-times-abrasive "I'm Olivier" quality in its younger students, but
with age, its performers become some of the most talented and unpretentiously
self-assured around. Adult intensive workshop classes range from four to eight
weeks long and run $150–$340.

Sarantos Studios, 2857 N. Halsted, Chicago, IL 60657 (312) 528-7114
I've known folks on the Chicago theater scene since 1988, and I still haven't
met anyone who's studied here. Go figure. Offers all-over-the-map acting instruction from a man fond of comedy and murder mysteries. Plan on spending
a little more than $125 a month for once-a-week classes in stage acting and
commercial technique. Three-hour seminars on the basics of the biz are $35 a
shot. And feel free to take a class that will allow you to appear in one of the
studio's murder mysteries. I just wouldn't put it on my résumé if I were you.

School of the Actors Gymnasium, 927 Noyes, Evanston, IL 60201
(847) 328-2795
This offshoot of the ultra-athletic and ultra-ultracreative Lookingglass Theater combines training in gymnastics, modern dance, mime, circus arts, and
puppet building. Eight weeks of one to two-hour class sessions run $63–$128.

Training Center for Actors, Directors, and Playwrights,
1346 W. Devon, Chicago, IL 60660 (312) 508-0200
Affiliated with the Center Theater Ensemble. A comparatively huge collection
of working Chicago theater folks teach classes in anything from musical theater to Shakespeare techniques to audition methods to on-camera work. Prices
are reasonable and variable.

Victory Gardens Training Center, 2257 N. Lincoln, Chicago, IL 60614
(312) 549-5788
Offers one of the most respected theater programs in the city at one of the
thriving grand old theaters of the Chicago scene. Classes are offered in monologues, how not to audition, Shakespeare, basic acting and directing, and
advanced scene study. Center offers eight-week classes (two to three hours
per week), generally running about $150.

Voice Over U, 640 N. LaSalle, Suite 535, Chicago, IL 60610
(312) 787-9384
Basically the brainchild of Chicago voice-over performer Sherri Berger, who's
worked on ads for McDonald's, Sears, Kraft, Amoco, and so forth. Offers lectures and labs in voice-over techniques and production. Private coaching costs
$65 per hour. Demo production costs $65 per hour.

Major graduate and undergraduate institutions with highly reputed programs in the field

Columbia College, Theater Department, 72 E. 11th, Chicago,
IL 60605 (312) 663-9462

Goodman/DePaul Theater School, 25 E. Jackson, Chicago, IL 60604
(312) 362-8375

Northwestern University, 1905 Sheridan, Evanston, IL 60302
(847) 491-7315

Getting Paid (well, almost)

All right, so you've taken a couple of classes, you've had a couple of
semisuccessful dates (if discussing Stephen Sondheim over a scone at Scenes
Coffeehouse can be considered successful), and you feel ready to step out into
that brave, acting world. Keep in mind that acting on the Chicago stage isn't
about to win you a hell of a lot of bread no matter how good you are. If you
want to make a living at it, you'll probably have to do some advertising or film

work (your agent can work on getting you those gigs). Even the best non-union actors in Chicago don't make dick. If you're not part of the Actors Equity Association, which allows you to perform in some of the bigger houses in town (Royal George, Briar Street, Goodman, Candlelight Dinner Playhouse), you should consider yourself part of a minuscule, lucky few if you're clearing one hundred dollars a week (off the books, of course, straight cash, no reporting to the IRS). That should cover one-way Amtrak fare to New York, provided you don't want one of those cushy sleeper cars. Success can come awfully slowly in this business. Good things, migraines, social security payments, and service industry jobs come to those who wait long enough.

Now it's time to bolster the old résumé with some key (or not so key) roles in shows around town. The logical next step is to take a spin on the old audition auto-da-fe. The major companies in town (ETA Creative Arts Foundation, Lookingglass, Goodman Theatre, Remains, Shakespeare Repertory, Steppenwolf, Northlight Theater) generally don't do cattle call auditions. Send them a picture and your résumé in the late summer or early fall (check with them for an exact date.) If you don't have a good black-and-white eight-by-ten glossy of yourself, find a professional photographer who will take one. Don't try doing it yourself (like I did) using a Polaroid or a snapshot. If you have a shitty picture, it's guaranteed that some snide director is going to cattily discuss you when your pic arrives in the mail. Also, send a *real* résumé, no padding with BS about how you played Laura in *The Glass Menagerie* in the New Trier High School production. If you don't have real, professional or college credits, don't make them up (unless you're really a great actor). As is the case on any other job résumé, bullshit looks like bullshit. If you're auditioning, however, keep in mind that you're not alone and that there has to be some way, without gimmicks or odd clothing choices, you can set yourself apart from the rest of the crowd. One great way is to make sure you don't do the same monologue that everybody before you has done. Refer to the list of nine audition pieces and/or authors so overdone that any casting director with a small attention span might send you hurtling into hyperspace should you deign to utter them.

The Audition Ouch List (stuff you really shouldn't do for your monologue)

1. *Danny and the Deep Blue Sea*, by John Patrick Shanley (come to think of it, anything by John Patrick Shanley)
2. Teach's monologue from David Mamet's *American Buffalo* (after you say "Fuckin' Ruthie, fuckin' Ruthie, fuckin' Ruthie," no one's gonna listen to anything more)

3. Pale's opening monologue from Lanford Wilson's *Burn This* (sounds a lot like Teach's monologue, only not as good)

4. Anything by Neil Simon (unless you're auditioning for community theater)

5. Anything by Eric Bogosian (it only sounds good if he's doing it, anyway)

6. Anything from any Southern playwright requiring a Southern belle accent (this is Chicago; we don't do those here, and yes, that means *Crimes of the Heart*, too)

7. Anything by Christopher Durang (especially that one about sticking a hamster in one's vagina; yuck)

8. Any monologue that you wrote about your own particular perversions (especially if you're a psychiatrist trying to break into theater taking yours from the words of your patient [Yes, this has happened before, more than once. You know who you are.])

9. Anything with a British accent if you can't do one—come to think of it, anything with any accent if you can't do one

To keep up on upcoming auditions, check out the *Reader* performing arts section in the classifieds. Audition information is also available via Performink or the 976-CAST line (see Publications and Other Resources). Although most any time is a good time to keep an eye on audition listings, the serious audition season begins round about August. Every year, a zillion new theater companies with funky names sprout up. Audition for them at your own risk. Usually you can get an impression at the audition if folks know what they're up to or not and whether you'd want to be a part of their group.

Eleven Warning Signs (flee the audition NOW!)

1. "Well, we don't know exactly where we're gonna be performing it, but I got someone working on that."

2. "Well, I thought we'd figure out our rehearsal schedule somewhere later down the line."

3. "We're gonna try our best to be paying people if we make back our costs."

4. "We're looking for someone who's gonna play a small part and do some stage manager and costume design work for us too."

5. "It's an original piece. I wrote it, directed it, put up the money for it, and did the set and the lighting design, too."

6. "How do you feel about late, late off-night shows?"

7. "Are you comfortable with your body?"

8. "Now I want you to read for the part of the prostitute; I'll be playing the customer."

9. "How badly do you want this part?"

10. "Do you like to party?"

11. "I have to call and see if Cafe Voltaire's available the nights we want it."

Theaters to Audition For (or not)

Barring the unknown factor, you know, theaters with names like Picklepuss Productions, I have provided a list of the more established theaters and theater companies in town to watch out for when auditions roll around. Rather than give background information about each, I have devised a handy but highly subjective grading system which will help you prioritize your list of audition possibilities. The grades are the composite result of a survey of five Chicago theater critics including Mary Shen Barnidge (*Chicago Reader*, *Windy City Times*), Lawrence Bommer (*Chicago Tribune*, *Chicago Reader*, *Windy City Times*), Jack Helbig (*New City*, *Chicago Reader*), Bill Williams (senior theater critic, *Chicago Reader*), and the schmo who wrote this book. Power ratings have been averaged from the five critics' ratings of five categories: originality of choices (Is the company pushing the envelope and doing interesting things or just Edward Albee and Tennessee Williams over and over again?), overall acting quality, overall technical quality, reliability, and attitude and ambiance (which allows a critic to gauge the overall atmosphere of a theater—whether a company really loves and is excited about what it's doing or whether it is peopled by licentious misanthropes). Not every theater company in Chicago has been included. Some are too itinerant and off-and-on to merit consideration. Others are pretty much the products of the same group of people, who don't necessarily invite newcomers into their midst. No rating system is scientific, and even I was surprised at how theater companies I like a lot, such as Zebra Crossing and Chicago Actors Ensemble, found their way so far down the list and how Lifeline wound up at the very top. Still, this should be a good indicator of the relative quality of theaters to get involved at in Chicago.

Point Distribution

A+ 4.3	C+ 2.3
A 4.0	C 2.0
A- 3.7	C- 1.7
A- - 3.6	C- - 1.6
B++ 3.4	D++ 1.4
B+ 3.3	D+ 1.3
B 3.0	D 1.0
B-2.7	D- .7
B- - 2.6	D- - .6
C++ 2.4	F 0

A Word or Two About Performance Art

The lines between theater and art and stand-up comedy are a bit blurry, to say the least. For some blurry artists, a lot of it deals with venue: If you're in a theater, it's a monologue. If they serve drinks there, it's a stand-up routine. If you're in an art gallery, well then, it's performance art. All the same, the city has a small but productive group of artists who have been making quite an impact on the local scene, even if their work isn't categorizable in any traditional sense. From monologuists and poets like Paula Killen, Lisa Buscani, and Jeff Dorchen to the experiments with theatrical form embarked upon by members of the Curious Theatre Branch and Doorika, the dissemination of performance art has grown considerably since its birth some twenty years ago at N.A.M.E. gallery. If you look to join this movement, here are a few venues to consider.

Chicago Filmmakers, 1543 W. Division, Chicago, IL 60622 (312) 384-5533

Gallery 2, 847 W. Jackson, Chicago, IL 60607 (312) 563-5166

Lunar Cabaret & Full Moon Cafe, 2827 N. Lincoln, Chicago, IL 60657 (312) 327-6666

N.A.M.E., 1255 S. Wabash, Chicago, IL 60605 (312) 554-0671

Randolph Street Gallery, 756 N. Milwaukee, Chicago, IL 60622 (312) 666-7737

Chicago Theater Power Ratings

Name	Address	Originality of choices	Overall acting quality	Technical quality	Attitude and ambiance	Reliability	Overall grade point average
American Blues Theatre	1909 W. Byron	3.54	3.25	3.075	3.15	2.575	3.118
Annoyance Theatre	3747 N. Clark	3.325	2.525	2.175	2.825	1.5	2.47
Apple Tree Theatre	595 Elm, Highland Park, IL	2.8	3.6	3.48	2.82	2.74	3.088
Bailiwick Repertory	1229 W. Belmont	3.54	3.08	3.25	2.94	2.66	3.094
Black Ensemble Theatre	4520 N. Beacon	3.26	2.4	2.2	2.92	2.54	2.66
Blue Rider	1822 S. Halsted	3.575	2.725	2.25	2.5	2.175	2.645
Candlelight Dinner Playhouse	5620 S. Harlem, Summit, IL	2.275	3.675	3.675	3.675	3.85	3.435
Center Theatre	1346 W. Devon	2.446	3.0	3.0	3.0	2.68	2.825
Chicago Actors Ensemble	941 W. Lawrence	3.8	2.38	2.42	2.72	2.46	2.756
Circle Theatre	7300 Madison, Forest Park, IL	3.08	2.8	2.4	2.6	2.28	2.63
City Lit Theatre	410 S. Michigan	4.17	3.5	2.85	3.5	3.2	3.44
Court Theatre	5535 S. Ellis	2.8	3.74	3.58	2.88	3.4	3.28
Defiant Theatre	Roving	2.7	3.025	2.925	2.675	2.7	2.81
Eclipse Theater	2074 N. Leavitt	3.26	3.2	2.88	2.68	3.14	3.032
ETA Creative Arts Foundation	7558 S. South Chicago	3.14	3.08	2.82	3.14	3.14	3.064
European Repertory Theater	615 W. Wellington	3.46	2.68	2.26	2.6	2.54	2.708
Factory Theatre	1257 W. Loyola	3.25	3.025	2.6	3.325	2.9	3.02
Famous Door Theatre	3212 N. Broadway	3.6	3.85	3.675	3.675	3.175	3.595
Footsteps Theatre	5230 N. Clark	2.98	2.85	2.85	3.0	2.9	2.916
Free Street Programs	1419 W. Blackhawk	3.575	3.2	2.33	2.9	3.13	3.02766
Goodman Theatre	200 S. Columbus	3.54	3.78	4.12	3.08	3.26	3.556
Griffin Theater Company	5404 N. Clark	3.06	2.48	2.28	3.14	2.34	2.66
Hidden Stages	500 W. Cermak	2.72	2.075	2.35	2.75	2.0	2.379
Illinois Theatre Center	400A Lakewood, Park Forest, IL	2.23	2.03	2.23	1.9	1.57	1.992

Latino Chicago Theatre	1625 N. Damen	3.46	2.92	2.86	3.08	3.22	3.108
Lifeline Theatre	6912 N. Glenwood	3.74	3.74	3.54	3.6	3.54	3.632
Live Bait Theater	3914 N. Clark	3.94	3.34	3.32	3.34	3.08	3.404
Lookingglass Theater	3309 N. Seminary	3.5	3.2	3.86	2.86	3.0	3.284
Mary Archie Theatre	731 W. Sheridan	3.28	3.28	3.4	3.2	2.74	3.18
National Jewish Theater	5050 W. Church, Skokie, IL	3.28	3.48	3.34	3.0	3.46	3.312
National Pastime Theatre	4129 N. Broadway	3.075	2.93	2.87	2.77	2.23	2.776
Neo-Futurarium	5153 N. Ashland	3.65	3.3	2.575	3.075	2.775	3.075
New Tuners Theatre	1225 W. Belmont	2.6	2.94	2.74	2.4	2.4	2.616
Next Theatre Company	927 Noyes, Evanston, IL	3.8	3.34	3.26	3.26	2.94	3.32
Oak Park Festival Theatre	Austin Gardens, Oak Park, IL	2.42	3.6	3.48	3.0	3.48	3.196
Organic Theatre	3319 N. Clark	3.54	3.22	3.28	3.22	2.54	3.16
Raven Theatre	6931 N. Clark	2.6	3.18	3.0	3.54	3.06	3.076
Roadworks Productions	1532 N. Milwaukee	3.6	3.1	3.1	3.35	3.1	3.25
Shakespeare Repertory	1060 N. Dearborn	2.52	3.88	3.94	3.2	3.68	3.444
Shattered Globe Theater	2856 N. Halsted	3.4	3.66	3.26	2.94	3.06	3.264
Splinter Group Theatre	1937 W. Division	3.54	3.18	2.86	2.72	2.575	2.975
Stage Left Theatre	3408 N. Sheffield	2.925	2.86	2.6	2.25	2.525	2.63
Steppenwolf Theatre	1650 N. Halsted	3.08	3.6	4.0	2.82	3.08	3.316
Strawdog Theatre	3829 N. Broadway	3.26	3.08	2.8	3.48	2.88	3.1
Torso Theater	2827 N. Broadway	3.075	2.575	2.075	2.925	3.0	2.729
Transient Theater	1222 W. Wilson	3.0	3.0	2.68	3.14	2.62	2.88
Trap Door Productions	1655 W. Cortland	2.075	1.67	2.43	1.57	1.33	1.82
Turn Around Theatre	3209 N. Halsted	3.16	3.5	3.175	3.075	2.9	3.162
Victory Gardens Theatre	2257 N. Lincoln	3.26	3.34	3.56	3.48	3.08	3.344
Wisdom Bridge Theatre	400 S. State	2.72	2.94	2.86	2.66	2.66	2.768
Zebra Crossing Theatre	4223 N. Lincoln	3.38	2.8	2.26	2.86	2.41	2.746

Publications and Other Resources

(312) 976-CAST

It's the lazy man's audition listings. Updated every day, it is the most current source for actors. It's also thirty cents a minute. You make the call.

Audition News, 6272 W. North, Chicago, IL 60639 (312) 637-4695
A slim monthly mag that sells for $1.75 at area bookstores and frequently contains information that is nearly out of date by the time you can track it down. However, it's probably the best place to look if you want to do murder mystery dinner theater or read your acting horoscope. Caveat emptor.

League of Chicago Theaters, 67 E. Madison, Chicago, IL 60603 (312) 977-1730
This cooperative organization was founded in 1978 to promote theater community. Offers co-op ads for bargain rates to theater companies in major newspapers, sales of tickets to your shows through central Hot Tix office, theater information hotline, newsletter, and workshops.

Performink, 3223 N. Sheffield, Chicago, IL 60657 (312) 296-4600
A free biweekly publication about the city's acting community that features the most comprehensive audition listings but is also a little insidery for these tastes. Listings of recent castings seem to serve mainly as a source for bragging and sour grapes gossip ("Can you believe *he* got that McDonald's industrial? I wonder who he slept with"). Available at bookstores like Act One and cafés like Scenes and Urbus Orbis.

The Reader, 11 E. Illinois, Chicago, IL 60611 (312) 828-0350
Once the prime source for audition listings, now offers merely a smattering, but it also features some of the oddball ones from people who don't really know how to go about placing theirs anywhere else. However, far too many auditions are along the lines of "Theme Park looking for masochist to remain silent for the summer in Yosemite Sam costume." But it's still the only reputable publication that will review pretty much every show in town.

Stagebill, 400 N. Michigan, Chicago, IL 60611 (312) 832-7160
Read it to kill time before a show begins, or make paper boats with it during the intermission. This slim program-magazine offers little new information about the Chicago theater scene other than actor bios, puffpiece articles, and navel-gazing columns. Still, you can't beat the price.

About Unions

If you're in the acting business in Chicago, there are pretty much only three acronyms you need to memorize: AEA (Actors Equity Association), SAG (Screen Actors Guild), and AFTRA (American Federation of Television and Radio Artists). Novice actors need have no particular interest in AEA. The membership process begins when a nonunion actor works in a union house. Once you accumulate a certain number of weeks working in equity houses, you are qualified for membership, which means you pay monthly dues that assure you of union base salaries when you work at equity houses and that you can no longer work in nonequity houses, which comprise about 80 percent of Chicago theaters. Equity minimums tend to run between $100 and $500 per week, depending on the size and type of the theater you're working in. In other words, turning union means you will be paid decently if you can attract the few people in town who do pay. Equity showcases allow union actors to strut their stuff for little-to-no compensation (below union dues) if the union is informed. A union actor may also try to obtain an equity waiver to appear in his or her friend's nonunion show.

SAG and AFTRA work similarly but pay better (ahh, the advantages of doing commercials for soap and Gatorade or getting work in low-budget exploitation horror flicks). Going rate for SAG actors is usually about $500 a day for speaking roles and $150 for extra work. And SAG is much more open-minded about granting waivers for performers who want to appear in low-budget or student films.

About Agents

When are you going to wind up needing an agent? When there's money to be made. Ninety-eight percent of the Chicago theater world exists without agency help, although some of the bigger equity houses like Goodman are beginning to look at them. If you want to break into TV, commercial, industrial, or film work, you'll rarely have a chance without one. There are good agents in town, but the business also has a meat market feel about it, and, whenever you walk through the door, you have to get used to the feeling of being sized up, magnified, and microscoped. It's part of the job. It's an image-oriented career. Deal with it, or don't. If you can survive on your own without auditioning by biting a Nestlé Crunch, smiling at a camera, and saying "Mmm," let's hear it for you. Some agents in town are real sleazeballs, too. They're not listed here.

Cunningham, Escott, DiPene, 1 E. Superior, Chicago, IL 60611
(312) 944-5600
Full-service commercial talent agency. Supplies voice-over talent for CD-ROM
and other interactive games, as well as for the usual stuff. Also has branches
in L.A. and New York. Cuts exclusive agreement with clients.

Harrise Davidson and Associates, Incorporated, 65 E. Wacker,
Chicago, IL 60601   (312) 782-4480
One of the more respected agencies in town, dealing with all aspects of the
business.

Geddes Agency, 1925 N. Clybourn, Chicago, IL 60614
(312) 348-3333
A very well-reputed agency, which has, over the years, represented John Cusack
and Dennis Farina. Deals in TV, motion picture, and theater work, not much
industrial work. Looks for "personalities" rather than best-looking folks. See
interview with Elizabeth Geddes for further information.

Shirley Hamilton Incorporated, 333 E. Ontario, Chicago, IL 60611
(312) 787-4700
Founded in 1962. This full-service agency (TV, film, theater, commercials,
modeling) has over 5,000 clients on file. Clients have included Shelly Long,
Mandy Patinkin, and Robert Urich. Send your picture or résumé, and two
telephone numbers.

Linda Jack Talent, 230 E. Ohio, Chicago, IL 60611   (312) 587-1155
Founded in 1992. Represents actors for TV, radio, and film. Specializes in
voice-overs, no modeling, no kids. Send your picture or résumé and/or voice-
over tape. Be prepared to wait months for a response.

Jefferson and Associates, 1050 N. State, Chicago, IL 60610
(312) 337-1930
Founded in 1981. Very small agency (fifty clients) for TV, voice-overs, and
film. Signs exclusive agreements with actors (no freelance talent). Looking
for younger actors with potential for success in L.A. Rarely responds to pictures or résumés. If you do enough theater, they'll find you.

Emilia Lorence Limited, 619 N. Wabash, Chicago, IL 60611
(312) 787-2033
Agency with strong reputation primarily deals with TV, film, and voice-over
work, specializing in "not just a pretty face" character types. There's a lot of
industrial work here.

Stewart Talent, 212 W. Superior, Chicago, IL 60610 (312) 943-3131
It's a TV, film, and print agency. Drop off your headshot or résumé with the
receptionist.

Voices Unlimited, 680 N. Lake Shore, Chicago, IL 60611
(312) 642-3262
This exclusive agency caters to voice-over talent. Send them a three-minute
tape.

You'll Need

Audition monologue book or play scripts
These might help you once you actually get your appointment for your audition and you need to prepare a monologue and familiarize yourself with the
play being done. Still the best place for these is Chicago's only full-service theater bookstore, *Act I, 2632 N. Lincoln, Chicago, IL 60614 (312)-348-6757.*

Cigarette
You don't mean you're actually going to pay for cigarettes, do you? Someone
else in the show has got to have a pack.

Elizabethan costume
You have to start out doing Shakespeare, don't you? Why does every novice
actor usually get cast in the hardest stuff? Find your tights, your tunic, and
your flouncy dress at *Kaufmann Costumes, 5065 N. Lincoln, Chicago, IL 60625
(312) 561-7529.* It's been there for over fifty years.

Get-out-of-jail-free card
Theater parties tend to get a little out of hand sometimes. If the cops come in
to bust it up, it might be a good idea to have one of these along. The best place
I know to get a game of Monopoly is still *Marshall Field & Company, 111 N.
State, Chicago, IL 60602 (312) 781-1000.*

Grooming kit
They say that all that matters is your performance. Wrong. If you don't look
half-decent, 90 percent of directors will tune out your performance. Let's start
out with a comb and a brush and some clippers. Try *Chicago Hair Goods Company, 428 S. Wabash, Chicago, IL 60605 (312) 427-8600.*

How to stop smoking handbook
It's a rough life since you took up smoking again, isn't it?

Makeup

Maybe that's why I stopped acting. That weird orangey base makeup stuff made me look like a jack-o'-lantern. I tried to say I was allergic, but somehow no one believed me. Bob Jones's makeup, the top-of-the-line stuff for actors is available through *Act I, 2632 N. Lincoln, Chicago, IL 60614 (312)-348-6757.*

Motivational tapes

Way, way back in the day, all you had to do to boost your self-confidence was *Looking Out for #1*. Not anymore. Now you need someone in your ear telling you that. Watch late night television on either WGBO, Channel 66, or WCIU, Channel 26, and you'll learn all you need to motivate yourself from the experts.

Professional photographer

You'd better get a good-looking headshot and be willing to cough up some money for it, not only because you want people to remember your face but because you don't want to wind up on somebody's dartboard, either. Check out the ads in *Performink* or, better yet, ask your friend with the cool picture where she got hers.

Puppet

Maybe you're not the in-front-of-the-scenes type. Maybe you want to don a black mask and do *Danny and the Deep Blue Sea* with puppets. Try *National Marionette Company, 1922 W. Montrose, Chicago, IL 60613 (312) 989-0308.*

Wig

Overheard once in a theater that shall remain nameless said by one actor to another, both of whom shall also remain nameless: "Aw man, you're so lucky you're bald, man. You can wear a wig and get so many different looks." Could be. Both Harpo Marx–style and Eva Gabor–style wigs, among others, may be purchased at *Wig Fashion of Chicago, 11 W. Washington, Chicago, IL 60602 (312) 236-2496,* or *Wigfield Boutique, 22 E. Adams, Chicago, IL 60603 (312) 263-6034.*

Interviews

Kate Buddeke on Just Doing It

Kate Buddeke came to acting later than most and struck gold far quicker than most as well. Appearing in Apple Tree's *Ourselves Alone*, she won a Joseph Jefferson Citation her first time out. She's appeared at Goodman in *Mill Fire* and in Robert Falls's excellent revival of Eugene O'Neill's *The Iceman Cometh*.

She's also appeared on Broadway in the Tony Award–winning *Carousel* and has had bit parts in films. Blink twice and you might miss her in bed with Aidan Quinn in *Blink*. Buddeke is also an artistic director at American Blues Theater.

Location: Kopi, A Traveler's Café

AL: Now, you started at this business from a kind of different way—you started in music.

KB: I was in bands. I was in England for seven or eight years. I had a great time and I came home, had a band here, and I just got bored. A friend of mine told me I should take some acting classes because I'd been out of town a long time and didn't know anybody. So I took classes with Kyle Donnelley at the Actors' Center, and she put me in my first show. I got a Jeff Citation [*Ourselves Alone* at Apple Tree] for that. It seemed really easy to do, to be an actor. Not easy on your emotions, but easy to do.

AL: Had you done theater stuff before?

KB: *Hair*, but that wasn't acting. It was all getting fucked up and going out having a good time.

AL: But there was no stage fright to overcome?

KB: Not at all. Kyle taught me about using your emotions, you being that person whoever you're acting. It's not becoming somebody else. It's always you that you're playing, and it was a lot of fun. The next show I did was *Mill Fire* at Goodman, and I know that I called David Petrarca on the phone at his house.

AL: Did you know him before?

KB: No, but I said I thought he ought to see me for this, and he said he'd met me in a bar and I'd been calling him short and stuff, being my usual obnoxious self, and he gave me an audition for it. A lot of people expect them to call you in, but you can't expect to be remembered, because there are so many of us.

AL: Did you ever send your pictures and résumés out?

KB: No, I have never done a mailing ever, because I have American Blues Theater and I look through head shots, and if they're not a person of color or older or a really incredible résumé, I don't really keep them. And people keep sending me shit. It's like "stop!"

AL: Just because it reeks of desperation?

KB: Yeah, and you've got to go to general auditions if you're not known. And you have to be really good. And then it's a Catch-22, because how do you get really good if you don't do the work? Actors only get better by doing it. You don't get better by doing the same monologue in an audition.

AL: What monologues did you do in auditions?

KB: I haven't done a monologue in years. I used to do one from *Cowboy Mouth* by Sam Shepard until I found out that everybody was doing it. I never do any classicals. Just 'cause they're really hard as an auditioner. It's hard to take Shakespeare out of context. And it's really hard to sit and listen to it.

AL: So if you wouldn't want to sit through it, you wouldn't bother doing it.

KB: Absolutely not.

AL: Do you have any sort of ritual before auditions?

KB: No. I go in, I read, and I leave. Even if I'm doing a show, I read the script once. I don't learn any of the lines. I don't want to know how I'm going to react. You build off each other and learn off each other.

AL: That saves you some work, too, doesn't it?

KB: Absolutely.

AL: How did you wind up getting an agent?

KB: I'm with Stewart Talent. I got an agent a long time ago. There are some agents that will take anybody, which is not really a good idea.

AL: You wind up in a big file.

KB: And you have to have the ability to go in and schmooze them. Stop in there once a week and say "Hi, how are you?"

AL: I never understood what the function of that was. People talk about going in to see their agents once a week. What are they doing in there?

KB: I always feel here that agents never really work for you. They're just the middleman. You need them, rather than they need you. Very weird.

AL: You started off with one that would take anyone.

KB: I lasted with them for two months. I went there with very clear goals. I don't want to be a commercial person. I don't want to do industrial films, which is snobby of me, but I just have no interest in that.

AL: Which disqualifies you for 75 percent of the work.

KB: I have no desire to go play a young mom. Maybe a drug commercial or something, fine. They weren't thinking of what I wanted. There are a certain number of people who do industrials and make a lot of money doing them, and more power to them, but I have no desire. I'm not in this business to make money at all.

AL: Have you had to work other jobs, though?

KB: No, never, because I got *Ourselves Alone* and then the next show I got was an Equity show. Chicago's unique in that what jobs you get are up to you. You have to pursue them. *Iceman Cometh*, at Goodman, I happened to be in the lobby waiting for a friend and I saw all these women who were my type coming out of an audition and I was like "What's going on?" So I didn't even know what the play was, and someone told me there was a part for a whore, and I was like "Why aren't I being seen for that?"

AL: Do most of the people you run across have the same approach as you do?

KB: No.

AL: You recently got to Broadway in *Carousel.* How did this gig come about?

KB: I met the casting director in a bar in Chicago.

AL: What bars are there where all these things happen for you?

KB: Actors go to certain places. They go to Joel's or Hopleaf. I drink, and I hang out, and I go to openings. And I met this casting director at a party for *The Skin of Our Teeth* at this bar. I was yelling at David Petrarca that he brought in this woman from New York and I told him I knew five other people in Chicago who could've done a better job. So this guy, two years later, remembered me being loud and drunk and boisterous. So he called me into New York; I didn't even read the script. I remembered seeing the movie and saying, "Ah, this sucks." I went into this huge room with like thirty people and I sat down and I said, "You know, I gotta tell you. I fucking hate musicals and I hate this one more than any." And that was basically my audition. We talked about why I hated it and the director, it turned out, wasn't fond of it either.

AL: Did you get to like it a bit more after you'd been in it?

KB: No.

AL: How does the New York theater scene compare to the Chicago scene?

KB: To me, New York is all about money, all about personality. It's not about the ensemble, it's not about the work, and it's certainly not about creating. It's all about revivals, Tony Awards, being weird. Here, people care more about the work and the community. After we did our number on the Tony Awards and won our awards, we weren't allowed to stay and watch. We were basically thrown onto the street. We were standing around 50th Street saying, "Well what the fuck do we do now?"

AL: That must've felt like crap.

KB: Oh, terrible, terrible. We were all waiting for our bus to come get us. We're like "This sucks." Here, at least, anybody can go and have fun.

AL: Do you get a certain reaction from people outside of Chicago because of Chicago theater's reputation?

KB: Yeah, people think we're really good for some reason. I don't know why. When I walked into rehearsal, they're all like, "Oh, you're the Chicago actor. Let's see you act." I'm like "You're the New York actor. Let's see you suck."

AL: Do you see a difference in the style?

KB: I think Chicago's ability is to create great ensembles. We do amazing ensemble work, as opposed to one guy. Everybody knows how to create together. I think we don't have money to produce big. We can't hide behind scenery. We can't hide behind star names. We have a chair and a bed and that's it. And space is close. You can't fake it here, because it's so small, which is good. Which is probably why we are better actors.

Elizabeth Geddes on Who Needs an Agent

Elizabeth Geddes is the founder of one of Chicago's highest reputed agencies for television, theater, and motion picture actors, the Geddes Agency.

Location: The Geddes Agency, 1925 N. Clyborn

AL: First, how does someone go about approaching you, and what are you looking for when they approach you?

EG: Actors who are looking for representation first need to send us a picture and résumé. And that's where it starts. How we have come to represent our clients is from recommendations from other clients, going to theater, somebody coming in to do a monologue that has just blown us away, watching people through schools. We get hundreds of pictures.

AL: On what criteria do you decide which pictures to pull?

EG: Something extremely unique, something special, something that shows a personality. The picture needs to intrigue. It needs to represent who the person is. You don't have to be gorgeous, you don't have to be ugly, you don't have to be tall or short or blonde or blue-eyed. There has to be something that's intriguing about the picture, and then you turn it over and you look at the résumé and there have to be some kind of credits. There has to be some kind of education or something that says that this person did not just decide to be an actor yesterday. I'm not interested in that. I can't represent somebody who just woke up and decided they could be rich by being an actor. It does not happen that way.

AL: How important is the quality of the picture and the résumé? Do you need to spend top dollar on it?

EG: If you're going to submit a picture, you better have the best thing that you can, because it's going to represent you. If you're going to have a shot that doesn't tell who you are or a snapshot or not a professional headshot, you might as well not bother. You really have to invest in what your career is going to be. If you can't invest in it, then why should I invest in it? This is a two-way street here.

AL: Okay, so someone sends you their résumé, an adorable picture, you say come on in and do a monologue.

EG: A two-minute monologue that represents who they are. I want them to come in and do their best work. From there, we decide if they're ready to be here.

AL: Do you care about the contents of the monologue?

EG: No. One of my clients came in and did a monologue that could have been offensive, if we had chosen to be offended by it. But it was so powerful and so moving that we chose not to be offended, and it just drew us in. He's now in L.A. and working. It's not the content; it's the presentation. If you're in the moment and your monologue has art and it is real, that's what it's about.

AL: So, it doesn't matter if you've heard the monologue fifty times before, as long as it's done well.

EG: No, but the most popular monologues should be put aside. Try to find something more suited for you. The one monologue we hate to see is one from *The Sure Thing* that John Cusack did. And a lot of young people do it. It's a wonderful monologue, but Cusack was a client and we did that film. Only he can do that monologue as far as we've seen.

AL: Okay, so the monologue blows you away. Then you sit down and do an interview process.

EG: One of the agents sits down and talks with them. We give them the procedure of how it's going to be.

AL: How is it going to be?

EG: Well, it's going to be about communication, in terms of a relationship. It's a partnership. They have responsibilities; we have responsibilities. And it's an open forum. If there are problems, you have to come in and discuss them. You have to keep up on your pictures and résumé. You have to be responsible about checking your machine. You have to be professional about going to auditions and responding to our phone calls. You have to participate.

AL: What is being professional about auditions?

EG: Being prepared, being on time, knowing what you're going to do and doing it, making a choice.

AL: Are there higher-echelon clients as opposed to lower-echelon ones? Some who get sent out more than others?

EG: It depends what's being cast at the moment. Lately, Generation X is going like crazy and the forty-year-olds don't get the auditions. You can't even it out. It's whatever category of actor is hot at the moment and what's happening at the moment, what the hot TV show is, what age frame.

AL: Who in Chicago needs an agent? When should someone take the step to approach you?

EG: For me, when there's training going on and you've completed your program at DePaul or Northwestern and you've been on stage and you're now really going to give it 150 percent, you're going to wait tables to support yourself and you want your career to go forward, you should have an agent. But if you're just getting into this, this agency won't be interested.

AL: Do you recommend training programs for people who just aren't ready yet?

EG: Sure. I'll pick up the phone and say, "We really can't represent you, but keep working on your craft." But we have to see something there, or if there's somebody there. We took a woman recently who was just sweet, charming, beautiful, and she had not much on her résumé. But she was so real that we decided to work with her, even though we thought she wasn't quite ready, that there was a lot of stuff that she was missing. But there was something engaging about her. You just have to follow your instincts in this business.

AL: In terms of training for actors, do you feel any program in Chicago has done a particularly good job of turning out good students?

EG: DePaul does. They have the best program. Columbia does some good work. Steve Scott teaches at one of the audition centers, and he does some incredible work. Glenn Haines does some nice private coaching. Mary Ann Thebus does some really good coaching. In terms of film and television, I don't think there's a really good class for cold reading in this town. If there is, I don't know of it.

AL: Can you immediately tell what sort of client it is you're looking for?

EG: I can tell you when one of my clients walks in this door. I can tell you an actor from a non-Geddes actor. We have people who call up on the phone and they say, "You've got to see this actor; he's a Geddes actor."

AL: How do you define that?

EG: I can't. They're extraordinarily talented and very unique, and they're usually not drop-dead gorgeous. They're full of personality and character and strength and insecurities.

AL: I had a friend in Chicago who signed up with an agent who would constantly hound her about her weight. Is that something you have to do at times?

EG: Sure. I'm the critical eye here. We're in a visual business. Los Angeles is not interested in heavy women. It's as simple as that. And it's not fair to women. It's terrible. It's just sexist. But unfortunately, that's the reality. You have to be as physically fit as possible, because the camera puts fifteen pounds on you, and if that's going to happen, you don't have to be skinny, but you have to be fit and healthy.

AL: Is it all right to register with a number of agencies?

EG: Yes, we have a multilisted system in this town. We have it here because it's very difficult to make a living here, and some agencies are stronger in industrials. And some are stronger in this category or that category. We try to cover most of the areas of business. If somebody is an industrial actor, that's not our strength; they should go over to Emilia Lorance's, who does a lot of industrial business.

AL: Is this town strongest as an industrial town?

EG: Theater. That's where our reputation comes from. It's the only place anymore where you can get trained. In New York it's difficult, because it's Broadway and off-Broadway, and it's almost impossible to put small productions up. We have over a hundred theaters in this town doing extraordinary and unusual and out-there work.

AL: You'd think though that theater is the one area where you wouldn't need an agent.

EG: That's a misconception. We have been very lucky that the Goodman Theater and the Court Theater and Steppenwolf and all the major theaters call us. As Steppenwolf grows and other theaters grow, it's important for them to use agents. It's hard for an actor to grow. If somebody asks actors to do something and there are other possibilities and they have to make decisions, it becomes too personal and they need someone to go in and lay the possibilities on and help them reach the decision.

AL: So you become entrusted with the responsibility of saying no so the actor doesn't have to.

EG: Certainly, and do it in a businesslike way, because it is business. There are no hard feelings on either side.

Jeff Sweet on the Easy Art of Playwriting

Evanston-born Jeff Sweet has authored a number of plays for Victory Gardens Theater, including *Porch*, *The Value of Names*, and *With and Without*. His *American Enterprise* appeared at Organic Theatre before a roundly applauded production off-Broadway. He's written quite a bit for television including a gig as script doctor for the Emmy Award-winning *Pack of Lies*. He edits the annual *Best Plays* collection and, in 1978, authored *Something Wonderful, Right Away* about Chicago's Second City.

Location: Higher Ground, 2022 W. Roscoe

AL: Do you think that people's roles in theater have become too specialized and that the roles of the director, writer, and designer have become overrated?

JS: We're in a new era of theater. Once upon a time, all you needed in theater were actors and audience, and then, somewhere along the lines, one actor started bossing another actor around and that actor became the first director-writer and started saying, "Move here. Move there. Tell the mastodon story now." The history of the theater has largely been about people taking prerogatives away from actors. The actors were the original set designers to the extent that somebody would say, "Oh, I'm gonna do my tiger imitation in front of the limpid pool."

What is happening, though, is we're getting more and more and more and more fragmentation and specialization. A hundred years ago, nobody would have known what you meant if you said you worked in theater as a sound designer. Nobody would have known what you meant if you said you were a graphic designer. For that matter, directors didn't have the status they have now. They were basically the actor-manager coming into the town to tell actors in the neighborhood not to get in each other's way while they were doing *Julius Caesar*. The cult of the director, the idea of the directors having this primacy, is largely a twentieth-century phenomenon.

What is interesting to me about Chicago is that with Second City, it brings you back to the idea that theater is still possible with just actors and audience, and when you look at all of the people who've come out of Second City and done this extraordinary stuff, it reminds me that improvisational acting is one of the best generalist kind of experiences you can have. If you can hold the stage in the moment and simultaneously act, direct, and write, you can spin off and do so many different, specialized areas of this business.

AL: But that's also a best-case scenario. Sometimes what you're talking about results in chaos.

JS: Oh, absolutely. Not anybody who can do this can go off and write great plays. I'm not saying that everybody who can improvise is going to be able to become a great actor or a great writer, but this is a way to remind people of where theater started and to acquire skills that can be useful in all disciplines.

AL: How has the specialization affected playwriting?

JS: It certainly affects people in the way their skills are marketed in this ridiculous business. It's assumed that if you write soap opera, you can't write comedy. If you write comedy, you can't write miniseries. It also happens when assignments are being made in the theater. Producers are behind a lot of the putting together of musicals, and a lot of people who could write decent musicals are not looked at because they've never done it before.

AL: Do you feel you've been typecast at all?

JS: I've had a relatively easy time of it. I've stumbled stupidly from genre to genre. People have put up with me switching.

AL: What's allowed you to do that?

JS: I hope it's just the merit of the scripts themselves and the fact that I often write plays that are very cheap to produce.

AL: Do you have to censor yourself or budget yourself as you write?

JS: Sometimes, unless somebody's paying me an enormous amount of money, in which case I will write what they pay me. When I think about what I want to do for the theater, I will alternate between practical and impractical projects. I won't write anything that I'm not in love with, because when you write on spec, why should you write anything that you're not in love with?

AL: What's your relationship to Chicago?

JS: I grew up in Evanston. I wrote four original shows that got put on while I was at ETHS. My parents were here until the mid-eighties, and even though I was living in New York, I would come back a lot. I was working on the Second City book. It was because of the Second City book that I got hooked up with Victory Gardens. Originally I left Chicago to study film at NYU, thinking that Chicago didn't have much to offer for living playwrights. Goodman produced you if you were European or dead or both. Second City had no use for me. Hull House was the only action going on in terms of original scripts. As I came back here, I saw that in my absence the Chicago theater movement was getting started. I was recommended to Victory Gardens. I gave them *Porch* and the next year they put it on, and my plays were put on there every year through 1983.

AL: Was *Porch* the first play you attempted to have produced professionally?

JS: My first professional production was sort of a fluke, actually. It was up at Milwaukee Rep, called *Winging It*, an adaptation of Aristophanes' *The Birds*. It had a cast of twenty-five. I was at the O'Neill center my senior year of college. I was sitting at a piano noodling around and somebody said, "I like that. Is that from something?" I said, "Yeah, it's a musical I'm working on." He said, "Play the rest." I played the rest and he said if he liked the book, he'd do it. It happened that quickly.

AL: What inspired you to go into playwriting?

JS: I always found that dialogue was easy to come by.

AL: You had a knack for it.

JS: Partially it's journalism. Acting and journalism are first cousins. The actor was society's original journalist. There's a reason why, after actors, the source for the major number of playwrights is journalists. I think journalists have typed up the way people actually speak, and other people's speech patterns have been turned into your physical behavior. You internalize and experience it. It's a great way to learn about how people really speak. If you write a hard news story, you know that in the first two paragraphs you have to isolate what the event is, which is terribly useful for playwrights. If you're writing a feature, you have to have a hook which will keep people reading through the whole article, and that's great for learning how to write a whole play.

I've done a fair amount of journalism and that feeds directly into playwriting. I was a professional actor as a kid, and that also feeds directly into playwriting. Acting is tremendously competitive. I know wonderful actors who never get any work, but I don't know too many wonderful playwrights who don't get productions. Actors also sit around waiting for other people to offer them opportunities. Playwrights make their own opportunities.

AL: How did you work in promoting yourself to get productions?

JS: I learned that inadvertently. Most of the things I've learned I've stumbled across and realized that there were principles I could use. The most useful thing in terms of promoting myself that I can pass on is that if you want to get a play done, sending a play to a literary manager is not likely to succeed. Literary managers can only say two things, No or Maybe. Neither one of those is what you want to hear. On the other hand, I've found that, if you forge alliances with directors whose works you like, the directors will go off and act as your de facto agent. They will call up artistic directors directly and bypass the literary manager.

Another thing that I've discovered is that most intelligent actors want to direct, and if you can find somebody who's got some profile in the business, who you think has directing talent, you can't get them to act in your stuff but you can get them to direct it. It's a social profession; you can't do it by yourself. And one of the reason people will want to put on your plays, aside from the fact that they like the work, is that they like you and want to work with you.

AL: Do you use other people to improvise a lot when you're writing?

JS: If I know the project's going to be really colloquial, I like to use improvisation. When you're writing by yourself, you have to throw yourself into three or four characters and usually the author favors one character or another and isn't heedful of keeping each character pursuing their objective. When you're improvising you have three or four people constantly thinking about what their objective is.

Also, improvisation is closer to the way we behave than playwriting. When actors pick up a script, they look at lines and they try to figure out what kind of behavior they can create to support the lines; their job is to try to make the audience think that the lines are an extension of the behavior, but they're really working backwards. They have to create behavior that makes the lines look like they're coming out of the behavior. In improvisation, you start out with behavior and the lines are a by-product of that. When you're writing that way, you don't have to make up behavior; it's organically there.

AL: Do you see any detrimental effect on playwriting that the improvisational process had, the rash of company-generated works that don't have one authorial voice in them?

JS: You have to have one authorial voice eventually; otherwise, you get anarchy. It's usually the director or the project leader. Otherwise it's just shapeless. It may have a lot of life, but it won't have a point or a structure. Someone has to be responsible for the structure and deciding which material is in and which is out, even if that material is delightful. You have to have someone who can say what does and doesn't belong, to act as an editor, at the very least.

AL: Writing is generally such a solitary activity, but everything you do, you seem to turn into a social event.

JS: Half of it is solitary; half of it is social. You can't improvise unless you have other people in the room. You want to write something because you've met somebody. The cliché is that writing is solitary. But you have to deal with people. You have to find ideas in common. *Porch* was written because I had a crush on an actress. There are very few playwrights who are associated with nonurban backgrounds. Novelists and poets can write in a cabin someplace, but the theater is an urban phenomenon, because you need enough people to constitute an audience. Theater is going to occur where there are enough people to get together to serve as an audience. You can write a poem or a novel very easily and never leave your town. You can't work that way as a playwright. I don't know any successful hermit playwrights.

AL: As people get older they tend to get more insular and self-referential.

JS: That's a real danger. You also see people who are afraid to write something that doesn't sound like them. The Hemingway syndrome, where at the end, Hemingway was afraid of writing a sentence that didn't sound like a Hemingway sentence.

AL: Do you think there is too much emphasis given to this aura of playwright?

JS: I think that most actors could at least write a decent one-act play if they had decent improvisational training and if they were selfless enough to listen to others. Most people who can write a one-act play can extend those skills to write a two-act play. I don't think it's mysterious. If people understood how unterrifying writing is, I would have a lot more competition.

Part II: Theater . . . Without a Script, or Improv

In very few cities do people have the privilege of saying that there, a new, original art form was created. Few new forms ever come around. Sure, maybe in Athens they can say it, or in Rome. Perhaps the people of the cradle of civilization in the Middle East can say they were responsible for the creation of music. The imprecise dating of cave paintings still makes it difficult to determine where the world's first visual artists were born. Maybe Adam and Eve and the snake were the first to do mime, but don't quote me on that. (My Hebrew school teachers would probably want to have my ass for saying that.) Yet, in Chicago, strangely, we're able to say that the art of improvisation was created here. Well, maybe not created here, but this is the first place where it was recognized as art.

Much has been written about the beginnings of the fabled Second City. How a group of U of C students turned a predilection for spontaneous wiseassness into a national industry. How David Shepherd, Paul Sills, and Eugene Troobnic founded the Playwrights Theatre Club above a Chinese restaurant. How Elaine May and Mike Nichols polished their crafts with the Compass Players, founded under the tutelage of Viola Spolin and story theater maven Paul Sills, before jetting off to Broadway and then to Hollywood. How in 1959, Sills, Bernie Sahlins, and Howard Alk founded the Second City in a shuttered Old Town Chinese laundry, which became the training ground for an entire generation of theater, TV, and film performers too numerous to be mentioned here. How in the seventies and eighties, longtime Second City director and improv guru Del Close refined the art once again, metamorphosing the Chicago-invented tradition of sketch comedy into long-form, spontaneously created plays based on the intricate interweaving of drills, exercises, and games, in which the mysterious Harold—that symbol of a perfect symbiosis and sense of cooperation—would sometimes appear.

At its best, improv represents the height of artistry, in which the audience can watch the generation of art onstage. At its worst, it is masturbatory theater for the lazy, those who are too lethargic to be bothered with the concept of memorizing lines, organizing themes, or creating characters. At its scariest, it can become a form of drama therapy, in which students refer to their instructors as one might speak of the leader of a religious cult and attribute their newfound growth in interpersonal skills to their improv training. Bearing this in mind, the Chicago improv scene is a fertile one, and not only because there's a lot of shit out there. While in the eighties every bar had a comedian telling blue jokes, in the nineties every café has an improv squad. Like members of an intramural sports scene, gaggles of young Chicagoans who'd rather not play volleyball or join the Chicago Social Club's tag football teams have signed up for improv classes with dreams of appearing on *Saturday Night Live* or at least on television selling detergent, or, if not that, at least finding a date. Says the expert Del Close of his ImprovOlympic classes, "they're a great place to get laid." The result of this, as in the case of comedy clubs, is a wildly divergent level of quality in the improv on the Chicago scene, from the old steam engines of the zillion different companies that Second City now runs to the exciting experiments of Close and Charna Halpern to ImprovOlympic, which has launched a number of television and film careers, to the sophomoronic noodlings of dozens of groups of recent college grads (they shall remain nameless) who have accrued the dollars to rent theater spaces, if not the talent to put audiences in them.

Getting Schooled

Improv companies don't just make money off of booze and admission tickets. If that were the only way they made coin, they'd be out of business quick. But usually, in order to get into an improv company, you have to get yourself roped into a series of rigorous and highly profitable (for you and the school) classes. They've got you screwed, because unless you want to wind up in some untried, weird late night show at Cafe Voltaire with a bunch of people who *a*) think they're too good for, *b*) couldn't get into, or *c*) flunked out of Second City or ImprovOlympic, you've got to shell out the cash. It's a scam. It's a sham. It's the way things are done in Chicago.

Annoyance Theatre, 3747 N. Clark, Chicago, IL 60613
(312) 929-6200
Beginning, middle, and advanced improv classes are available here from the always outlandish and inventive (and sometimes a wee bit sloppy) company that brought you the *Real Live Brady Bunch*, *The Miss Vagina Pageant*, and so forth. Eight-week classes cost $275.

ImprovOlympic, 3541 N. Clark, Chicago, IL 60657 (312) 880-0199
If you can get past the cliquey, testosterone-infused boys' club atmosphere here, you can find your way into one of the hottest improv training programs

in Chicago. Led by Del Close, who practically invented long-form improv, and Charna Halpern, who institutionalized it, eight-week class sessions ($180) take you through four levels, from basic to advanced improv games and techniques, leading ultimately to your participation on one of the ImprovOlympic teams that perform here on a semiregular basis for no compensation. Says one ardent follower, "It's 90 percent bullshit and 10 percent brilliant, but the 10 percent brilliance makes it worth it."

Players Workshop, 2636 N. Lincoln, Chicago, IL 60614
(312) 929-6288
Founded in 1970 by Josephine Forsberg as one of the city's first improv training centers, the workshop, though often jeered by local wags as the place you study when you don't get into Second City, has placed many members eventually in the Second City company, as well as on national television. Among those who have studied with Forsberg are Shelley Long, George Wendt, Robert Townsend, and Homer Simpson voice Dan Castellanata. There are six levels of classes, each level lasting a total of twenty-four hours (not all at once), beginning with basic improv skills and ending with a performance at Second City. Each twenty-four-hour level costs $190.

Second City and Second City Training Center, 1616 N. Wells,
Chicago, IL 60614 (312) 664-3959
This Chicago institution could put you into one. Sometimes it seems that you could finish grad school or become an astronaut in the time it takes to get from beginning classes here to the main stage of Second City. But, since appearing on the main stage is pretty much the main goal of anyone going here (for those who aren't here to get laid, right, Del?), it may well be worth it. Five levels of eight-week classes ($190 per level) are required before you can be admitted to the conservatory program, a series of six terms of eight-week classes ($175 per level) culminating in a performance (wow). Completion of this program gives you eligibility to audition for the resident companies (suburban, E.T.C., main stage, and so forth). But Second City stresses, "THERE IS NO GUARANTEE THAT ACCEPTANCE INTO THE PROGRAM WILL LEAD TO A POSITION IN ONE OF OUR PERFORMING COMPANIES." Admission into the conservatory program requires an audition and sometimes completion of a basic acting course.

Interview

Del Close on the Method Behind the Mad Art of Improvisation

The mad genius Del Close is quite simply the guru of Chicago improv as a longtime performer and later director of Second City. He's lauded as an innovator in the field, having essentially invented the concept of long-form improv and the so-called Harold. He currently teaches at the Del Close Theater at ImprovOlympic and is coauthor of *Truth in Comedy*, a volume explaining improv techniques. As an actor, he's appeared at Goodman in *The Misanthrope* and Peter Sellars's *The Merchant of Venice*, and onscreen as a shifty alderman in *The Untouchables*.

Location: Jeanny's Chinese Restaurant, 1053 W. Belmont (Close likes the broccoli.)

AL: Before I go and take a class with you, what do I need to do to prepare myself?

DC: Go and see a couple of shows. If you feel the pull to get involved, sign up for classes. If you feel repelled or you just want to stay in the audience and have no impulse to jump in the ring and start fighting the bull, then don't sign up.

AL: What is the first thing you tell your students?

DC: "You already know how to do this." One of my favorite openings is, "The hard part of the day is over. You got here. You dealt with a really complicated world out there and this is a simplification and an abstraction of human behavior. You've been doing the hard stuff. You've been doing human behavior; now we're going to take human behavior and turn it into an abstract art form."

Improv is not a very abstract art form like chess is an abstraction of warfare. It's not as much of an abstraction as music is an abstraction of human emotion. We're using human behavior to abstract from human behavior. What nobody knows how to deal with is what happens when you get in front of an audience. All your training can turn to shit. And your IQ goes down as a result of self-consciousness. And there's no way you can deal with the sudden hypertrophy when your ego metastasizes under the public scrutiny.

There are ways of dealing with it, but they are all spiritual exercises—like investing consciously more concern in the other person than in yourself to make various choices—and if you don't do those, you will be swamped. The endorphins go out of whack and all kinds of stuff. That's one of the reasons why we teach people various techniques that, if they actually follow them, even when they're under the terrible baleful scrutiny of that big black giant that looks and listens with thousands of eyes and ears, they won't fuck up so badly.

AL: What's fucking up in improv?

DC: Playing below your potential. Forcing things. Going for the laughs instead of the revelations, which create bigger laughs. Giving each other's ideas and characters insufficient respect so that trivial things happen. They're still entertaining and get a lot of laughs and it's good improvisation, but Harold doesn't appear. When the group intelligence meshes to the point that a group mind or the gestalt intelligence emerges, it's almost as if there's a spirit that's holding it all together. And, from inside the experience, it's quite powerful because you're able to predict the future. You train out jokes and wit; you train in oblique thinking and nonsequitur thinking. You train in the ability to think on more than one level at the same time. As you're engaged in what may appear to be completely spontaneous human behavior, you're also trying to figure out what element you're creating within a larger pattern and what you are creating and what you are aiming toward.

AL: What draws people to improvise?

DC: I've always had a bunch of theories about why improvisation is culturally important. It's a game that people can play, men and women, professionals and nonprofessionals, actors and nonactors, on pretty much an equal basis. Being a really good actor does not necessarily guarantee that you will be a very good improviser. Sometimes that's the case, but sometimes it's not the case. Being an actual, complete, hopeless, wretched geek in real life doesn't disqualify you from being a solid improviser, either. We've got a couple of those. You go "Holy shit, where do they come from?" I think there's something about what we do that I like to think appeals to the citizen poet. It's an odd thing to do to get up and improvise. In our culture, we are so trained to be passive, to leave the activity to experts.

AL: Is there a spiritual element to it?

DC: Definitely. There's the sense of part of a community finding its own voice. Everybody gets told that they're spokesmen and women of their generation, but few get up and speak. There's also something kind of daring about it. The most frightening thing for people in the United States is getting up and speaking. That's precisely what we're doing—not only getting up and speaking, but creating and working together and going out into an unknown situation for an extended period of time, depending on nothing but our innate ability and our training and each other.

There's something culturally valuable about doing that. It's not even like we're not building bombs. We are creating relationships between people, because in order to make improvisation work as theater or comedy, you have to deal with each other in a way that, if people behaved this way socially, the world would be a nicer community—and not in a namby-pamby way. It's a way to participate in these group rituals we've lost, or if not precisely that, it's at least something that has a dim, distant echo of it. These are some of the reasons why somebody like me will continue to do improv over a lifetime. There are many worse things that I could be doing with my life.

AL: Do you see it as having a therapeutic value as well?

DC: Oh, fuck yes. It will change you, and not always for the better. Sometimes people turn into monsters of ego when they discover the kind of power they really have. They develop a whole new self-image. But, on the other hand, yeah, at the minimum people will say that they are no longer nervous in auditions, or not as nervous.

AL: A lot of people call you the guru of modern improv, a kind of spiritual leader.

DC: Sure, but where does that get you? What was once this huge, history-making artistic breakthrough is now "Okay, what else have you got? What have you done for me lately?" In the old days, there was no example of what I wanted. You couldn't say, "Okay you do it like that." Now, of course, you can. There's lots of examples.

There used to be clichés in the world, and I like to disprove as many as I can personally with my own life. Like "Those who can, do; those who can't, teach." Obviously I can do both. Another is "No art is possible by committee." That is to say, a group of people cannot get together, at least not on the spot, and create something interesting, nay, even wonderful. I rather chose to not take these clichés as cultural givens or truths of our lives, but as problems to be solved. Suppose you did want to create art by committee. What would you do? How would you change your behavior? First, maybe let's go back to great thinkers who told us how we might make a better world if we treated each other better, take care of our brothers, put their interests ahead of our own.

What does this advice mean in terms of art? I realized that in giving advice to student improvisers, I was actually quoting all these great religious leaders, and I thought, well, who were they? Were they not only great religious leaders, but also improvisational instructors?

AL: Is improv a religious experience?

DC: The self must disappear to some extent in order to do this work, and it does. And when it does, there's this enormous charge of energy that comes from the right hemisphere of the brain, as a dimension of spiritual enlightenment—a phenomenon which is widely experienced in various kinds of ecstatic religious experience from voodoo to the Bali trance dancers.

AL: How do you define it as an art form? Is it the spontaneous creation?

DC: It's the order that is imposed on it—nay, not imposed, discovered within it. There is no art without order. There is no art without structure. Art is not the moment of free expression—anybody can do that. That's just masturbation and free association and therapeutic purging. There's no art in that. Where the art comes in is in the control, in taking this material that could spew off in any direction and imposing on it, or discovering within it or revealing, the inner order of this seemingly random, disordered, or unordered behavior. I remember trying to get people to improvise something in a checkerboard pattern, and they're like "What the fuck do you mean?" It was clear to me. I think I could have done a light scene and then a dark scene and then an oblique scene that was neither light nor dark, but they were still hung up on some other level.

AL: How do you go about creating a new art form? How were you able to accomplish it?

DC: I have a feeling that I've been ahead of my time for a long time. I stole many of the ideas that I wanted to see on stage from movies—the rapid intercutting, the use of narrative voice and montage and conceptual overture.

When I first started developing this kind of form, my improvs were done by tons of people, twenty to thirty people at a time, and all the issues were extremely important to the people involved in them, like the Vietnam War. We did one at a high school graduation in California. We pulled in a painter's scaffold to give us different levels and there was action all over the basketball court. And then when one of the actors was shot down, one of the performers ran over there and so did three audience members, without realizing that they'd done anything unusual. And I was watching this whole thing and I thought that this was an insane breakthrough.

Artaud talks about the healing, therapeutic theater, and he does this by torturing his actors in the presence of the audience; Grotowski basically did the same thing, Theater of Cruelty. Ours is a theater in which the fourth wall is not permeable from the audience side. We don't go out and bother audience members like the Living Theater and so much of the rest of sixties theater. We allowed the audience to come through the fourth wall to join us and go back without having felt they'd committed a great aesthetic breakthrough, which it really was, for audience members to join the action and rejoin the audience without feeling at all disoriented. And I realized that Artaud was wrong; Grotowski was wrong. You don't heal an audience by torturing the performer in their presence; you heal the audience by healing the *performers* in their presence or by allowing the performers to heal themselves and having the audience go along with the process.

Things Every Artist Needs to Know

EIGHT

Doing It Yourself

Of course, if these methods of getting to the top of your profession prove unsuccessful or if the just-plain-irritating grind of it all (auditions, gallery schmoozes, and the like) begins to wear and tear on your artist's psyche, there is, of course, the wonderful world of do it yourself . . . or have someone do it for you. If you're in an art class, maybe that guy next to you actually has a trust fund and an uncle with a loft space. Hopefully, if you're an actor, somebody in one of your audition classes has a great idea to start a new theater company. One bozo I was in a play with tried to start up what he called the Naked Lunch Theater Company. He didn't get much further than the logo, which featured a stick figure drawing of a guy with a sandwich between his legs. If you encounter such an individual, maybe you should be the one at the head of the operation. The venture is risky (I know, actually, of one poor soul who started up a theater company in town called Shattered Globe Theatre, but the details are far too grisly to get into here), but if you've got a play and a group of willing citizens, or a new dance and a troupe of performers, or an idea for a gallery show, there are a number of ways you can do it for next to nothing.

American Blues Theatre, 1909 W. Byron, Chicago, IL 60613
(312) 929-1031
Incredibly airy, well-located, 150-seat home base for the American Blues Theatre Company. Difficult to nab during prime time, but often available during

summer months for reasonable and highly negotiable rates. Contact the theater directly.

Angel Island Theatre, 731 W. Sheridan, Chicago, IL 60613
(312) 871-0442
Home of the Mary Arrchie Theatre, with many a late night and off night space available for rental. Rents usually run $50–$75 per night. Theater companies are also invited to participate in the annual, ongoing "Abbie Hoffman Died for Our Sins" theater festival/marathon.

Athenaeum Theatre, 2936 N. Southport, Chicago, IL 60657
(312) 525-0195
Almost too good to be true; maybe too good for you. A 900-seat performance space with a balcony and red cushy theater chairs. Like something out of an old-style downtown theater. A new 60-seat studio space also available. Prices are negotiable. Send a one-page proposal to the theater manager.

Blue Rider Theater, 1822 S. Halsted, Chicago, IL 60608
(312) 733-4668
A 100-seat, roomy, fully-equipped theater space with padded folding chairs in an ultra-groovy neighborhood. Founded in 1985 and used primarily for theater, Blue Rider has been branching out to become a collective performance space incorporating dance, music, performance art, and so on. Availability is spotty for long runs, but if they've got the time and you've got the $600 a month, "unless you're a neo-Nazi" they won't say no.

Cafe Voltaire, 3231 N. Clark, Chicago, IL 60657 (312) 528-3136
A paradise for the agoraphobic in all of us. Certainly the busiest, if not the comfiest, bare-bones theater space in town. If you don't mind low ceilings, indescribably mushy couches for your audience, and the likelihood that you will be sandwiched between two other shows, come into the café to fill out an application with a one-page synopsis of your play/performance proposal. $100 deposit. Thirty-five percent of your ticket sales go to the house.

Chicago Dramatists Workshop, 1105 W. Chicago, Chicago, IL 60622
(312) 633-0630
A spic-and-span, fully equipped, 75-seat performance space in a small pocket of an artistic no-man's-land. The theater is usually booked well in advance. Call or send your proposal to the managing director. The negotiable rent usually winds up around $400 a week (or $15 an hour for daytime rehearsals).

Greenview Arts Center, 6418 N. Greenview, Chicago, IL 60626
(312) 508-0085
The former Kesser Maariv synagogue (vintage 1957) and community theater transformed itself into a performing arts center for both established professionals and fledgling companies. Offers complicated cooperative rent agreements for those aspiring to be resident companies, which amount to approximately $500 a month plus box office percentage for a 60-seat lab space, and $800–$1000 a week plus box office percentage for the main stage 200-seat space. The center will handle all the PR for a greater box office percentage. Send a very detailed artistic and marketing proposal to the managing director.

International Performance Studio, 1517 W. Fullerton, Chicago, IL 60614 (312) 281-9075
A wonderful bargain if you can get it. Charges $100 a night for the 100-seat black box theater with complete lighting and sound equipment and vintage comfy theater seats from the old World Playhouse. The former home to the highly controversial, Grotowski-influenced Dreiske Performance Company. Preferences for productions run toward the multicultural, multilingual, and nonnaturalistic. In other words, if all you want to do is do another damn Shanley or Mamet play, find yourself another space. Address a one-page-maximum, basic proposal to the general manager.

Links Hall, 3435 N. Sheffield, Chicago, IL 60657 (312) 281-0824
A 75-seat dance studio with a thirty-by-thirty performing area and no wing space. Has a basic lighting and sound system. Rent is $150 per night and $100 each additional night. Anybody can rent it, as long as you do your own publicity, box office, and technical work and make sure everyone knows that you're an independent production not associated in any way with Links Hall's production season.

O Bar, 3343 N. Clark, Chicago, IL 60657 (312) 665-7300
A cleaner Cafe Voltaire–style basement space with a lower ceiling and nicer chairs. Seats around sixty. Charges $50 for Friday or Saturday prime time shows, $40 for all other shows, and $5 an hour for rehearsal space. Book two months in advance. Call first.

Organic Theatre Greenhouse, 3319 N. Clark, Chicago, IL 60657
(312) 327-2427
A couple of great, cheaply priced spaces are available if you can deal with the headache of scheduling here. There's the ultra-comfy 75-seat Greenhouse

space and the more basic 50-seat theater studio. If you can convince the managing director that you don't want to perform Sundays at 4:00, this is very well located and a good deal.

Sheffield's Wine and Beer Garden, 3258 N. Sheffield, Chicago, IL 60657 (312) 281-4989
Not the most conducive place for theater or, well, anything else that might be drowned out by excessive bar noise. There's no sound system and rudimentary lights. But, if you like a challenge and a bargain and you're not into complicated sets and so forth, you're all set.

Theatre Building, 1225 W. Belmont, Chicago, IL 60657 (312) 929-7367
Not for the faint of heart or the slim of wallet, this is one of the premier rental houses in the city and the price shows it. Has three 148-seat black boxes (one proscenium, two thrust). Send your proposal to the theater manager, but the credit check will probably be more important. Costs $1,350 a week. Reserve one to two months in advance.

Turn Around Theatre, 3209 N. Halsted, Chicago, IL 60657 (312) 296-1100
A weirdly shaped 75-seat theater. More a comfortable alleyway than a traditional theater space in a seemingly perfect yet somehow cursed location that has spelled the end of such businesses as Stars, Guzzlers, and the Lakeview Jazz Club. Likes to work with Equity companies, but doesn't always. Primetime performances cost $175 per night; late nights and off nights are $100.

Urbus Orbis, 1934 W. North, Chicago, IL 60622 (312) 252-4446
Cool, groovy space in the back of the fabled café with very basic sound and lighting equipment. Seats about forty if you're lucky, fifty if you're nuts. Costs $80 a night. Has a very conducive if somewhat flaky performance schedule. Book way in advance and make lots of follow-up calls to avoid headaches.

Victory Gardens Studio, 2257 N. Lincoln, Chicago, IL 60614 (312) 549-5788
Very well located, almost too well located as far as parking is concerned. The cozy 58-seat performance space comes with lighting equipment, sound system, computerized box office, and house manager. Partial to new plays by authors the theater is familiar with. Books about three to four months in advance. No late nights. Costs $700 a week, firm.

Zebra Crossing Theatre, 4223 N. Lincoln, Chicago, IL 60618
(312) 248-6401
An 80-seat, air-conditioned space in a neighborhood with (this is very important) good parking. The resident company produces four works per year and leans toward one-person shows and out-of-the-mainstream authors for rentals. Main stage rental costs $600 per week. Off nights and late nights are negotiable.

A Word on Rehearsal Space

If you're a nomadic dance or theater troupe, rather than spending a whole big chunk of change on studio time or some ritzy rehearsal hall, probably the best bargains going in the city are the Chicago Park District's fieldhouse spaces. There are lots of club rooms and even auditorium spaces available, and they usually cost no more than $20 a night. Best bets are *Sheil Park, 3505 N. Southport, Chicago, IL 60657 (312) 929-3070; Chase Park, 4725 N. Ashland, Chicago, IL 60640 (312) 561-4887;* the slightly scuzzy *Gill Park, 825 W. Sheridan, Chicago, IL 60313 (312) 525-7238;* and, if you can get it, the really nice basement, dance floor, or top floor of *Indian Boundary Park, 2500 W. Lunt, Chicago, IL 60645 (312) 674-7648.*

How to Promote Yourself

The cool thing about being an artist in Chicago (apart from the lucrative TV bio offers) is that it costs virtually nothing to get the word about your project out there. All you need is paper, a typewriter, a roll of stamps, envelopes (or a computer with a fax/modem, if you must), and the appropriate names in the media. Virtually every newspaper offers free listings for arts events, and if you get yours in two to three weeks before the time when you want your information out there, you can throw word of your event in front of literally hundreds of thousands of people. Don't bother sending it to every mom and pop newspaper in the neighborhood. If I saw your art exhibit mentioned in *Inside Lincoln Park* or the *Hegewisch Hometown Economist,* I'd probably think it was something lame and community oriented, and I wouldn't go at all.

Keep in mind that nice stationery is always good. So is a nice ten-by-thirteen envelope. Printing your announcement on shitty paper and jamming it into a letter envelope frequently shuttles you into the trash bin—not fair, but the way things work. As far as getting your work reviewed (unfortunately one of the only ways to get publicity for your work), the "squeaky wheel gets the grease" theory applies. Don't be an asshole or anything; just call the person in charge of assigning reviews a couple of times until you get a satisfactory response. Call preferably way early in the morning or way late in the day, when the person you want to get ahold of is unawares or when the intern who's been trained to deal with people like you isn't in yet. Or, better yet, if you are uncomfortable about hyping your own work, get a friend to do it for you. There's nothing lamer than getting a press release in the mail that says "Art Opening Featuring the Work of Joe Schmo. Press Contact: Joe Schmo." Everyone wants to have PR director on his or her résumé somewhere under "Special Skills," right? Or I suppose you could use a different name and pretend you're your own PR director. Make sure you're good at disguising your voice, though. And be certain that you're comfortable talking about yourself in the third person like famous athletes do. Practice saying phrases like this one to get accustomed to it (by inserting your name in the appropriate place): "What's most important is not what the media thinks, but what Michael Jordan thinks. I've got to be looking out for Michael Jordan."

What to Put in Your Press Release

A press release is not a novel, nor is it a stand-up comedy routine. Save the witty anecdotes for when people actually agree to come see your performance or exhibit. Make your press release as basic as possible and easy for an editor to understand. Divide it into the *who*, *what*, *where*, *when*, and *how*, making sure that the title, address, phone number, and price are prominently displayed. If you want something specific to be published about your art, come up with a catchy two- or three-sentence sound bite to summarize. Editors are lazy, and if you phrase things well or cleverly, they're liable to just print whatever you write verbatim.

Where to Send Performance, Gallery Opening, or Other Listing Information

Chicago Magazine, 414 N. Orleans, Chicago, IL 60610
(312) 222-8999

Classical Music: Ted Shen

Pop Music: Dan Kening

Theater Listings: Jeanne Rattenbury

Dance/Performance Listings: Gale Kappe

Theater/Film Critic: Penelope Mesic

Chicago Reader, 11 E. Illinois, Chicago, IL 60611 (312) 828-0350

Gallery Listings: Bonnie McLaughlin, Joel Score

Dance Listings: Laura Molzahn

Theater Listings: Albert Williams

Music Listings: Renaldo Migaldi, Peter Margasak

Art Criticism: Fred Camper

Dance Critics: Laura Molzahn, Maura Troester

Music Critics: Peter Margasak, Bill Wyman

Theater/Performance Critics: Mary Shen Barnidge, Lawrence Bommer, Jack Helbig, Justin Hayford, Achy Obejas, Albert Williams

Chicago Sun Times, 40 N. Wabash, Chicago, IL 60601 (312) 321-3000

Comedy/Performance Criticism: Ernest Tucker

Pop Music Critic: Jim DeRogatis

Theater Critics: Hedy Weiss, Avis Weathersbee

Theater Openings: Joe Pixler

Chicago Tribune, 435 N. Michigan, Chicago, IL 60611 (312) 222-3232

All Listings: Room 400

Art Criticism: Alan Artner

Comedy Criticism: Steve Johnson

Music Criticism: Greg Kot

Senior Theater Critic: Richard Christiansen

Theater Critics: Lawrence Bommer, Sid Smith

Theater Openings: Lawrence Bommer

Gallery Listings: Lori Gray

Performance: Achy Obejas

New Art Examiner, 314 W. Institute, Chicago, IL 60610 (312) 649-9900

Editor: Ann Wiens

New City, 770 N. Halsted, Chicago, IL 60622 (312) 243-8786

Listings: Liz Pawelko, Gil Kaufman, James Porter

Music Critics: Ben Kim, Gil Kaufman

Theater Critics: Chris Jones, Lucia Mauro, Jack Helbig

Art Critics: Lisa Stein, Michael Weinstein

About Posters

Walk down Clark Street and every window is crowded with posters—theater events, art gallery showings, bands. The light posts are covered with bumper stickers and wheat-pasted fliers. A good use of your time and energy? Well, think about it; when was the last time you went to a concert or show because you saw it advertised in the window of the Bagel? I thought so. Posters are stupid. Postcards are ten times better and cheaper. They're small, handy, fit on a refrigerator secured with a ladybug magnet, and give that personal touch when they're received through the mail. If you're starting out, the sad truth about the arts is that most of the people who are first going to come check your work out and start the word of mouth traveling are friends, friends of friends, family, friends of family, and people you've met in bars. A postcard is probably the best way to lure them in. If you're a bartender with a stack of postcards, you've got a couple steps up on everybody.

Grants, Awards, Contests, and Additional Resources

It's a sad fact of the modern artist's plight that if you rely on your art to make your living, you may well have to spend just as much time writing applications for grants and awards as actually working on cultivating your art. I know folks who view working at Kinko's and Easy Copy as their personal application for an endowment rather than engaging in the arduous, frustrating, and sometimes downright demeaning world of grant proposals. But, if the grant search is the route you choose, there are several ways to go about it. Though the rapidly shrinking National Endowment for the Arts isn't helping matters any, there are a number of other money sources for artists. Playwrights might want to check out the Center Theater International Playwriting Contest or the annual Cunningham Playwrights' Award from DePaul. The Center for New Television has opportunities for film and video artists, and the Illinois Arts

Council offers grants for every sort of artist imaginable. Listing all of these here would not only be a pain in the ass but unproductive. No one likes reading a phone book. A better idea is to check out the city's best resources for grants information.

Chicago Artists' Coalition, 11 E. Hubbard, Chicago, IL 60611
(312) 670-2060
This artists' resource organization will give you a personal consultation on which grants to apply for. It also offers grant writing and proposal writing workshops.

Donors Forum, 53 W. Jackson, Suite 430, Chicago, IL 60604
(312) 431-0264
Located in the beautiful and historic Monadnock Building, the forum has all the information about grant and loan opportunities that you could ever hope to get your mitts on and is open from 9:00 A.M. to 4:00 P.M. The forum also hosts seminars and workshops about grant proposal writing and publishes *The Directory of Illinois Foundations* (sixty bucks, pal), *The Members and Partners Directory* ($25 on computer disk), and other helpful volumes.

Illinois Arts Council, James R. Thompson Center, 100 W. Randolph, Suite 10-500, Chicago, IL 60601 (312) 814-6750
A major state arts funding source offering fellowships of up to $10,000 in choreography, crafts, media arts, music composition, photography, poetry, playwriting, prose, screenwriting, and visual arts, as well as other grants programs.

What to Say in Your Interview

It's bound to happen someday soon, and if it's gonna, you'd better be prepared. Realize that the interview is an art form and not just some irritating obligation. Realize, too, that your image is often every bit as important as your work. You might create great art, but, if you can't create good, memorable quotes along with it, it's going to be a lot harder to get somebody's attention. Here are ten questions some boneheaded journalist (perhaps even me) might be inclined to ask you, along with a multiple choice of boring, clichéd responses you might want to eschew and some more thought-provoking responses you might be inclined to try—if you have the nerve. A good technique if you run across a question you don't want to answer, is to say in a testy voice "What do you mean?" Repeat this until your interviewer goes on to a different question. If you've ever read interviews with Bob Dylan or Miles Davis or Liz Phair, masters of this art form, you'll notice that their responses are a brilliant combination of testiness and the elliptical nonsequitur.

Question: So, where did it all start for you? What got you into the business?

Boring answer: Well, it was always something I was good at, and, one day, I figured "Hey, let's just try it." I never thought of this as a career.

Clichéd response: I never thought of doing this until, one day, my friend went to this audition/exhibition/competition [choose one] and he asked me to go with. Strangely enough, I was chosen instead of him.

Better: It's like I hear voices, strange disembodied voices, that sound like Elmer Fudd, which tell me what to do and those are kind of like my muses. They drive me to the edge, sometimes even over the edge, if you know what I mean. I mean, when you've seen the edge, there's no way to get back.

Question: When was the first time you realized you wanted to be an artist?

Boring answer: I can't remember that far back, no way.

Clichéd response: I had this really great teacher, Mrs. Wozniak, and she kind of took me under her wing and entered my work in competitions.

Better: In which lifetime do you mean, man?

Question: What motivates you to create art?

Boring answer: My paycheck.

Clichéd response: I'll tell you something, it's not any one thing. I think it's a combination of a lot of different things.

Better: Pain. Have I shown you the dungeon where I work?

Question: As an artist, what is your role in society?

Boring answer: You know something? I've never really thought about that. I'm really kind of tied up in my own personal stuff right now.

Clichéd response: I'm basically trying to give a voice to the voiceless. I was voiceless until I started painting/acting/dancing/reciting [choose one], and now it's like the work talks for me.

Better: I don't live in a society. There's no such thing. What do you mean by *society*, man?

Question: If there were one thing you could say to people through your art, what would it be?

Boring answer: Well, I'm not sure if I'm trying to say anything specifically. . . .

Clichéd response: Just basically be yourself and express yourself, respect yourself, and respect others, and they will respect you.

Better: That question you asked me right now, just that. That's perfect.

Question: If you couldn't be an artist, what would you be?

Boring answer: An accountant, like my parents.

Clichéd response: I think we're all artists, so I don't see how I couldn't be one. I know I'd be expressing something in some way.

Better: I'd be you. And I'd make my money talking to me.

Question: Who's your greatest influence?

Boring answer: God/My parents/My lover [choose one].

Clichéd response: John Lennon/Andy Warhol/Mikhail Baryshnikov/Simone de Beauvoir/Djuna Barnes/Jesus Christ/Gandhi/St. Francis of Assisi/Mother Teresa [choose one].

Better: Does it have to be a human?

Question: How do you deal with mental blocks?

Boring answer: I just work through it.

Clichéd response: I ride my bike a lot, I go to the gym. Sometimes I call people up on the phone and bug them until it passes.

Better: I've got a gun.

Question: What do you think about criticism of your work?

Boring answer: Everyone's entitled to his or her own opinion.

Clichéd response: I don't read it. Well, I read some of it, but I don't pay attention to it. Well, I pay attention to it, but I don't take all of it seriously. Well, I take it seriously, but I don't read it. No, I don't care about it. I don't read it. Really, I don't. Except that one time. Nah, I don't read it.

Better: I've got a gun.

Question: Do you have any advice for young artists just starting out?

Boring answer: There's room for all of us; the more the merrier.

Clichéd response: Just keep plugging away. Someone's bound to notice.

Better: Just steer clear of me, man, if you know what's good for you.

Things to Repeat to Yourself Every Morning (or afternoon) When You Wake Up

I never wanna work for nobody.

I'm never gonna wear a suit. Well, almost never. Well, only when I want to.

I'm never gonna ride the Metra downtown.

Everyone who criticizes me is jealous.

In the words of Quentin Crisp, "Other people are a mistake."

Today I'm going to do something no one has ever thought of before.

I don't care about my paycheck.

NINE

Where the Artists Are (or, city of neighborhoods, my ass)

It's that time again, the time when I'm tempted to fling any guidebook about Chicago or any other damn city across the frigging room, the time for me to say something about Chicago being a city of neighborhoods. Then we've got to stick in a melting pot metaphor. Or maybe even an ethnic stew. Well, screw it. Sure, there are a lot of neighborhoods here, and they also have lots of nice names with lots of relatively interesting (or at least not mind-numbingly boring) history to them. And we can say all kinds of things about Chicago being segregated, and, yeah, it's all probably true. But artists don't live in neighborhoods. There aren't neatly bordered artists' territories where a Starbucks to the West, a Coffee Chicago to the east, a sweaty jazz bar to the north, and a seltzer factory to the south marks your entry into Arts Town, Illinois.

Artists don't live in neighborhoods; they live in clumps. They position themselves in spokes, in squiggly lines, in amorphous shapes resembling popcorn balls or mutant dodecahedrons. And, like capitalistic Cheshire cats, as soon as rent prices start zooming upward, they disappear, leaving only a security deposit behind. If you are a true, true tortured artist, you may in fact not want to live or work or eat around any other artists at all. You might want to nose your way into Hegewisch where you'll be the neighborhood iconoclast. But, if you hunger for the company of other revolutionaries such as yourself, if you long for those evenings of brandy and unfiltered cigarettes, if you hope desperately to get into another conversation over squid ink linguini about grant writing procedures, here are some of the places where you might want to move, live, work, and eat. Keep in mind, though, these helpful hints if you want to be taken seriously and not as the dilettante some may think you are.

1. Never eat at a restaurant with the word *artist* in it (anything called Cafe Des Artistes is definitely out).

2. Never move into a place that describes itself as an "artist's loft." This will only guarantee that your floorboards will creak and your landlord won't be around.

3. Never ever be seen reading anything that has a pun on the word *art* in the title (as in, *Getting to the Art of the Matter*).

4. Never go anywhere with a phony-sounding French name (see 1).

5. Goatees are out.

6. So are berets.

It's hard to believe there was a time that Old Town was considered this city's arts pocket, that that's where any groovy people lived, that David Crosby, in the sixites, when he could still fit through a door, considered Old Town his home. I'm sure in about ten years we'll be saying the same thing about Wicker Park. To longtime neighborhood residents, the announcement of the erection of this neighborhood's first cash station, at North Avenue and Milwaukee, was the signal that this could very well be the beginning of the end. Representing the transitory step between the downfall of a neighborhood and its upswing toward gentrification, artists necessarily lead a nomadic lifestyle. We will use old neighborhood names as benchmarks so that the city folk will know where we're talking about, but just to identify the new artist clump, we'll endow each with a new name: the name for artists; the name for people in the know; the name for people like me and you and the rest of the world.

A Dozen Artistic Clumps

The Bathhouse District (Boring old name: South Loop)

How's that again?
This neighborhood was always a natural. It had Al Capone, bathtub gin, cheap-as-dirt rent, train tracks, Chinatown bordering one end, the School of the Art Institute and Columbia College on the other, the offices of *Streetwise* nearby.

South of the Loop between, oh, about 13th and 22nd Streets, and from Lake Shore Drive to Canal Street lies a burgeoning series of artistic outposts where gangsters, Hollywood-sanitized murderers, and other assorted creeps and thugs once ruled the land; where shady First Ward aldermen John "Bathhouse" Coughlin and John "Hinky Dink" Kenna redefined politics as the art of hosting sleazy balls attended by well-heeled drunks and the Everleigh sisters, noted purveyors of ladies of the evening; where backroom deals were cut in the Chicago Coliseum to appoint presidential candidates at Democratic and Republican national conventions; where Music Row used to be; and where Chuck Berry and Muddy Waters cut their classic albums at Chess Records.

One hesitates to call this an artistic community. There is no true sense of community here. No parks in which to gather, no restaurant or street-side café in which to while away the hours, no theater, no neighborhood arts coalition. For years, rumors have abounded about the coming wave of gentrification. Mayor Daley's moved in nearby, and the Prairie Avenue Historic District of century-old homes like the Glessner House brings in the tour bus crowd. Still, though, this area remains desolate, attracting more folks awaiting trial at the Circuit Court than real estate speculators.

But, for the tortured, isolated, alienated soul in all of us, this area is way cool. A walk through vacant lots and destruction sites past abandoned buildings with tattered "For Sale" signs on them leads up the stairs to the best dance hall reggae parties in town. A longer walk leads to a peculiarly located center for elegantly dressed steppers to revel in the sounds of some of Chicago's best jazz musicians. And, over the canal, over the train tracks, past abandoned factories bathed in the kung pao aroma of nearby restaurants stand some of the city's most secluded artists' work spaces and residences. Art galleries like N.A.M.E. have already settled into the neighborhood, but not in any overzealous sort of way. Music video producers like H-Gun Labs, 3-D computer animators like Runandgun!, and graphic arts studios are already here, too. The Bathhouse awaits.

Where will I live and what will it cost?

Lofts, lofts, lofts aplenty. And there are so many damned vacant ones around here that you can wind up paying, basically, whatever you want. Prices in this up-and-coming area run anywhere from $250 for your rawest, most termite ridden roach motel to $1,200 for the more finished, tuckpointed, well-heeled-artist-ready loft. Best way to find a place is to walk up and down Michigan and Wabash all day. If you can find a landlord, you'll be all set.

Where's the post office?
2035 S. State.

Where's the nearest police station if someone tries to rob me?
You're in luck, because you're right by the main headquarters, 1121 S. State, and the Central district office, 11 E. 11th (nonemergency (312) 747-6230).

What's there to eat?
Like Chinese food? You're all set. You don't? Well, you better eat at home or walk to the Loop or try your luck at the fast-food soul food joints that line Cermak. My Chinatown recommendations? The champions remain Hong Min (221 W. Cermak) and Three Happiness (209 W. Cermak). It's not something I'd eat, but I know plenty of people who swear by Three Happiness's barbecued pork chow-tai. For something healthy, try veggie dishes at Mandar-Inn (2249 S. Wentworth). For something delicious but not quite as healthy, head further east on Cermak for soul food.

What will I do at night when I'm bored?
Despite the apparent desolation of this neighborhood, there's been a growing nightclub and artist hangout scene ranging from the casual and subdued (the Culture Club, 1351 S. Michigan) to the fancy and subdued (the Cotton Club, 1710 S. Michigan) to the isolated and subdued (Hidden Stages, 500 W. Cermak). If you're not into subdued, you might be best off taking the mile or so walk into the Loop.

Where should I go for a beer?
I'm a fan of the ambiance at the Strictly Business Cocktail Lounge (1355 S. Michigan).

Where should I go after I've had a few too many?
Try breaking into the ruins of the old, abandoned Lexington Hotel on Michigan and 22nd. Maybe you can find out what Capone kept in the vault.

Are my neighbors cool?
Sure, a little insular maybe, but basically cool.

But where will I do my shopping, man?
Not the easiest question to answer. Chinese food items are readily available. Just stroll down Wentworth and you'll get all the bamboo shoots, ginseng, and pressed duck you'll need. Beyond that, you're in trouble. I suggest buying a car.

Where are the artists?

They're all over working in their studios and their offices. They're working on videos at H-Gun Labs (2024 S. Wabash) and Runandgun! (2239 S. Michigan). They're exhibiting at N.A.M.E. (1255 S. Wabash). They're grooving it up at the Culture Club and the Cotton Club.

The Gap-Toothed Clark Street Jack-o'-Lantern
(Boring old name: Andersonville)

How's that again?

Clark Street is weird. It slices schizophrenically through town, changing its personality every mile or so. Here's a gang hang out. Here's an artsy strip. Here's a cemetery. Here's another artsy strip. Here's a bunch of thirty-something guys with frat haircuts—wait, there's another little artists' enclave over there. If you were drawing a map of Clark Street for the artists, it would resemble rows of teeth with every other tooth or so blacked out. The most interesting tooth in the Clark Street skull, at least as far as artists are concerned, would have to be the neighborhood known as Andersonville, that one-time stronghold of Swedish-American immigrants centered around the intersection of Clark and Foster.

Sure, vestiges of the Swedish influence remain from Erickson's Fish Market to the venerable Ann Sather's to the Swedish American Museum and Swedish Bakery on Clark, but if you were keeping score, you'd probably find that, lately, a small lesbian community has begun to replace the Andersons and Johannsens of this area. Either way, despite being rather inconveniently located as far as public transportation is concerned, the jack-o'-lantern smile has begun to seduce artists of all ethnicities and sexual orientations with its infinite charms. The drawing power of this neighborhood is largely the result of surprisingly reasonable rents for surprisingly large amounts of space, a generally safe environment, and a variety of ethnic groups, including Turkish and Arabic families, all living in relative harmony.

Where will I live and what will it cost?

This is a family kind of area, so there aren't a whole lot of bachelor pads and miniature efficiency studios in faceless high rises. Wood floors, fireplaces, and small family houses pretty much predominate. If you don't want to live above a bar and you're not averse to having a roommate, you can do pretty well by splitting the cost of incredibly spacious two bedroom apartments, which generally run in the $800–$1000 range. Another option is to head a bit west into the even quieter Ravenswood community and snag a cheaper loft space or floor of a family home there.

Where's the post office?
Ravenswood, 2522 W. Lawrence.

Where's the nearest police station if someone tries to rob me?
The 19th District, 1940 W. Foster.

What's there to eat?
Being a slob, I've always favored the pizza slices from Primo Pizza (5600 N. Clark). For people with slightly more than grease on their minds, this is a very good, cheap, ethnic dining area. Fans of Turkish cuisine swear by Konak (5150 N. Clark); decent Greek salads and spanikopita may be had for a song at Andie's (5253 N. Clark); the fruit soups at Ann Sather (5207 N. Clark) are kind of fun; there are a couple good falafel stands around; and, though I've never really gotten into it, I know folks (my old barber, for example) who rave about the Persian barbecued chicken at Reza's (5255 N. Clark).

What will I do at night when I'm bored?
Well, if you're going to stay in the area, you might wind up getting bored anyway. Past ten o'clock at night, the mouth of the pumpkin is pretty much closed. The Griffin Theatre (5404 N. Clark), located in an old restored movie theater, is a friendly and respectable theater company. Sometimes there's not bad acoustic music at the neighborhood bar Kerrigan's (5355 N. Clark) or Kopi, A Traveler's Café (5317 N. Clark). But, as I said, pickings are slim. You might want to check out Specialty Video (5225 N. Clark) for a good collection of films that don't necessarily feature Mel Gibson, Sharon Stone, or Michelle Pfeiffer.

Where should I go for a beer?
Soul Jam (5240 N. Clark).

Where should I go after I've had a few too many?
The Round Table Restaurant (5721 N. Clark) is a weird piano bar trip, like something out of 1962.

Are my neighbors cool?
Sure, but they go to bed early.

But where will I do my shopping, man?
For straight-ahead groceries, the Jewel on Clark and Bryn Mawr will do quite nicely. Specialty cuisines are available at Erickson's Delicatessen and Fish Market (5250 N. Clark).

Where are the artists?

Some are hanging out getting bombed at Hopleaf (5148 N. Clark) or sipping java at Kopi, A Traveler's Café. Some of the granola-crunchy ones are trying to hawk their work at Woman Wild (5237 N. Clark) or One Touch of Nature (5208 N. Clark). Others are browsing through the bookstores like Women and Children First (5233 N. Clark). The rest of them are somewhere away from here or they're at home. Don't wake them.

The Twisted Bicycle Wheel (Boring old name: Wicker Park/Bucktown)

How's that again?

The intersection of North, Damen, and Milwaukee is the rusty hubcap from which shoots jagged diagonals of streets veering off from one another in a spinning fit of confusion. Consider this your starting point, your epicenter, ground zero, if you will. No one around here seems to know where the exact borders are between Wicker Park and Bucktown, so I won't bother to explain. Neighborhood histories are almost always boring, anyway—settling of prairie land, Indian trail, path for buffalo, influx of farmers, German immigration, wealthy landowners, dadadadadadada. Suffice it to say that people lived here, then came the artists, then came the real estate speculators, then came the townhouses, there go the artists. (Some of them, anyway.)

The rest find themselves in disjointed elbows of the bicycle wheel, camping out in unrehabbed apartments on dead-end streets and in brownstowne buildings beside quaint $400,000 homes. The spokes of the wheel move ever outward, angling through Humboldt Park, Logan Square, and Ukrainian Village, trying to keep one step ahead of Starbucks and Century 21.

Despite the cries of gentrification, existence along the spokes of the bike wheel remains an exciting and fulfilling one for the artist. And, were it not for the influx of BMWs and briefcases, what else would there be for a community to form itself around? The groups that always seem to unite the best are the ones that join against something rather than for something. So the graffiti artists spray out their articulate objections to the new robber barons of the era; the politically active, many of whom don't vote (who can blame them?), loft their rocks through the windows of the new developments; and the painters and the poets gather in Urbus Orbis, in Earwax, and in Quimby's comic book shop to bitch about the latest harbingers for the end of a once-thriving arts community. Things were never as exciting here as they are right now.

Where will I live and what will it cost?

Wicker Park and Bucktown rents can get awfully absurd because of the influx of townhouses and fancy-ass loft buildings. It's certainly becoming one of the most expensive neighborhoods in the city that's not in walking distance of the lake. The slightly more adventurous are turning down the opportunity to live above greasy spoons or in walk-ups with rapidly escalating prices to move east to deserted former industrial spaces along Elston Avenue or west toward North and California and Humboldt Park. Although not as "safe" or "hip" as the more-traveled areas, the western region offers dirt cheap deals on coach houses, huge loft spaces, and apartments.

Where's the post office?

Wicker Park station, 1635 W. Division.

Where's the nearest police station if someone tries to rob me?

You should probably run into the nearest bar instead; police stations are few and far between around these parts. District 13 at 937 N. Wood (nonemergency (312) 746-9350) is probably your best bet.

What's there to eat?

There's not a bad selection of eating joints here, from the upscale and trendy like Cafe Absinthe (1958 W. North) and Avanti Popolo (1616 N. Damen); to the midscale and trendy like Soul Kitchen (1576 N. Milwaukee) and Cafe Du Midi (2118 N. Damen); to the cheap and trendy like Earwax (1564 N. Milwaukee) and Urbus Orbis, (1934 W. North); to good and hearty but not so trendy like Northside Cafe (1635 N. Damen) and Silver Cloud (1700 N. Damen); to the scrumptious and ethnic like Papajin (1551 N. Milwaukee) and Frida's (2143 N. Damen). For breakfast there are always the yummy dumplings at the Busy Bee (1550 N. Damen) or the omelets at Bongo Room (1560 N. Damen). And for dessert, the venerable Margie's Candies (1960 N. Western) is nearby.

What will I do at night when I'm bored?

Red Dog (1958 W. North), open until 4:00 A.M., is probably the wildest dance club in the city. The Bop Shop (1807 W. Division), one of the most reliable music clubs in town, is just a hop, skip, and a jump away. Double Door (1572 N. Milwaukee) can always come up with loud, innovative rock acts. Latino Chicago Theatre (1625 N. Damen) and Eclipse Theater (2074 N. Leavitt) are two of the more reliable and adventurous theater companies around.

Where should I go for a beer?

Don't go to the Rainbo Lounge. Leave Liz Phair alone. Check out the just-as-hip but not quite-as-well-traveled Holiday Club (1471 N. Milwaukee).

Where should I go after I've had a few too many?

How about the Russian and Turkish baths on Division for a massage to cool down before you drive?

Are my neighbors cool?

Yeah, there are still a lot of artists and down-to-earth family folks, particularly the further you get away from the loft complexes. But remember the frightening cry "The real estate speculators are coming! The real estate speculators are coming!"

But where will I do my shopping, man?

General groceries are available at Rama Mart (1520 N. Damen) or the Jewel on Milwaukee and Division. For dessert items, try Las Villas Bakery (1959 W. Division). WaxTrax! (1653 N. Damen) is a pretty good, nonmainstream CD shop. And if you need a comic book, there's always Quimby's Queer Store (1328 N. Damen).

Where are the artists?

All over the Flat Iron Building you can find galleries and studios, including Aron Packer's outsider gallery (1579 N.Milwaukee). Milwaukee and North is right in the middle of the so-called West Side gallery district, which includes Gallery 1633 (1633 N. Damen), Gallery 203 (1759 N. Milwaukee), David Leonardis Gallery (1352 N. Paulina), Wood Street Gallery (1239 N. Wood), Idao Gallery (1616 N. Damen), and InsideArt (1651 W. North). The more adventurous Uncomfortable Spaces galleries of Beret International (1550 N. Milwaukee) and Ten in One (1542 N. Damen) are also here. You can also find artists hanging out at Urbus Orbis, Rainbo, and the "Abraham Lincoln" bar (1443 N. Elk Grove).

The Vertical Rehearsal Space
(Boring old name: Lakeview)

How's that again?

Some neighborhoods are best observed from street level. You need to walk around to get a feel for the area. But take a helicopter ride over Wrigley Field and its southern environs and you'll have a better idea of where the city's actors and dancers are. From Sheridan on the east to Racine on the west, bounded by Diversey and Addison, you'll probably find more faceless highrises and mid-rises per square inch than anywhere else in town. This is a transient area where every building seems to have a "For Rent" sign on it and is loaded with that concept of the seventies and eighties, efficiency apartments.

Which still means what it always meant: your kitchen is practically in your bed, which is great if you crave a beer in the middle of the night, but not so hot if you have company.

You won't find many visual artists around here. Painters and sculptors usually require a bit more room than is offered in the usual swinging bachelor or bachelorette pads. Somehow, though, even though you'd think being an actor or dancer would require a lot of space too for rehearsal, tons of them have sequestered themselves into the cardboard box apartments that abound in this neighborhood. Perhaps it's the frugal lifestyle or the obsession artists need to have with themselves that makes it possible for budding thespians to exist in closed quarters. Or maybe it's the need to create an inhospitable environment so that they will want to leave the apartment as quickly as possible.

Whatever the underlying psychological motive, there are decided advantages to depositing yourself so near the lake and Wrigley Field. The jogging trail, the harbor, the el, and the lake are oh, so close. Nightlife is popping constantly. There are disadvantages too—like parking. Like, if you have a car, where the hell are you going to put it? This is an area that has more Denver boots per square inch than children. Also, the jogging trail around here can sometimes suck and be a safety hazard as sleekly lycra-clad, would-be triathletes zoom past you on expensive mountain bikes screeching "Your left! Your left! Your left!" Yuck.

Where will I live and what will it cost?

In a cardboard box. Well, not really a cardboard box but most likely, some sort of efficiency studio on Briar or Barry or Melrose or Aldine, for anywhere from $350–$550 per month. This place will most likely be in an elevator building that's clean, well kept, and perhaps the most boring and faceless thing this side of a Red Roof Inn. The further away from the lake you go, however, the roomier your place will get. But once you're up to Racine or beyond, it becomes more expensive, as well.

Where's the post office?

It's at 909 W. Fullerton, but I'd be very leery if I were you. The 60614 and 60657 zip codes are notoriously the worst for mail delivery in the city. If you don't mind having only 90 percent of your letters arrive, go for it. If not, take a drive or a walk to some other neighborhood and do all your important mailings from there.

Where's the nearest police station if someone tries to rob me?

The 23rd District, 3600 N. Halsted.

What's there to eat?

Surprisingly, by Wrigley Field on Clark Street lies one of the most reasonably priced and delectable ethnic food restaurant selections south of Devon. Ethiopian cuisine at Addis Ababa (3521 N. Clark) rocks; the burritos at La Canasta (3511 N. Clark) are key; the sushi at Matsuya (3469 N. Clark) is better than average; and the broths and pickled vegetables at Noodle Noodle (3475 N. Clark) rock the house. Excellent veggie fare is available at the Chicago Diner (3411 N. Halsted). Decent veggie fare may be had at Cafe Voltaire.

What will I do at night when I'm bored?

Depends on your sexual orientation. Well, it doesn't have to. But right in the middle of the Vertical Rehearsal Space lies Boys' Town, the predominantly gay nightlife strip on Halsted featuring bars like Bucks (3356 N. Halsted) and the Manhole Club (3458 N. Halsted), which rock on weekends 'til dawn. There're lots of theater companies in the area; on any given night, there's some sort of play (not always the greatest ones) in the basement of Cafe Voltaire (3231 N. Clark) or at the Turn Around Theatre (3209 N. Halsted). There is also usually a good selection of plays upstairs at the Organic Theatre's Greenhouse (3319 N. Clark). The usually adventurous and intelligent Bailiwick Repertory is close by (1229 W. Belmont). There's only one movie theater in the area, the slightly scuzzy Broadway Cinema (3175 N. Broadway). If you're not into sports bars, you might have some problems with the nightclub scene, but as a tonic, there's a pretty wild dance atmosphere at Berlin (954 W. Belmont). The dating scene at Sluggers (3540 N. Clark) is relatively repulsive, but the batting cages upstairs are good, cheesy fun for a drunk evening out. Music ain't that easy to come by in the general vicinity, with the exception of B.L.U.E.S. Etc. (1122 W. Belmont) and the venerable but usually far-too-crowded reggae bars like the Wild Hare (3530 N. Clark).

Where should I go for a beer?

I certainly wouldn't go to Yak-Zie's or any other of the area's many meet markets. I'd probably go to Sheffield's Beer Garden (3258 N. Sheffield).

Where should I go after I've had a few too many?

I'd just hang outside Wrigley Field and groove to the Dixieland band.

Are my neighbors cool?

Sure, and a lot of them have really friendly, adorable dogs. Very few, however, have families. And if they do, they're not telling.

But where will I do my shopping, man?

Treasure Island (680 N. Lake Shore), the Market Place (521 W. Diversey), Jewel (3531 N. Broadway), and Dominick's (3012 N. Broadway) are all nearby, in descending order of quality. And if you're looking for a White Hen Pantry or a 7-Eleven, there are probably more convenience stores per square inch here than anywhere else in the city.

Where are the artists?

If they're not at the theaters, they're at the neighboring bars like the Gaslight Corner (2858 N. Halsted), longtime hangout of the old Steppenwolf clan, or Sheffield's. Some of the neighborhood writers inhabit the bookstores like Barbara's (3130 N. Broadway) or Unabridged Books (3251 N. Clark) and the cafés like Coffee Chicago (2922 N. Clark) or Scenes (3168 N. Clark). The rocks by the Belmont Harbor also are a good place where artists congregate, but I wouldn't necessarily bother them there.

The Butchers' Blocks, or Slaughterhouse Row
(Boring old name: West Loop)

How's that again?

If you come here looking to snap your picture in front of the statue of Michael Jordan, you're in the wrong place. Or maybe you're in the right place, but you're the wrong kind of person to live here. You're the kind of person who views these streets out of your side-view mirror and says, "Hey, I don't mind driving around here for a game, but who lives around here?"

Well, some artists do. Just east of Chicago Stadium, east of Damen, say, and west of Halsted, in the area bounded by Grand to the north and Madison to the south lies a burgeoning, occasionally tony artists' community—well, I wouldn't quite say *community*—um, enclave in a neighborhood heretofore known only for its industrial and manufacturing plants and its fish and meat markets. The markets are still here, and if you walk around here around four o'clock in the morning you'd swear you walked into either something out of a Rocky movie or a George Romero cinematic nightmare. Gone are the stock-yards, but their bloody legacy remains. Men in white, fresh from the slaughterhouses, cart gigantic bovine carcasses and squid into the markets to sell to restaurant buyers who wander out of here still before dawn with enough vegetables, fish, and beef to feed that evening's customers.

For those not vegetarians by moral choice, this is a very unusual, if some-what isolated, area to live and to work. If Chicago ever becomes a broadcasting giant again (not bloody likely), look for rents to skyrocket. But for now, Oprah

Winfrey's Harpo Studios, Christian television broadcasting outlet WCFC, Channel 38, UHF broadcaster WCIU-Channel 26, and a few too-slick-for-words loft buildings are the only harbingers of yuppification.

Where will I live and what will it cost?

This area is something of a crapshoot, with fancy-schmancy, rehabbed loft spaces with high ceilings and brick walls on Washington going easily into the four-digit range. On the low end, there are dirt cheap, abandoned industrial loft spaces on Randolph above some of the markets and restaurants. From what I've heard from folks who've dug themselves into these $350-a-month shambles, you'll spend more than double your rent for a year's worth of Raid and Roach Motel purchases. In other words, when picking a place on a budget to settle in around here, be vewy, vewy careful if you're the least bit squeamish.

Where's the post office?

Main post office, 433 W. Van Buren.

Where's the nearest police station if someone tries to rob me?

The 12th District, 100 S. Racine.

What's there to eat?

The best restaurant in the area is undoubtedly the down-home, southern cuisine of Wishbone (1001 W. Washington), providing it's actually open when you want to go. Just a hop, skip, and a jump away is Greektown. I've never been big into gyros (baaaaad experience one late night at the twenty-four-hour Greektown Gyros on Halsted and Jackson), but the red snapper at Courtyards of Plaka (340 S. Halsted) and Greek Islands (200 S. Halsted) is usually top-notch. For the slightly more chichi crowd, the French bistro–style party place Marché (833 W. Randolph) is the place to be seen wearing something ultrasleek and black reminiscent of the Porsches parked outside. At the northern edge on Grand, Cafe Fresco (1202 W. Grand) is a good late night Italian eatery.

What will I do at night when I'm bored?

Tough call. Past sundown, unless you're into watching the trains go by or waiting for the meat packers to drive on through, this area is really dead, so dead that it's hard to find even a neighborhood tough or a gangbanger around to make life adventurous. This ain't exactly a neighborhood for walking around. The nearby UIC campus, with the exception of the occasional video screening or speaker, isn't exactly rocking, either. Dancing at the the

Warehouse III nightclub (738 W. Randolph), checking out belly dancers in Greektown, going to see a game at the United Center (I know, really artistic), or having dinner are your only real neighborhood options.

Where should I go for a beer?
The United Center. To fit in, drink and repeat the following phrase: "What is this? Miller? I can't drink this shit."

Where should I go after I've had a few too many?
Cook County Hospital.

Are my neighbors cool?
You won't have that many neighbors, and some of them have four legs. Feed them cheese.

But where will I do my shopping, man?
Grocery stores are few and far between, but Isaacson and Stein Fish Market (800 W. Fulton) and a couple of the butcheries and produce markets are open to the public. Some of the best bread and homemade pizza slices may be found at D'Amato's Bakery (1332 W. Grand).

Where are the artists?
They're sipping coffee in the café in the 954 W. Washington building, exhibiting in Exhibit (724 W. Washington), Ezell (954 W. Washington), Ab Imo (804 W. Randolph), and nearby Fassbender and Tough galleries (both 415 N. Sangamon). A lot of them are hanging out, dining, or waiting tables at Wishbone. Still others are hanging out by the bar at Marché.

Tortilla Flat (Boring old name: Pilsen)

How's that again?
Long predicted as the next area to undergo the ubiquitous transformation from ethnic neighborhood to artists' neighborhood to genrtified yuppiedom, it never really happened for Pilsen. In the late eighties and early nineties, galleries, theaters, and arts organizations settled in here waiting for an avalanche that never came. Several gave up or closed shop and moved north, most notably the very highly reputed Interplay Theater and Joseph Holmes Dance. Others never came and headed to Wicker Park or the nearby South Loop instead.

This is bad news for real estate speculators and folks who want to say they live next to artists, but good news for real artists looking for a cheap, electrifying urban living experience. This formerly Bohemian and now predominantly Mexican area centered at 18th and Halsted and jutting out west, east, and south to Damen, Halsted, and Cermak is a vibrant neighborhood, which, though certainly no paradise, is safer than lots of people would give it credit for. Tough-as-hell, rowdy bars blasting Latin music are what attract attention as you walk through the neighborhood, but there are an equal number of classier, more subdued watering holes and restaurants more suited to arriving artists. And, though there aren't really many galleries around, the walls under and over viaducts contain as lively outsider art as you'd find in most River North spaces. And still, this is mostly a family neighborhood.

Some rock musicians occupy houses on the western edges of Tortilla Flat, and there is some spillover from the largely Caucasian bohemian South Loop Bathhouse District scene along Halsted and slightly west of it. But if you are not of Latino heritage and you really want to make this your living choice, it might be a good idea to brush up on your Spanish.

Where will I live and what will it cost?
It'll be very cheap if you live in the dead center of the area. If you are not a clean freak, you can get away with $500 for a two-bedroom in a walk-up on Loomis or Allport. Things get more livable and more expensive as you move east toward Halsted and beyond.

Where's the post office?
1859 S. Ashland.

Where's the nearest police station if someone tries to rob me?
Marquette District Station, 2259 S. Damen.

What's there to eat?
Excellent and dirt cheap Mexican cuisine at longtime Chicago favorite Nuevo Leon (1515 W. 18th). A walk down 18th Street will eventually lead you to Bishop's Chili (1958 W. 18th), which serves its eponymous food in more than a dozen varieties and has the South Side's excellent Fillbert's Root Beer. A short walk north down Halsted will lead you to Jim's Polish, a legendary Maxwell Street twenty-four-hour polish sausage stand, which is, to borrow from author William Burroughs in *Naked Lunch*, "indescribably nauseating and delicious." Also as a side note, in the summer there are usually a good number of fruit and Popsicle vendors selling excellent cheapo products.

What will I do at night when I'm bored?
There's a little bit of experimental theater around at Blue Rider Theater (1822 S. Halsted) and occasional jazz or Latin music at La Decima Musa (1901 S. Loomis).

Where should I go for a beer?
La Decima Musa (1901 S. Loomis).

Where should I go after I've had a few too many?
Home. Find someone with a pushcart and a coconut Popsicle and snarf it down on the way.

Are my neighbors cool?
Yes, if you can speak the language.

But where will I do my shopping, man?
Decent baked goods available at Paraiso Bakery (1156 W. 18th) and Francisco Bonilla (1844 S. Blue Island). Buy groceries at Fruteria la Garra (1759 W. 21st), Fruteria la Mundial (1900 S. Blue Island), or the major supermarket La Casa del Pueblo (1810 S. Blue Island).

Where are the artists?
If they're not sipping java at the Blue Rider Theater's café space, they might be in Cafe Jumping Bean (1439 W. 18th). They could well be exhibiting at Calles y Sueños (1900 S. Carpenter) or the Mexican Fine Arts Center Museum (1852 W. 19th). Then again, the younger, more rebellious ones might well be under a viaduct with a can of spray paint.

The Seventies Past Blast
(Boring old name: East Rogers Park)

How's that again?
Sometimes it seems as though everyone who was a hippie in the sixties turned either maliciously or benevolently corporate. They shaved off their cheek warmers, sliced off their bushy pony tails, and went into medicine or personal injury law. Or they kept their hair (while they could), changed their wardrobes, and headed up right-minded, megamonied, new institutions like ice cream companies, alternative newspapers, natural foods industries, or theater complexes and donated proceeds of their incomes to whales and rain forests.

Then you walk around Rogers Park by the Morse el stop and you realize what happened to everyone else. Not to diss this 'hood. It has its aspects. It's cheap to live here, there're lots of creative folks wandering the streets, the beach is nearby, it has some all right theaters, and there's plenty of healthy food. But this has to be the most unconsciously uncool region in the city of Chicago. In other words, you'll see the occasional 'fro, lots of sandals (the brown worn leather kind), lots of cut-off shorts, lots of acoustic guitars, lots of New Age jewelry, and lots of folks in sparse apartments with big, droopy pot plants and excessive record album collections. That is to say, it's still 1974 around here.

Where will I live and what will it cost?
This is a pretty cheap area. Decent, basic one-bedroom apartments near the lake and the Morse el tend to run about $500. Of course, the closer you get to the el, the cheaper you get, which isn't something I'd actually advise. This neighborhood has grown seedier over time, and it has a creepy, transient, crack-addict feel to it sometimes. And, every time you walk around here, it seems there's a new police sketch of some neighborhood criminal affixed to a light post. If safety is of prime interest, I'd recommend either going east of Sheridan, where apartments are a bit more expensive, or closer to Loyola University, which is also a bit more expensive, unless you wind up in a September-May relationship with a college student, and then you can just stay at his or her dorm.

Where's the post office?
1723 W. Devon.

Where's the nearest police station if someone tries to rob me?
The 24th District, Rogers Park, 6464 N. Clark (the cool-looking one).

What's there to eat?
It's not exactly a diner's paradise around here. Heartland Café (7000 N. Glenwood) serves average to decent natural food dishes in a pleasant atmosphere. There are a couple of good taco joints around here, and the soups at Captain Nemo's (7367 N. Clark) are all right. Leona's (6935 N. Sheridan) and Giordano's (6836 N. Sheridan) chains have restaurants around here. But, if you're really hungry for something good, you're probably best off taking the Devon Avenue bus or a long walk to West Rogers Park and snarfing down the city's best Indian and Pakistani cuisine.

What will I do at night when I'm bored?
It hasn't been the same around here since Ashkenaz, the city's once-greatest deli, shut its doors long, long ago, but there's still stuff to do around here. The Lifeline Theatre (6912 N. Glenwood), voted the best in the city by this book, is right by the Morse el. The always-respectable Raven Theatre (6926 N. Clark) usually is running a revival of a play you've heard of but maybe haven't seen. The Factory Theatre (1257 W. Loyola) usually is a pretty reliable BYOB source

for low-budget, amusing entertainment. Midnight shows at the Village North (6746 N. Sheridan) of the *Rocky Horror Picture Show* and *Bladerunner* are good for a snicker or two. Decent bands play at Morseland (1218 W. Morse). And then again, you can always put on your dashiki and check out the folk entertainment scene at Heartland Café or the occasionally aptly named No Exit (6970 N. Glenwood).

Where should I go for a beer?
Roy's Bar (7006 N. Glenwood).

Where should I go after I've had a few too many?
If I were you, I'd go home.

Are my neighbors cool?
No. Next question.

But where will I do my shopping, man?
You'll find excellent natural foods shopping at Morse Avenue Natural Foods (1527 W. Morse) and then, of course, further east, there's always Osco (1425 W. Morse).

Where are the artists?
You might find a few of them at Ennui Cafe (6981 N. Sheridan) or at Heartland or No Exit. But, if there are any very successful artists around here, they're going to be on the beach. Surf's up, dude.

The East Side Stagger
(Boring old name: South Shore)

How's that again?
In the olden days, they used to call the focus of African-American culture at 47th and South Parkway (now Martin Luther King Drive) The Stroll. Up until the sixties, the South Side was a vibrant haven for artists and musicians who plied their trade at venues like the Regal Theater and the Tivoli. These venues hosted some of the country's finest talent, including Duke Ellington, Smokey Robinson, and even The Jackson Five.

Time has not been kind to the city's predominately black neighborhoods, as years of city neglect, racism, and poverty have resulted in a vast expanse of fast-food restaurants, small, dingy shops, and urban blight. Attempts have been made to try and liven up the South Side, from plans to revitalize the historic corner of 35th and State as the entrance to Black Metropolis to efforts to create artists' residences on 71st Street. Little of this has reached fruition, but small pockets of artistic creativity seem to be slowly sprouting in the area known as South Shore.

From 67th to 79th, from Stony Island to the lake, every now and again, you'll see a music venue, a café, or a gallery in and among the profusion of fried fish shops. Let's be honest, it's not really a "stroll," though. It's more of a stagger.

Where will I live and what will it cost?
It'll be way cheap. Faceless apartments and attractive courtyard buildings, when you get a few blocks west of the lake, can run as cheap as $450 for a two-bedroom. Wow. Keep in mind, though, that despite the fact that this is a relatively safe and walkable part of the South Side, it still ain't perfect. And burglary is heavy. An extra couple hundred bucks here or there will get you into a restored vintage apartment closer to the lake and safer territory, or will at least buy you a set of burglar bars.

Where's the post office?
2207 E. 75th.

Where's the nearest police station if someone tries to rob me?
Not as close as you might like: Grand Crossing, 7040 S. Cottage Grove. But there usually are cops patrolling the South Shore Country Club where the mounted police's horses are kept.

What's there to eat?
Other than fried crap, there are some decent options, most notably at the Dining Room (2131 E. 75th), which features decent soul food, and the far superior but farther away Army & Lou's (422 E. 75th), the city's classic soul food restaurant and favorite of the late mayor Harold Washington. For those with little consciousness of health, Leon's BBQ (1640 E. 79th) still features some of the best hot links in town. Gross but delicious.

What will I do at night when I'm bored?
There's usually some sort of music or theater entertainment (often of a community level) at the South Shore's jewel, the South Shore Cultural Center (7059 South Shore), a park-district-owned palace that houses one of the city's most beautiful and extravagant-looking ballrooms. Alexander's Steak House (3010 E. 79th) has been a steady jazz venue for years. A drive a mile or two west will lead to slightly less cozy territory but high-quality entertainment, including the New Apartment Lounge (504 E. 75th), where sax legend Von Freeman

still holds court every Tuesday, and Artis' (1249 E. 87th), which features blues on Sundays and Mondays with a seventies high school prom atmosphere. Also a bit west of South Shore but still in spitting distance, are two of the city's best little-known theater companies, ETA Creative Arts Foundation (7558 S. South Chicago) and the Chicago Theater Company (500 E. 67th), both of which offer high-quality, innovative plays whose quality rivals many of their far-better-known North Side competitors. And national acts frequently grace the stage of the New Regal Theater (1645 E. 79th), a restored classic movie palace.

Where should I go for a beer?
Me, I'd go a little bit west to Lee's Unleaded Blues (7401 S. South Chicago), a rocking honky-tonk featuring raucous blues entertainment.

Where should I go after I've had a few too many?
Rainbow Beach, to watch the sun rise over one of the best skyline views this city has to offer.

Are my neighbors cool?
The ones who hang out on the front steps and talk to you are cool, and there are lots of friendly families around. Just don't go tipping or cocking your hat at a rakish angle around the groups of young men gathered in the abandoned parking lots under the viaducts or in the park at night.

But where will I do my shopping, man?
Not a whole lot of choices here. There's a Dominick's on 71st and Jeffrey and the well-stocked Delray Famous Fresh Market on 73rd and Stony Island.

Where are the artists?
A lot of them can be found either exhibiting or performing at ETA Creative Arts Foundation. Some of them are plying their trade at Mojo Hand Studio (1805 E. 71st) or sipping java at Beanies Cafe (1949 W. 71st). Others are browsing the titles, getting wise at the Knowledge Bookstore across the street. And, if you want to get known or know somebody in the dance hall reggae scene, you better head over to Tallas Records (1921 E. 79th).

Pysanka City (Boring old name: Ukrainian Village)

How's that again?
Chicago's Ukrainian Village has always been one of the most tightly knit ethnic communities, and, if such a thing is possible, it became even more so during the fall of the Soviet empire and the Ukrainian independence movement some

years back. This is village life, a place where everybody knows everybody's grandmother, everybody knows what a *pysanka* is (a Ukrainian easter egg), and folks sit on the front porch sipping lemon vodka and gossiping in Ukrainian about who's getting married to whom.

The community is a small one, bordered by Western, Damen, Chicago, and Division. This neighborhood is suspicious of outsiders at times, being located uncomfortably close to what denizens perceive is the danger of gang life at Roberto Clemente High School. There was a time when, if you wanted to live here, it was good to have a Ukrainian name or Ukrainian friends who could recommend you without reservations. Times have changed since then, to be sure, as many of the young folks, feeling too much of the pressure of the Old World, have moved out, leaving prime virgin territory to be despoiled by settling young artists, eager for the insular, quiet, everybody-knows-everybody family feel that still exists in Pysanka City.

Where will I live and what will it cost?
Unlike many of the emerging artists' communities, here you will most likely not be dealing with a real estate company. Probably you'll be dealing with an old couple who wants to rent the first floor of a beautiful, spic-and-span brownstone to someone reliable, trustworthy, and clean. It's cheap here ($400–$700 for a very spacious one-bedroom), and all prices are negotiable, but as in the past, sometimes it's best to know somebody or speak the mother tongue.

Where's the post office?
It's a toss-up. Use either the Midwest Branch, 2419 W. Monroe, or the Wicker Park one, 1635 W. Division.

Where's the nearest police station if someone tries to rob me?
The 13th District, 947 N. Wood.

What's there to eat?
Not a whole heck of a lot, but there are excellent Ukrainian specialties at Saks (2301 W. Chicago) and Galan's (2210 W. Chicago). If that's too stuffy for you, there's the ultrahip, roadhouse-style cuisine of Twilight (1924 W. Division).

What will I do at night when I'm bored?
Community life still thrives here thanks to the local Ukrainian dance groups at the Ukrainian Cultural Center (2247 W. Chicago) and the church groups in Pysanka City's incredibly ornate churches. Still one of the hottest music spots in the city, The Empty Bottle (1035 N. Western) rocks on most nights. Or you can try taking a dip at Smith Park Pool (2526 W. Grand).

Where should I go for a beer?
Saks.

Where should I go after I've had a few too many?
The private Mardon Billiard Club (2115 W. Chicago) and see if they let you in.

Are my neighbors cool?
Yes, the young ones definitely are. And the older folks can be incredibly wonderful—once they've stopped being suspicious of you.

But where will I do my shopping, man?
Probably at the Ukrainian Village Grocery (2204 W. Chicago).

Where are the artists?
Those who aren't hanging out at the Ukrainian bars have probably settled into one of the area's hipper drinking establishments, such as the rather cool Club Foot (1824 N. Augusta), The Empty Bottle on an off night, or J & L (1808 W. Chicago).

Sconetown
(Boring old name: Roscoe Village and environs)

How's that again?
The quaint name Roscoe Village has always seemed to me to be one of those inventions foisted upon a part of the city by real estate developers rather than something that formed organically out of some historic importance. The rehabbing of single family homes and loft buildings in this relatively quiet, residential section of the North Side of the city near the Ravenswood community did not, in fact, lure wealthy and influential moguls. What it did bring, however, were scone eaters.

I don't know what it is about the area of the city bordered by Diversey to the South and Addison to the north, between Western and Ravenswood, but I find it hard to get into a conversation with anyone who has lately settled into the neighborhood without discussing scones somewhere down the line. What has resulted is a sort of three-pronged neighborhood atmosphere, with decidedly unhip families peaceably sharing this old, European-style community with up-and-coming artists who have come for the solitude and with speculating yupsters who seem to be here only for the scones. I don't even like scones. What are they? Are they dessert? Are they breakfast? Are they ever really fully cooked? How can you tell, when they still taste like dough?

Scones aside, much-anticipated gentrification has not fully hit this place, allowing it to maintain a pseudo-bohemian atmosphere. A number of dancers and homebody members of a couple of well-known rock bands that shall remain nameless have settled in and around Sconetown. If I were looking for the next ultrahip, rockin' neighborhood where energetic, emerging graffiti artists were settling, I doubt I'd move here. But if I were a writer or a performer of some kind looking for a relatively cheap rent for a comparatively large amount of space and a calm, convenient, low-profile lifestyle, I would definitely look into it. I don't know everything I'd do here once I moved in, but I could tell you straight out what I wouldn't be having for breakfast.

Where will I live and what will it cost?
A year or so back, I really wanted to move into this ultracool, reasonably priced, rehabbed Masonic temple on Damen a bit north of Sconetown near Irving, but it filled up too quickly for me. Bummer. These days, I'd settle for one of the top floors of what look like but aren't always single-family dwellings on Roscoe or Cornelia near Hamlin Park, which tend to run in the $600 to $800 range for quite a good deal of space.

Where's the post office?
It's a tough call. Depending on where you are, it's a toss-up between the Ravenswood office (2522 W. Lawrence) and the Lakeview branch (1343 W. Irving Park).

Where's the nearest police station if someone tries to rob me?
Belmont Station, 2452 W. Belmont.

What's there to eat?
There's not a whole heck of a lot in the immediate vicinity worth writing home about. Brett's Kitchen (2011 W. Roscoe) is a bit snooty and overpriced but serves excellent brunch, truly. The Village Tap (2055 W. Roscoe) has really good hummus and falafel. For the grumbling-bellied insomniac, this area is rife with late night greasy spoons.

What will I do at night when I'm bored?
There are limited but not entirely unpleasant options, which range from the cool and bohemian, like smoking and listening to grooved-out Irish folk at Augenblick (3907 N. Damen), to the cool and old-fashioned, like checking out the waiters and bartenders who work magic tricks at nearby Schulien's Restaurant (2100 W. Irving Park). There's good rock music at the Beat Kitchen (2100 W. Belmont) and off-and-on quality tunes at Bedrocks (2125 W. Roscoe). And the Jazz Buffet (2556 W. Diversey) is a somewhat staid venue featuring top jazz talent in a dinner theater environment. But the real thing that makes

this 'hood worthwhile is the bowling. I can't frigging stand bowling, and still I dig this place. Here you are right on top of Waveland Bowl (3700 N. Western), one of the nuttiest twenty-four-hour bowling scenes in Chicago. Come in here at 4 A.M. and it is still ear-splittingly loud. To the south, Diversey River Bowl (2211 W. Diversey) provides a mellower counterpart.

Where should I go for a beer?
The Village Tap. It's one of the friendliest bars I know in the city, and it even has good food. It's the kind of place where you can go by yourself and either *a*) people will be nice to you, or *b*) they'll just leave you alone.

Where should I go after I've had a few too many?
Bowling.

Are my neighbors cool?
Yeah, really cool, integrated and unpretentious.

But where will I do my shopping, man?
The blight of the Riverview Plaza on Western between Addison and Belmont, which replaced this city's most fabled amusement park, has absolutely huge Dominick's and Jewel branches. For more home-style and less intimidating grocery shopping, there's the Cardenas Supermarket (2153 W. Roscoe). Old-style, European baked goods like breads and sweet rolls are available at Philip's Bakery (1955 W. Belmont). And, if you're looking for furniture, Belmont around here is this city's antique row.

Where are the artists?
Some of them are sipping java at Higher Ground (2022 W. Roscoe). Sixty or so of them are working late into the evening in the studios of the Cornelia Arts Building (1800 W. Cornelia). Dancers are rehearsing at the Zephyr Community Center (4401 N. Ravenswood) and the Hamlin Park Fieldhouse (3035 N. Hoyne), where Nana Shineflug's Chicago Moving Company is headquartered. A few of them are eating scones, but late at night, the rock and rollers are bowling.

Jekyll and Hydeville (Boring old name: Hyde Park)

How's that again?
Well, it is kind of a two-faced neighborhood, really, or, at least it has its incongruous aspects. This quiet—yeah, too quiet—and even racially integrated 'hood of scholars, academics, and beards seems separate from the crumbling businesses on 47th Street, 63rd Street, and Cottage Grove. The neighborhood

has been called an island, but that is deceptive, for it is the neighborhoods that surround Jekyll and Hydeville that are isolated, cut off from the quiet serenity of Hyde Park. People there are forced to live in squalor while the well-heeled students and faculty of the University of Chicago luxuriate in clouds of pipe smoke thinking great thoughts.

Though the days of sixties radicalism and artistic invention have long since passed this neighborhood, the abundance of bookstores, cafés, and solitude make it a good choice for the budding artist. There is a decided reputation for geekdom around here, and it is somewhat well-founded: the most rocking place on a Saturday night is, without a doubt, the Regenstein Library. But, if you don't mind a long ride on the Jeffrey express bus to get to downtown or to any other burgeoning artists' community, you could do a lot worse.

Where will I live and what will it cost?
You have a couple of options. If you don't mind living with students or grad students, check the Ida Noyes Center (1212 E. 59th) or the International House (14714 E. 59th) for shared housing opportunities. If this turns your stomach, there are always cheap rentals (approximately $500 for a one-bedroom) available a bit north of campus in courtyard buildings on Woodlawn and other neighboring streets. An intriguing option, also, is a rise in the number of hippie-style co-op living arrangements in Jekyll and Hydeville (as in, "You're baking the bread this week, man"). I won't give these folks away by printing their addresses or numbers, but this is a relative bargain for the right person. Ask around or look for their fliers at local bookstores. You'll find them.

Where's the post office?
4601 S. Cottage Grove.

Where's the nearest police station if someone tries to rob me?
Police stations aren't real nearby. You're best off grabbing one of the emergency phones that are planted all over the U of C campus.

What's there to eat?
Your main choices involve the local branches of high-quality restaurant chains like Ann Sather's (1329 E. 57th), the not-Chicago-style-but-still-quite-good Pizza Capri (1501 E. 53rd), Edwardo's (1321 E. 57th), or the original Medici (1327 E. 57th). Local folks still swear by the ribs at Ribs 'n' Bibs (5300 S. Dorchester), and Caffe Florian (1450 E. 57th) ain't bad for a coffee and a pastry.

What will I do at night when I'm bored?
The cliché is that the area is totally dead after dark. The truth is that it's only partially dead. Although the area rivals a Mormon settlement for evening

entertainment, there are a few choices. U of C (5801 S. Ellis) ain't exactly a wild place, but its film societies, including DOC films, have some of the best, most inventive programs of high-quality (but sometimes of poor print quality) films in town, screening at the Law School Auditorium (1111 E. 60th), the International House, and Ida Noyes Hall. The Court Theatre (5355 S. Ellis) is a very reputable if somewhat stodgy producer of classic stage works. And sometimes there's live entertainment, or at least good conversations for eavesdroppers, at noted neighborhood watering hole Jimmy's Woodlawn Tap (1172 E. 55th). Beyond that, though, you're on your own, pal.

Where should I go for a beer?
Make it a mai tai or something else that comes in a pineapple and have it at the cocktail lounge at House of Tiki (1612 E. 53rd).

Where should I go after I've had a few too many?
Go to the Museum of Science Industry's huge 70-millimeter screen Omnimax Theater (57th and Lake Shore), sit in the front row, and feel the sensation of riding in a plane or exploring the ocean floor. And then prepare to sleep near the toilet bowl at home.

Are my neighbors cool?
Not really, but they're so uncool they're cool, if you know what I mean.

But where will I do my shopping, man?
Folks around here love the independent Mister G's Finer Foods (1226 E. 53rd) for groceries.

Where are the artists?
If they're not acting or in the audience of the Court Theatre, chances are you might find them at the Hyde Park Art Center (5307 S. Hyde Park). If it's June, they might very well be exhibiting at the 57th Street Art Fair. Most likely, though, they're working on getting inspiration for their next work of art at one of the many great area bookstores like Powell's (1501 E. 57th), 57th Street Books (1301 E. 57th), or the massive labyrinth of Seminary Co-Op (5757 S. University). Either that, or they've snuk into Regenstein Library. It's not easy, but with the proper amount of chutzpah it can be done.

Berwyn (No funky nickname—this is just too weird)

How's that again?
Ask people in the arts where the next burgeoning artists' community is and they're liable to give you the predictable answers the Bathhouse District or

the Twisted Bicycle Wheel (well, they're not calling them that, at least not yet). But, lately, I've been getting a really strange answer: Berwyn. At first, I thought people were putting me on. Like the time a friend of mind suggested that she was going to open up a Starbucks in Pullman.

You'd think Evanston, maybe. That's a given. You'd think Oak Park. You'd maybe even think Kenosha if you were in a particularly open-minded mood. But Berwyn? But after five different people give you the same unsolicited answer, it's time to look the thing squarely in the eye and figure out what the deal is. After years of being the punchline in any Second City joke, this still largely Italian suburb due west of the city centered between Harlem and Oak Park Avenues near Hinsdale, Oak Park, and (God help us) Cicero, Berwyn seems to be garnering serious attention from artistic folks looking for cheap rents in a safe, slightly urban atmosphere.

Where will I live and what will it cost?
One look at the local paper *Berwyn Life* reveals a wide array of cheap, clean apartments in (can we say this?) downtown Berwyn. Even the hugest and nicest one-bedroom apartment here will rarely run you over $500.

Where's the post office?
6625 W. Cermak.

Where's the nearest police station if someone tries to rob me?
6647 W. 26th.

What's there to eat?
Excellent Italian food abounds and so does great junk food. Try the malts at nearby Parky's (7021 W. Roosevelt), the Italian Ice at Gina's Ice Cream (6737 W. Roosevelt), and the slices at Gino's Pizza (1547 S. Oak Park). A walk to the local White Fence Farm branch in Riverside (3604 S. Harlem) will snag you a dozen corn fritters for ten bucks.

What will I do at night when I'm bored?
Not all that much, but your options aren't bad, either, for a suburb. The roadhouse Fitzgerald's (6619 W. Roosevelt) usually offers high-quality national blues, country and western, or rock and roll acts. The Harlem Avenue Lounge (3701 N. Harlem) also is a pretty good blues venue. It's hardly my favorite, but the Candlelight Theatre (5620 S. Harlem) in Summit ain't far, either.

Where should I go for a beer?
The Weinkeller microbrewery (6421 W. Roosevelt).

Where should I go after I've had a few too many?
It's the suburbs, man. What do you have in mind?

Are my neighbors cool?
Your guess is as good as mine.

But where will I do my shopping, man?
Any of a thousand Jewels, Dominick's, and White Hen Pantries in the surrounding areas.

Where are the artists?
They're coming, they're coming.

TEN

Your Day Job

It ain't going to happen over night, this artist thing. And even if it does, it might not start paying the bills just yet. Besides, you're going to need to do some job where you get to meet people and encounter those who will inspire your works of art. And what better place than a job that pays well and doesn't require that you use incredible amounts of brain power? You can read the "Help Wanted" section of the *Tribune* and the *Reader* as well as I can to find yourself a slew of telemarketing and temporary jobs. Or, you can look below and find a list of twenty potential places for people just like you where your body can be occupied with work while your mind is occupied with art.

Arthur Andersen Accounting, 175 N. Harbor

Bally's Health Clubs, 2828 N. Clark

Barnes & Noble Bookstore, 659 W. Diversey

Best Buy, 1700 N. Marcey

Borders Bookstore, 830 N. Michigan

Chicago Motor Coach Company, 750 S. Clinton

Chicago Public Schools, 1819 W. Pershing

Coffee Chicago, 3323 N. Clark

CompUSA, 7011 N. Central, Skokie, IL

Crate & Barrel, 646 N. Michigan

The Gap, 3033 N. Broadway

Gourmet Cup Coffee, 2531 N. Clark

Kaplan Educational Center, 6427 N. Sheridan

Kinko's, 2300 N. Clybourn

Lettuce Entertain You Restaurants, 5419 N. Sheridan

Loftus and Meara Temporary Service, 199 E. Superior

Princeton Review, 2847 N. Sheffield

Starbucks, 105 W. Adams

Target, 2656 N. Elston

Tower Records, 2301 N. Clark

Or, you could just be a critic!

Acknowledgments

Special thanks to *Subnation Magazine* (John, Chip, Andy, et al.), my mother the proofreader, Rabbi Dan Epstein, Bill Williams, Paul Creamer for all the shirts, Kate Steffes for the mango salsa, Claire Pensyl, Ira Bell, Cara Jepsen, Phil Koch, Bill Gillmour, Nathalie Van Straaten, Joel Leib, Jeff Abell, Bob Koester, Joy Gregory, Aron Packer, Byron Roche, the cast of *The Blank Page*, Covert Creative Group, Shirley Mordine, Mary Shen Barnidge, Larry Bommer, Jack Helbig, Nathan Mason, Al Cohn, Ned Schwartz, Sam Hwang, Jeremy Freeman, everyone who went on the record and everyone who didn't, "Don't Think Twice; It's All Right."

Index